STRATEGIC LEADERSHIP

STRATEGIC LEADERSHIP

Managing the missing links

Expanded and improved second edition

Richard S. Handscombe

Philip A. Norman

McGRAW-HILL BOOK COMPANY

London · New York · St Louis · San Francisco · Auckland
Bogotá · Caracas · Hamburg · Lisbon · Madrid · Mexico
Milan · Montreal · New Delhi · Panama · Paris · San Juan
São Paulo · Singapore · Sydney · Tokyo · Toronto

Published by
McGRAW-HILL Book Company Europe
Shoppenhangers Road · Maidenhead · Berkshire · England
Telephone 0628 23432
Fax 0628 770224

British Library Cataloguing in Publication Data
Handscombe, Richard S.
  Strategic Leadership: Managing the
  Missing Links. — 2Rev. ed
  I. Title II. Norman, Philip A.
  658

  ISBN 0-07-707763-6

Library of Congress Cataloging-in-Publication Data
Handscombe, Richard S.
  Strategic leadership: managing the missing links / Richard S.
Handscombe, Philip A. Norman. — Expanded and improved 2nd ed.
    p. cm.
  Includes index.
  ISBN 0-07-707763-6
  1. Strategic planning. 2. Technology—Management. 3. Customer
service—Management. 4. Management audit. I. Norman, Philip A.
II. Title.
HD30.28.H3668   1993
658.4'012—dc20
                                                              92-43218
                                                                  CIP

1234 CUP 9453

Typeset by BookEns Limited, Baldock, Herts.
and printed and bound in Great Britain at the University Press, Cambridge

To our ever-patient wives Joyce and Ria

CONTENTS

INTRODUCTION TO SECOND EDITION

The task of managing businesses to achieve strategic leadership in the 1990s is recognized as imperative and daunting. The first edition of *Strategic Leadership: The Missing Links*, published in 1989, was conceived to provide practising managers with guidelines for achieving strategic leadership and an understanding of what this means to their specific business.

It is believed that the new updated and expanded second edition will prove to be an even more useful process guide and workbook for practising directors and managers as well as consultants, academics and management students than the first edition. The second edition not only highlights the missing links in much strategic management practice, but also provides practical advice and guide-lines for their active management. This is reflected in the title *Strategic Leadership: Managing the missing links*.

Since the publication of the first edition, developments of considerable importance have occurred which support and enrich our original ideas and their practical application. The strategy in preparing the second edition has been to update the first edition in a manner that:

- provides practical guide-lines for improving and extending strategic management processes and practices, building towards achieving strategic leadership
- updates the background against which the concepts and ideas are presented, recognizing that many of the business developments and visions projected in the first edition are becoming realities
- highlights the wide acceptance of the concepts contained in the book and their relationships with related management issues such as innovation and total quality management
- enriches and extends management process ideas and innovations as a result of a further three years experience assisting organizations to evaluate and implement the contents of the book in practical situations
- expands on the issues of strategic supplier relations and the environment, strategic customer relations, and the vital enabling issue of corporate culture in achieving best business and management practice
- expands the number of audit questionnaires, improves the presentation and content and integrates them into a far-reaching and comprehensive

diagnostic process for reviewing existing company corporate management practice against industrial best practice

- increases the number and range of examples using practical application of ideas throughout the book, particularly in a new ultimate chapter 'Making it happen'.

Practising senior managers will find many concepts and ideas related to:

- auditing and improving management processes, and their management
- building a realistic vision of the future that takes full account of customer needs and technological capability
- creating a common sense of mission to drive strategic planning performance towards clearly defined strategic performance indicators
- committing top management to practical action plans towards that vision
- developing the top management team on an achievement centred basis
- watching, analysing and accessing customer, technological and supplier opportunities and risks on a continuous basis
- improving commercial astuteness and adaptability to significant changes in market and environmental trends and events
- establishing a sense of direction and framework of policy guide-lines within and against which to evaluate subsidiary business unit and product group strategies
- developing an appropriate corporate culture as the facilitator of eventual change
- quantifying progress in achieving strategic change in business results and management capabilities.

The needs for such changes are increasingly recognized by companies in view of the complexity of the competitive market-place and the many external initiatives. The DTI Innovation Programme and Department of Employment Investors in People programme in the UK, The Baldridge Awards in the USA, the ISO9000, and environmental initiatives of the EC and United Nations, and — most urgently — the move to market conditions in Central and Eastern Europe as well as the technology-led strategies of South East Asia that continue the drive towards global excellence in products and services all indicate the necessity for change.

Readers will find the updated and expanded text provides practical guide-lines for a Total Strategic Management (TSM) programme.

The flow diagram at the beginning of each chapter links *Strategic Leadership* into a cohesive framework for analysis and action towards a strategic leadership position.

Richard S. Handscombe
Philip A. Norman

PREFACE TO SECOND EDITION

Today's strategic decisions continue to be taken on shifting sands stirred by the strong economic and competitive tides resulting from the globalization of business and emergent changes in the relative industrial power of the US, EC, Japan, the Pacific Rim and Central and Eastern Europe.

The business environment of the next decade will be a tough one. New complex pressures on businesses and business leaders, particularly the chief executive, will require a deeper awareness of a number of newly emergent strategic issues. Existing management processes will need to be speedily adapted if the opportunities and risks associated with new issues are to be grasped and managed to competitive advantage. Innovations in the use of both management and science-based technology will be essential, supported by innovations in the manner in which winning teams are developed for tomorrow. The changing business scene in Europe arising from the single European market and the consequent inward investments from Japan, the US, etc., can only lead to heightened competition in what is the largest and fastest growing market in the world. The planned European Trade Area linkages with EFTA and the re-emergence of Central and Eastern European countries as suppliers, customers and areas for business investment will ensure an accelerated pace in global competitive pressures. This picture has emerged with frightening clarity since the first edition of *Strategic Leadership — The missing links* was published.

This book was originally stimulated by our joint practical experience and observations in a wide range of business situations within the UK, the European Community and, internationally, in some 40 countries. This is still relevant. Our observations continue to demonstrate that many management teams have yet to prepare thoroughly for the future. In our work we have identified 10 fundamental business phenomena, each important in its own right and interrelated. All provide essential sources of vision and vitality to aid the development of competitive strategies for the future.

The 10 phenomena are listed below and expanded upon in detail throughout the book in an integrated manner. Audit check-lists are included to aid personal analysis and appropriate action planning for development at key points in the text.

1. The 1990s demand that companies return to seeking significant improvements in the profit and cash flow generated from competitive products and services as the major source of shareholder value, as opposed to opportunistic sales of surplus land and divestment of businesses which are a mismatch with core business streams. This implies a return to genuine trading performance, objectives and standards.

2. The development of tomorrow's competitive products and services will require greater attention and anticipation of the strategic, as distinct from operational, needs of key customers, both in the corporate and personal markets. The strategic needs identified may be for improved products or services. However, increasingly they will include the need for profit-effective and faster access to new enabling and/or support technologies — the technologies required by the customer to remain competitive in the future. Suppliers can play a critical role, often contributing the difference between strategic reality and dreams.

3. The companies that recognize and exploit the most significant business opportunities in the 1990s are likely to be, in many instances, those with access to relevant and timely technology and an effective process for its management. The effective management of technology is a strategic asset alongside people, finance, property, plant and natural resources.

   EC programmes such as Commett, Jupiter and Europace are designed to help Europe reassert its technical prowess *vis-à-vis* the US and Pacific Rim countries. In turn, their national and regional initiatives are designed to make progress tough. One example of this is regional grants to low technology industrial areas.

4. The base of proven product, service, process, distribution and systems technology is growing exponentially, nationally, regionally and worldwide. Yet much remains largely under-exploited, often waiting to be recognized, accessed and exploited in synergy with home-grown company technology. For many companies, grasping the opportunity will require a significant intellectual reappraisal. It is already happening among global giants as well as small start-up businesses.

5. The approach to managing the use of technology in the future needs to go beyond, and be fundamentally different to, the process used by many companies for the management of scientific and technological research and development. Much work needs to be done to develop

the practices for the management of technology. However, we believe that a common strategic vision and sense of direction for the management of the total technology of a business is required today to sustain productivity and genuine bottom-line results. This is critical at a time when functional budgets for research, product development, process development, information technology and continuing technological education can each be several percentage points of sales turnover and can in most cases not be diminished without risk.

In many companies today, the management of the use of technology is piecemeal, with decisions on priorities for internal or external investment programmes being made at a subordinate functional, as opposed to a corporate, level.

6. Often, much strategic thinking at board level remains shallow and is merely a coordination of functional or national viewpoints. This situation is unlikely to be successful in generating competitive products and services which match the strategic needs of future customers and hence establish a strong basis for strategic customer/supplier alliances. Further unique strategic insights will be required for global success, not a 'follow the leader' application of generic strategies.

7. Leading companies now have a total technology strategy in place. It is integrated with the overall business strategy, and goes way beyond traditional information technology and research and development in its focus on the use of technology for value-added versus cost-competitive advantage. Other teams of directors and senior managers fail to spend the personal time, effort and resources necessary to identify, interpret and understand the technological opportunities and risks inherent in the future strategy of key customers. This observation reinforces the growing concern, particularly in the UK and US, that in spite of the continuous growth of scientific achievement and the socially and environmentally visible impact of science and technology, perhaps as few as one in five people are scientifically literate. Being small is no protection in this case as leading companies will progressively seek similar standards from all companies that they use as suppliers — eventually the missing link in the chain reaches the smallest business.

8. The issues outlined require the availability of appropriate knowledge, skills and intellectual capacity to ensure relevant and timely analyses and decisions. They require the role and culture of top management to be reviewed, together with a reappraisal of the knowledge and skill base for future success.

Analysis of how companies review the future suggests that some can be described as prospectors or market drivers, and others as reflective analysts or market followers. This book is designed to help both types: the prospectors by helping them sharpen their existing continuous search for market opportunities and timely innovative responses to achieve and maintain a lead; the more reflective companies by maintaining their drive for operational efficiency and enriching their ability to prosper with tomorrow's more turbulent market and technology.

9. Novel but practical approaches to the development of individual employees, teams and corporate culture will be required. An approach to culture audit and development that achieves a balance between essential output and input factors is required. In turn this has major consequences for the practices of companies, consultancies and business schools.

10. In many companies, a spectrum of quantified performance indicators is absent. The indicators required for monitoring the successes and failures of strategic development programmes against best management standards go beyond the traditional financial indicators developed progressively from the 1920s.

    Without quantified performance indicators it is difficult to design, launch and implement a corporate change programme in a professional manner and with a high probability of success.

Strategic Leadership is primarily aimed at chairmen, chief executives, top management and business teams. It is intended to be used by companies of all sizes. The book provides much more than an update on important management concepts. It introduces a number of vital new concepts, and provides a framework for self analysis and action in the face of a challenging, but realistic, vision of the future business environment. This second edition expands on the concepts and, more particularly, on the management processes and related skills involved in a practical manner.

However, practising managers at all levels, consultants, students of management and business studies and their academic tutors will find many ideas of interest for both application and further research. The concepts and processes outlined start from, and build on, a broad strategic base. Their application in practical situations is expanded on in this second edition throughout the book and in Chapter 10.

The book emphasizes the need for directors to be fully involved in establishing and steering the implementation of business strategy and, in particular, to ensure that:

• more emphasis is given to understanding tomorrow's customer needs, supplier capabilities and the potential for strategic relationships
• the use of technology is managed in a more comprehensive, creative

and strategic manner than hitherto. Technology is highlighted as a vital corporate link within strategic management processes

- the supplier network is developed in a strategic manner to optimize what the company does and what is delegated to suppliers in terms of product, process and technology development
- strategic management processes are audited and updated to ensure they achieve the insight, innovation, focus, flexibility, culture, commitment and behaviour essential to continued success
- the necessary people capabilities are developed integrally with, and in support of, strategic change programmes
- change programmes are focused on and driven towards specific and timely strategic performance indicators.

We emphasize the need to integrate decisions to invest in accessing and developing technology for new products, services, processes and systems within the framework of a corporate strategy as opposed to treating them as functionally sponsored sub-strategic or operational decisions.

These processes are essentially practical and based on the authors' experience as senior executives and consultants rather than on pure academic research. The book provides a blend of new and matured ideas which, in strategic combination, break new ground.

We believe that this book fills a vital gap in the development and use of the strategy formulation process and provides a stimulus towards more comprehensive strategic decisions and actions — actions which can lead to sustained competitive success for both customers and suppliers. Neither can live long without the other.

The book is structured to be used as the basis for active in-company strategic audit, analysis and action planning as well as a support text for management seminars and MBA-type programmes. The integrated audits provide a basis for practical reviews and updates based on best practice. They will be found to be vital inputs to Total Strategic Management (TSM) and Total Quality Management (TQM) programmes as well as being complementary to Innovation Tool Kits. As such it provides a worthwhile read and source of ideas for both directors and academics world-wide.

Chapter 1   reviews the critical issues and implications for the strategic management process which are likely to face top management in the future. The background and views expressed in the first edition have been updated and expanded upon.

Chapter 2   highlights the need for a more strategic approach to customer alliances and relations, with alliances based on customers' strategic needs and the potential of available proven technology.

Chapter 3   reviews the concept of the management of the use of technology
             as a vital competitive force, and highlights the need for top
             management's involvement and integration in the strategic
             management processes of analysis and decision-making at
             corporate and individual business level.

Chapter 4   emphasizes the need to strengthen strategic and operational
             relationships with suppliers of products and services if a
             company is to achieve its own strategic ambitions.

Chapter 5   reviews trends in the evolution of the processes of strategy
             formulation and implementation, and provides valuable
             ideas for strengthening existing processes, including the
             incorporation of stronger customer, supplier and technology
             dimensions.

Chapter 6   presents a new and balanced view of the importance and key
             dimensions of company culture in facilitating timely changes
             in corporate strategy, capability and implementation of cor-
             porate development programmes. A new corporate culture
             audit is included.

Chapter 7   outlines the impact of the changes implicit in previous chapters
             on the role, practice and culture of chairmen, chief executives
             and top management teams.

Chapter 8   considers the integration of the processes for the develop-
             ment of the supportive knowledge and skills required by
             directors, top management and business teams with those for
             the successful implementation of strategic decisions.

Chapter 9   establishes a firm and novel basis for planning, monitoring
             and controlling the strategic development of the business
             and company culture in an integrated manner.

Chapter 10   demonstrates how the concepts, management processes and
             skills presented and discussed in earlier chapters have been
             applied in practice by a range of companies, educational
             establishments and government agencies.

Each of the chapters includes a number of new concepts, ideas and an
integrated series of diagnostic audit check-lists. We wish our readers an
interesting read and fruitful audits, and hope that — in combination —
they lead to sustained future competitiveness. In the Postscript a help line
is offered to readers seeking further practical guidance.

Richard S. Handscombe
Philip A. Norman

ACKNOWLEDGEMENTS

This book owes its existence to the many associates, clients, seminar participants, earlier employers and international friends who have shared with us their achievements and apprehension regarding the quality of the strategic management process. We acknowledge their preparedness to test ideas in practice and their belief that things rarely stand still in a competitive world.

Further, we acknowledge the support of management and academic readers, and commentators world-wide to the first edition. Also acknowledged are the valiant attempts of new entrepreneurs in Central and Eastern Europe to translate and apply many aspects of the book in creating and tackling emergent market economies. Many have indicated a concern that the real issues for tomorrow are not being given sufficient consideration, and that the strategy process is still too often based on management concepts and processes relevant to the early 1980s rather than the 1990s.

Since the first edition in 1989, the subsequent South East Asian International edition in 1990 and the Spanish edition in 1992, many national and international initiatives have been taken which integrate with, and give additional support to, many of our propositions. In this edition we provide an enriched starting point for developing solutions for tomorrow, and acknowledge with thanks the broad spectrum of accumulated wisdom that has challenged and stimulated our thinking.

CRITICAL ISSUES FOR TOP MANAGEMENT TEAMS IN THE 1990s

The achievement of competitive success in tomorrow's international business environment will continue to be tough. Success will require new skills in several dimensions of Total Strategic Management (TSM). Increasingly, practical top management teams recognize the vital need for enriched strategic insights, processes and skills.

What are they? What do they mean in practice?

Where does your business stand today? Are you prepared to exploit tomorrow's opportunities?

The top management challenge

Top management teams around the world face a period of unprecedented business opportunities — but also unprecedented risks. Tomorrow will not be the same as yesterday in the private or public domain for large, medium or small business enterprises. Top management must recognize, grasp and achieve 10 fundamental objectives to secure a firm basis for competitive success in national, international and global markets.

1. The achievement of *sound business performance standards* and concurrent strategic development ahead of national and international competitors.

2. A continuous watch on trends and cross impacts for *early warning of new opportunities and risks* and *prompt responses*.

3. The creation of *committed strategic relationships or alliances with key customers*.

4. The *effective access and use of technology* to satisfy customers' strategic needs, improve productivity and establish or maintain environmental standards on an economic basis.

5. The *effective leadership of suppliers* to secure optimum risk interfaces between what the company does and what suppliers do.

6. The development of a *comprehensive but flexible Total Strategic Man-*

agement (TSM) approach geared to the achievement of best practice standards that transcend many Total Quality Management (TQM) programmes.

7. The use of *competitive and time effective management processes* to review, update, integrate and implement visions, decisions and plans for tomorrow, whether in expansionary or recessionary times.

8. The development and maintenance of *productive and dynamic roles* for the top management triumvirate — the directors, general managers and product/service business managers.

9. The effective use and development of more competent, worldly, aware and *business driven top management and support teams.*

10. The establishment and *continuing evolution of a balanced company culture* that, through corporate and individual achievements and behaviour, satisfies the challenges, beliefs and business values of customers, employees, suppliers, financiers and other stakeholders.

At first sight, the 10 objectives may not look entirely new. As individual statements they are not. But they are new in the context of the business environment of the 1990s. Taken together in context, their impact on future business strategy, and the complexity of the tasks involved, will present many top management teams with new issues to be considered and acted upon with diligence. For many, implementing the tasks will be onerous. Top management teams need to consider them and start to take appropriate action now with a recognition that only best business and management practice is now good enough. Even for today's successful management teams the tasks represent a substantial additional work-load. For the less successful companies, they represent a substantial, exacting but essential corporate development challenge and also represent areas of significant risks if not managed in an objective and systematic manner.

The 1980s and early 1990s saw major developments in the business environment for world-wide companies, particularly in Western Europe and the US. Present indications are that the 1990s will see additional substantial further developments as Europe adjusts to the competitive conditions of the post-1992 Single European Market and the desires of the increasing number of countries applying to join the EC before the year 2000.

In South East Asia, companies will need to adjust to increases in cost base and a tightening of business controls and ethics. In parallel, Eastern and Central Europe will make valiant attempts to start to catch up with leading industrial nations. However, at the same time leading nations are driving themselves towards tougher management, business and environmental standards. For developing countries, enormous challenges remain in both the industrial and agricultural sectors. The mix of opportunities and risks has never been as extensive and complex. Change is seen to be here to stay.

Change needs to be managed in a pro-active manner. Top management must, therefore, modify existing management practice and culture, and take on methodologies more appropriate to tomorrow's highly competitive and changing environment. Firstly, a deeper and even more determined sense of strategic mission or purpose will be required. Second, a close integration between the key aspects of operational and strategic management and their effectiveness must be secured. Third, significant investment in manager and management team development will be required to establish an essential practical conscious competence in areas such as strategic decision-making, opportunity and risk management, and innovation — including lateral thinking and team leadership of realistic strategic implementation plans.

The development and day-to-day use of the above competences by all levels of management on a continuous and consistent basis provide the essential cornerstones of tomorrow's corporate culture. It is accepted that many successful companies have now made progress in moving towards a corporate culture built on the foundations of competence in strategy formulation and implementation, the management of innovation, and management development. The culture of an organization needs to be developed in support of the process of strategy development and implementation, and not vice versa. Also, it is contended (and will be demonstrated) that the changes of the 1980s and emerging critical issues for the 1990s give rise to requirements for new key capabilities at individual, team and corporate levels if competitive standards of performance are to be set, achieved and sustained. Among the many business issues facing top management, three stand out as the most critical as a consequence of their impact on business strategy and the consideration and resolution of other issues.

1. The need to establish strategic alliances with key customers.

2. The need for integrated strategies for the effective access and use of relevant technology in all areas of the business.

3. The need to consider strategic contracts with key suppliers.

The issues are interrelated and, in later sections, we outline the additional management dimensions concerned with the effective management of customers, the use of technology and suppliers. We propose that the three issues must be incorporated into established approaches to strategy in a unified and integrated manner. This will result in a major reappraisal of the top management skills required for tomorrow. The needs identified

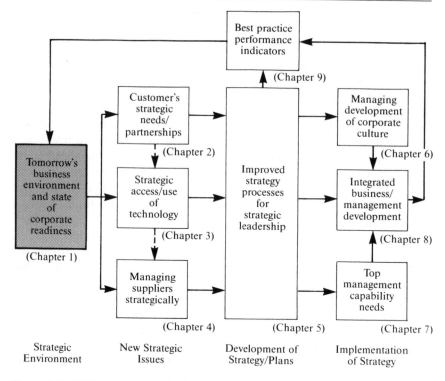

Figure 1.1 1990s management process issues

will have a major impact on management development plans and processes.

Figure 1.1 provides a framework for this evaluation of corporate readiness and for the book as a whole. Each box relates to a specific issue and chapter. Chapter 10 provides application examples related to each chapter.

The succeeding sections of this chapter develop the following topics:

- the reasons for giving emphasis to customer strategies, the effective strategic use of technology and suppliers
- the impact on corporate management concepts and style with particular reference to new dimensions in the leadership role of the chief executive officer and board of directors
- the introduction of the concept of strategic profiling. This is a concept designed to help identify and respond to the missing links in your business management practice compared with the criteria for competitive success in the future. The chapter concludes with a basic audit questionnaire which provides an assessment against the levels of management practice required for success in the 1990s. The audit is

expanded in scope and scale in subsequent chapters to provide a comprehensive statement of best practice and a diagnostic view of the
strengths and weaknesses of the business.

The emerging role of customer strategy

Significant market developments have taken place, and continue to take
place, which highlight the need to form strategic relationships and under-
standings with key customers and suppliers. The following seven major
developments point companies in this direction:

1. The shortening of product life-cycles, coupled with a significant speci-
    fication upgrading at each change in product design, can only be har-
    nessed by close customer/supplier strategic relations, e.g., the impact
    of micro-electronics on the white goods industry, compact disc *v.* digital
    tape, the design of the automobile, etc.

2. The global development of markets in key product areas in which
    only the best international products are the winners. The number of
    products which are truly international is growing as a percentage of
    total trade. For example, most quartz watch movements sold world-
    wide are of Japanese creation, the large-scale ROM/RAM chips are
    principally Japanese, the global on-line financial services offered by
    the major international banks, and so on. The removal of technical
    barriers will open up markets, but the successful companies are likely
    to have jumped the barriers already by pre-emptive competitive
    moves on an international basis.
       Good product packages exhibit fitness for purpose, productive bene-
    fits for the customer, quality and reliability of delivery, commissioning
    and total customer service.

3. A focus on the total quality of the product or service as a key inter-
    national marketing priority. Again, Japan has understood this problem
    from the point of view of the product but can only remain successful
    by strategic integration of priorities and objectives with suppliers.
    Deregulation has prompted a number of airlines and banks to make
    major efforts to sustain service initiatives on a long-term basis. The
    Quality Awards and Marketing Quality Assurance Certification now
    attracting international interest will accelerate action.

4. The increasing number of strategically minded customers who are
    looking for strategic relationships with suppliers who have the desire
    and capability to match their strategic intentions. For example, the
    aerospace contractors who require their sub-contractors to match

their strategic marketing objectives in terms of future specification improvement and overseas/offset manufacturing, and the international retail chains who become more demanding in terms of design value for money.

The impact of Japanese car manufacturers on raising the quality aspirations and performance of local suppliers in Europe, the US and Pacific Basin is a vivid example. This is being repeated in other industries in which Japan is becoming the lead nation.

5. Dealing with the competitive pressures of over-capacity in Western industry. The UK and US have had to face these problems in the 1980s, but the emergence of the Single European Market in 1992 and Central and Eastern European developments will ensure that this issue is extended across the EC in the 1990s. Only the best prepared and coordinated businesses will survive to prosper from this rationalization, and close customer/supplier strategic relationships will be crucial to both. The successful will gain and sustain the benefit of exposure to some of the world's most demanding but best customers. Having dealt with over-capacity in the 1980s will not exempt US and UK companies from the pressures of the 1990s.

6. The emergence of new trade blocks represents a challenge to many industries with global consciousness. The establishment of direct international trading coupled with, in some cases, industrial investment in competing blocks makes close strategic understanding of customers and suppliers essential.

7. Since the publication of the first edition of this book, a seventh development has occurred which strengthens our view that no top manager can take comfort from historic achievements. Many small and large, particularly high tech, companies are failing in the early 1990s. But this is not a repeat of the early 1980s. While poor businesses were caught out in the 1980s it is now *good* companies which are failing because of the inexorable build up in competition. As emphasized throughout the text, only best practice companies can be reasonably sure of survival.

The major issue facing businesses is, therefore, how to be competitively successful in a time when products/services have to be the best internationally, and be profitable, with shorter life-cycles and rapid specification change, while over-capacity in Western industry and the competitive pressures of Japan and other Eastern countries are increasing. It is clearly crucial to develop a strategic relationship with the company's prime customers and become dedicated to making them more competitive in their own chosen markets. This is increasingly true for consumer and financial service industries as well as for manufacturing industries. A common issue is the increasingly open availability of basic enabling technologies — if one looks with open and enquiring eyes.

The effective and strategic use of technology

The 1980s saw the emergence of a number of new technologies from trial applications to global use. Technology is now recognized as the source of major improvement to the effectiveness of a wide range of products/services, e.g., in micro-electronics in consumer products and wide PC application in businesses, synthetic yarns in textiles, new ingredients in foodstuffs, diagnostic agents and equipment in healthcare, and so on.

As a consequence, leading companies are widening their vision of what constitutes relevant technology and its inherent business opportunities. The past decade has brought the realization of a wide and widening gap between 'available technology' and 'technology in use' — as illustrated in Fig. 1.2. Successful companies are now increasingly looking beyond

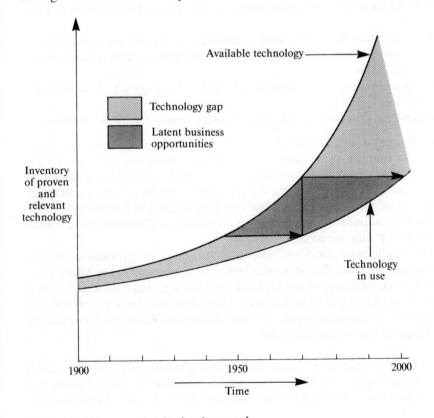

Figure 1.2   The emerging 'technology gap'

traditional in-house research and development and exploring the possibility of accessing external technology on a national and world-wide basis. The competitive opportunities thus opened up are very significant and the risks associated with being late in the game potentially very high.

In the 1980s many companies started to use well-proven (somewhere) technologies that first emerged in the 1960s for new products and processes. For instance, the following technologies were available but not widely used in the period 1950–70: composite materials, superconductivity, genetic engineering, electronic super chips and lasers. This phenomenon has continued in the 1990s. Examples include biotechnology testing and diagnostic equipment, intelligent electronics, smart card, recycling of plastic bottles, engine emission systems and intelligent packaging.

The principal issue for any business, therefore, is how to make more effective use of the appropriate available technology in products/services/processes/systems at the right time, irrespective of sources. This will require strategic company-wide initiatives to:

- build awareness of trends, potential sources and availability of technology
- make better use of the total technology in current use somewhere in the world, whether in industry, government, research institutes or universities
- take advantage of accessible relevant technology which is available but not yet in use
- develop processes to review technology needs across the business.

As discussed earlier, the dimensions of this critical issue are much broader than the management of R & D and demand treatment as a key element in the processes used for strategy formulation and implementation. The issues also have important implications for the selection and development of top management and this is discussed in Chapters 7 and 8. However, of immediate importance is the degree of technological awareness of top management.

In parallel with the developments identified in the previous section on customer and supplier strategies, other developments have taken place (or are taking place) which highlight the strategic importance of striving for the effective use of technology. The following seven major developments are considered among the most important. Each has an impact on a range of important industries.

1. The demonstrated ability of developing countries to exploit outside technologies to gain a strong market position in selected areas in a short timescale by effective management of the use of existing technology.

2. A recognition by governments and industry in developed countries of the 'real' benefits to be obtained by effective management of future key technologies such as information technology, biotechnology, advanced materials and nanotechnology, in an integrated manner.

3. Changes in the structure of industries and industrial companies to strengthen and focus activities in key technology areas for developing future high added-value businesses, e.g., European restructuring moves in telecommunications between GEC, Siemens, Plessey; establishment in USGE of *specific* technology groupings in future key technologies, Nestlé and Rowntrees in ingredient, process and distribution technology.

4. The rapid development of the science/technology park concept in Europe and the US to expand and accelerate the rate of transfer of applied science into usable product/process and system technology. In parallel, Japan and Taiwan are attempting to form a permanent association between university-based applied research in key technologies and industrial/government research and industry within the Technopolis concept.

    Other investments are gaining pace following the pioneering French developments of Sophia Antipoles. Major countries have competing projects, and leading science parks compete as business locations on the basis of access to technology, university educated work-force, international communication, costs, leisure facilities and a clean environment. Among the smaller nations, Malta competes as a strategic product development and distribution base linking the four axes of the Mediterranean for the twenty-first century. The number of UK projects expands — international companies often being the first to grasp the opportunities. Time waits for no one in today's business environment.

5. The pressures of international competition are resulting in shorter product life-cycles and bigger step-changes in technology at each stage. This reinforces the need to understand customer strategy and to invest in the effective management of the use of technology, and includes making full use of strategic technology partnerships with suppliers as an important means of access.

6. The search for higher added-value, while still remaining price and specification competitive, places heavy emphasis on making full and effective use of technology already available to develop manufacturing/operating processes and systems. For many industries, improved use of technology, and not labour reduction, is the major contributor to increased competitiveness.

7. The pressures in developed countries to deal with social and environmental problems, and the pressures from the Third World to solve their survival problems, are growing. Enabling technology is available to deal with these problems. However, substantial improvements in effectiveness of introduction are required for solutions to become politically affordable and within the perceived scope of business social responsibility. Where there's a will. Technology has been found waiting in the wings for biodegradation, CFC replacement, catalytic converters, disease free plants, etc.

The emergent key issue is that of *making effective use of available and emerging technology for products/services/processes/systems* across the full spectrum of business activities. The base of available world technology is growing exponentially, and every year the gap between the technology being used and the technology available is widening. In theory, *there is no limit* to technology as a resource. There is, therefore, an urgent need to establish processes and practices that enable business to increasingly penetrate the present gap between available and used technology in a controlled manner. Recent history in a number of developing countries would suggest that they recognize the power of effective use of technology in closing their specific gaps in an objective way. In this respect, could China provide tomorrow's future competitive shock, on a 25-year time perspective like Japan or one of the Central European countries with Japanese or German support? Where does your company stand today? Are you fully prepared? Ask yourself the following five basic questions:

1. What are the relevant new technologies today and tomorrow for your customers, the company and suppliers?

2. When were the technologies first developed and what has delayed their application? Are there still external or internal bottlenecks?

3. Are the needs being managed and satisfied in an integrated manner?

4. Who in the company is accountable for technology management?

5. Who in the company is managing the issue professionally?

Undoubtedly, the *effective use of technology* is emerging as a key issue for the 1990s within many companies. Yet only recently did reference works on strategy, creativity, innovation, entrepreneurship and intrapreneurship start to deal more than superficially with the topic. Those companies with foresight are recognizing technology as a strategic resource that ranks alongside people and finance. Technology is a facilitator, enhancer and interpreter of competitive opportunities and impacts on all competitive aspects of the business in terms of:

- product technology
- production process technology
- raw material technology
- distribution technologies
- information and promotional technologies
- customer service and administration technologies
- customer support technology
- product service technology
- supplier technology
- environmental technology.

With such importance, technological analysis and decision-making must play a part in all facets of strategic decisions, action and control. The point may seem obvious, but, throughout our extensive research, we found it difficult to believe how very few publications on corporate strategy and competitive strategy deal with the issue of technology, or even include the word in the index. Equally astounding was the distinct absence of reference to customers and their strategic needs, including technology, in spite of the growing interest in total customer care pro-grammes, total quality programmes and Quality Awards.

In the last five years some initiatives have been taken but most indications are that there is a world-wide lack of awareness of the importance of these issues remaining within businesses and a lack of sense of purpose in taking them on board.

There is a significant interest in Japan and a nervous awakening in the US and EC, but to date too few Western companies appear to have grasped the value of the effective use of the total spectrum of global tech-nology (as distinct from reliance on in-company creation of technology) in their competitive situation. How then will companies deal with the technological business environment of the 1990s? What emergent con-cepts and processes can help? Those companies searching for new ideas and taking them on board have the opportunity to establish a firm base to become industrial leaders. Such companies are likely to develop the effective use of technology as the 'ethos' of the company for the 1990s.

A strong corporate culture with a firm dedication to the effective use of technology can be a winning competitive strategy. Strategic technology is critical to many customer–supplier relationships. Technology enables timely responses to emergent market opportunities.

The process of developing the effective use of technology on a stage-by-stage basis is shown in Fig. 1.3 and illustrates the phases of the use of technology in the following order:

Operational and tactical — internal short-term improvements through operating or manufacturing processes and systems which, in due course, begin to impact on strategic decisions in products and services.

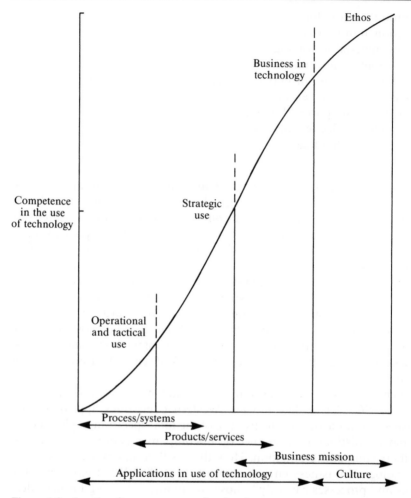

Figure 1.3 Levels of management of technology

Strategic — largely concerned with applying technology in new products and services focused on improving customer competitiveness or providing total quality or lifestyle benefits through products or services supplied to the ultimate end-user.

Business in technology — the effective management of technology can provide major opportunities for those companies which recognize that they are in the 'business' of technology management, e.g., contract product development, technology management consultancy, engineering conceptual design, or as a route to diversification, etc.

Ethos — where the mission of the business and its culture are dictated by the effective use of technology as the key area of business activity, and where no market sectors are barred from successful exploitation for technological reasons. At this level of managing the use of technology, a company can be considered to be technology *driven*. However, in such a situation, professional marketing cannot be ignored. A visionary marketing approach is essential if key customers' strategic needs are to be stimulated and satisfied in a timely and profitable manner. More technology-led businesses are likely to emerge from major manufacturing groups in the 1990s, beyond the drives for least cost production and total quality management. The customer dimension is discussed in depth in Chapter 2, the strategic use of technology in Chapter 3, and the development of culture in Chapter 6. Each has major implications for chief executives and top management teams.

The impact on top management and their development needs

So far, we have discussed the reasons for the addition of the following management tasks:

- leadership of continuous change process by the ongoing audit, challenge and integration of operational and strategic management practices
- managing the strategic dimensions of customer and supplier relationships and effective use of technology.

These two tasks represent a substantial addition for today's successful management teams and a substantial development challenge for less successful companies and teams. It will be argued later in the book that the additional management dimensions, concerned with effective (strategic) use of technology, give rise to substantial tasks in both manager and organization development.

In responding to the needs for change outlined in earlier sections, the following issues need to be addressed by top management:

- how should a business be directed and controlled in the future and what, therefore, is the role of the chief executive, chairman and top management team?
- how to create the necessary broad experience to be pro-active and successful in business — adding the new dimensions of customer strategy and technology
- how to motivate, organize and develop people at all levels to respond to the rapidly changing competitive situation
- how and when to use higher education or training to develop not only generic MCI-type competences but also customer and technological awareness
- how to recruit and retain enough of the right graduates with the potential

to become future top managers and functional specialists. A broad general awareness of how their specialism relates to other specialisms in achieving corporate competitiveness has become vital in organizational productivity.

- where will essential technology come from: in-house, by collaboration, or by buying in? Who will access the 'right' technology at the right time?
- where will future chief executives come from?

In view of the key role of the chief executive, this last point is particularly important and it is necessary to consider the following influences on the way the role, style and key capabilities of both chief executive officers (CEOs) and top functional managers have developed over the last 20–30 years, particularly from a UK viewpoint:

- the development environment and priorities of the 1960s–1980s
- progressive developments in the role and activities of boards of directors and the rising role of the non-executive or independent director
- the development of chief executives via peer groups/action learning and coaching by non-executive directors and company advisers
- the role of company boards in dealing with strategy, customer and supplier analysis and major problem solving
- the treatment of technology as a regular board issue
- the role of legislation and government business policies as an impact on UK business development over the past 20–30 years
- trends in UK business success and failure over the past 20–30 years including decline in manufacturing market shares and balance of payments.

1. THE DEVELOPMENT ENVIRONMENT AND PRIORITIES

Most senior CEOs and functional heads have passed through formative stages in their personal development in various periods of changing priorities in business, for example:

Period	Practical emphasis in UK
1960–1970	Project management Cost control Marketing productivity and technology
1970–1980	Cost containment People management Strategic planning Industrial relations and productivity

1980–1990	Total quality
	Strategy
	Creativity
	Innovation
	Culture and productivity
1990–	Strategy implementation
	International technology
	Customer/supplier chains
	Leadership development
	Competitive culture

The essential change has been the shift in emphasis from the *operational* approach in the 1960s to *strategy* in the late 1980s and the emphasis on making things happen quicker and more securely in the 1990s — not everyone has kept pace!

An almost inevitable consequence is that the formative years of most senior managers in the UK and US have been dominated by operational skills and hence they often find the conceptual tasks of creativity, innovation and strategy difficult to undertake in many small as well as large companies. The authors' training courses for directors from Eastern and Central Europe indicate that their problems are even greater. How, then, can CEOs and their colleagues face the new challenges of the 1990s and beyond?

Initially, the gap has to be closed (and can only be closed) by an objective approach to strategy formulation and implementation. In some industries the task is very tough since leading South East Asian competitors recognized, developed and exploited some of the vital competences earlier than their Western counterparts.

2. THE PROGRESSIVE DEVELOPMENT OF THE BOARD OF DIRECTORS

There is an established view that board effectiveness means corporate effectiveness, and that, in turn, means management effectiveness. The board is, therefore, the key instrument, and in an environment of change has to steer/direct the affairs of the company with relevant skills and care.

It was in the 1980s that the role of boards first became a dynamic issue, stimulated by the competitive need to survive recession and to build beyond this survival. However, one can question whether many boards have really grasped their new role in relation to strategy and their proactive responsibilities in promoting future change and the growth of professional competence required to compete in key market areas. The role requires new skills in the boardroom and a new approach to collective accountability. Generally, the approach to the use of outside directors in the 1980s is not a solution to this problem, and, while remaining valuable for independence and specific experience, their role must change for the future. They must become visionary contributors or even agents for change — as distinct from a source of (historic) accumulated wisdom. This has major implications for the selection of directors and also for the manner in which boards are used.

3. THE DEVELOPMENT OF CHIEF EXECUTIVES

This has been a difficult issue to deal with for the last 20 years. Continuing dilemmas include:

- the relative merits of internal indigenous growth (with inherent potential tunnel vision and lack of worldliness) and outside/mobile development (with the problem of lack of contact with company culture)
- how to develop CEOs from management who are experienced mainly in dealing with constraints and national markets when tomorrow's needs are for a pro-active management and global vision
- how to achieve the continuous personal development of the chief executive as the business needs change
- who does the chief executive discuss problems with? The chairman, non-executive directors, external consultant? Do networking and action learning provide help?

None of these issues have clear-cut answers, but in our experience most chief executives find them to be problematical and exacerbated by periods where the business has major problems, or where the outside world (competition, markets, customers' technology, etc.) is changing rapidly. In this respect, the 1980s were difficult and the 1990s will be even more so.

4. THE ROLE OF COMPANY BOARDS IN STRATEGY, CREATIVITY AND INNOVATION

All these activities require multi-functional analysis, judgements, opportunity analysis and decision-making. Most boards are unable to act this way and rely heavily on specialist reports from either consultants, company specialist departments or problem-oriented task-forces. The decisions are often *taken* following ill-informed, unbalanced or very brief discussions, with the consequent implicit acceptance of the risks that follow. At best, many companies still rely on a five-year-plan without a real strategic framework with the flexibility to exploit unplanned opportunities that can occur at any time, even following a thorough strategic analysis. The world never stands still and corporate oyster catchers watch eagerly for titbits of intelligence that offer competitive advantage.

5. TECHNOLOGY AS A BOARD ISSUE

The boards of many companies do not yet identify with and treat technology as a major strategic asset. There are three main reasons. Firstly, because technology is often regarded as synonymous with R&D activity; second, for secrecy reasons R&D is often divorced from other functions in terms of communication, location, focus and culture. Third, because the technical directors are often regarded as not commercial and, therefore, unable to contribute to the discussion and decisions related to broad market issues.

At best, the boards in many companies receive an annual report from the board member responsible for R&D or technical affairs. The document usually aims to present a picture of past technical achievement plus isolated future objectives. Too often, boards do not regard themselves as required to, or capable of, setting or evaluating technology strategy. Certainly, too few company boards regard the acquisition and competitive use of technology as a board issue. It is interesting to note that the leading Japanese chief executive officers claim that their boards spend 70–80 per cent of directors' meetings envisaging and evaluating customer and technological opportunities. Financial management and control are largely dedicated through strict guide-lines and commitments to a second tier of management who have authority to act.

In summary, we conclude that:

- the development environment for most current chief executive officers and top managers has been based on operational priorities and culture
- serious questions need to be asked regarding the effectiveness of current board concepts for the future
- the process of creating chief executive officers and their future development is ill-defined, and probably inadequate for the future
- boards generally do not deal sufficiently well with general issues of strategy, creativity, innovation performance and technology: yet they need the ability to capitalize on change and chaos — the best will have benefited from the Black Monday of October 1987 and the global recession of the early 1990s
- the role of the chairman and chief executive in strategy formulation needs to expand, i.e., they need to establish an effective process and ensure that directors and senior managers are literate in the strategy process and in all corporate functions at senior management level:

technologists must understand finance, marketing, production, etc., and vice versa. Only then can full participation be achieved in board decision-making as an intellectual and creative team process. In particular, there is an urgent need to make senior management 'technology literate' in all areas relevant to the *use* of technology across all company/ business activities, and they must be willing to access and evaluate technology from all and any source

- management in the 1990s will need to exhibit many new characteristics and achieve results in areas where they are not measured today; in particular, in the establishing and monitoring of the achievement of corporate development objectives.

The level of change required to respond to the challenges of the 1990s remains substantial in most companies, in most functions, and at many levels of organization.

Overall, the quantum change requires that the future is approached on a well-prepared basis. In this way, change can be grasped as an unexploited opportunity. The audit that follows provides a first opportunity.

Identifying the missing links in your business: an initial audit

An initial audit to enable your top team to review the current position of your business in relation to the critical issues identified and discussed in Chapter 1 is provided on the pages that follow.

The audit process suggested is:

Step 1   The completion of the basic audit questionnaire presented in Tables 1.1–1.5 and the audit summary of Table 1.6.

Step 2   The plotting of the results of Step 1 on the company/business strategic profile chart, as shown in Table 1.7. A completed and blank chart are provided with an explanation.

Step 3   Evaluation of the implications of the strengths and weaknesses of the profile identified by the strategic profile to identify areas of opportunity and risk.

Step 4   Start to develop an action plan to build on the strengths, and remove critical weaknesses identified. The audit questionnaires included in Chapters 2–9 will help you add detail to the action plan as you read further chapters. Use the book as your personal workbook and record.

The audit documents are designed around five company/business key areas:

1. *Business results* — an assessment of the current business results and the state of the strategic development of the business.

2. *Customer strategy and competitive situation* — an assessment of the readiness of the company in terms of the quality of customer base, customer intelligence and response, and competitor intelligence base.

3. *Use of technology* — an assessment of the effectiveness of the process of identifying and using available technology in a strategic manner.

4. *Effective use and development of people* — an assessment of the effectiveness of the way the company/business uses people and the actions taken to promote their personal and team development.

5. *Management of company culture* — an assessment of the match and support provided by the company culture to the development of the business and its people, and the achievement of leading business results.

This basic audit satisfies five fundamental needs:

1. The basis for a reflection on the issues raised in Chapter 1, before reading and considering the implications of the remainder of the book.

2. A preliminary identification of important strengths and weaknesses as the background to establishing priorities for the application of the management concepts and process described in later chapters of the book.

3. A stimulus to complete the related audit questionnaires included in Chapters 2–9.

4. A significant input to the 'SWOT' (Strengths, Weaknesses, Opportunities and Threats) or 'SOFT' (Strengths, Opportunities, Faults, Threats) analysis required as a key input to any strategic management process. It could well be part of individual work, prior to a strategy review (as discussed in Chapter 5).

5. The definition of the levels of achievement in the audit charts are designed to facilitate use by both service and manufacturing organizations.

The diagnostic approach is critical if new approaches to strategy formulation and implementation are to be tailored to the needs of the business. No single prescriptive approach can be valid. Unique business strategies and above average teams rather than generic strategies and average teams are essential ingredients of future corporate success.

Guidelines for analysing and interpreting the results of the audit commence on page 30.

Table 1.1 Basic audit questionnaire

Key Area A. Business results and overall strategic development

Business: _____ Prepared by: _____ Date: _____

Issues and questions	Situation appraisal		Assessment/Description of our current situation								What action could we take to resolve identified problems?
	Current strengths and recent successes	Current weaknesses and recent failures	Poor 1		2		3		4 Excellent		
A1. *Growth record* What is our growth record in profit before tax over the last 3 (or 5) years?			Profit declining in all product and service sectors		Profit declining in existing business and static in new areas		Profit static in existing products and growing in new areas		Profit growth in all product/service areas		
			(a)	(b)	(a)	(b)	(a)	(b)	(a)	(b)	
A2. *Customer focus* To what extent is our strategy driven by the strategies of key customers?			No conscious effort to identify and interpret customers' strategies		Strategy driven by short-term competitive situation		We have knowledge of key customers' strategy with dependence on customers' product 'champions' to set priorities		We have organized programmes to identify and support key customers' strategies for medium and longer term and joint ventures are in place		
			(a)	(b)	(a)	(b)	(a)	(b)	(a)	(b)	

	Statement 1		Statement 2		Statement 3		Statement 4	
	(a)	(b)	(a)	(b)	(a)	(b)	(a)	(b)
A3. *Product/service quality* What fraction of our sales are based on overall quality of product/service package *versus* keen low pricing?	Sales based solely on competitive product pricing		Good margins on competitive products in most established areas of business		Conscious drive to create product packages which sell on overall product quality — good margins on competitive sales		Significant part of sales in products where pricing based on product/service quality and added value package	
A4. *Strategic investments* Do we have future investment support assured for strategic development?	Rarely an issue which is raised at board/senior level meetings *Ad hoc* action if essential		Operating results and short-term projections reviewed with shareholders, banks, etc. Sometimes not full commitment		Regular internal contact with shareholders, banks, etc. on strategic matters, generally support achieved		Full and open reviews with shareholders and other sources of funding, backed by agreements	

Instructions: Review each of the questions in turn, complete a key point situation appraisal, assess which of the statements 1–4 best describes the current situation of the business, and tick the appropriate box (a). Indicate in box (b) the direction of the current trends. Lastly, plan appropriate action.

© Management of Technology Partnership 1992

22

Table 1.2 Basic audit questionnaire

Key Area B. Customer strategy and competitive situation

Business: _____ Prepared by: _____ Date: _____

Issues and questions	Situation appraisal		Assessment/Description of our current situation				What action could we take to resolve identified problems?
	Current strengths and recent successes	Current weaknesses and recent failures	Poor 1	2	3	4 Excellent	
B1. *Customer base* Do we have market leaders or trend-setters as our key customers?			We do not pursue market leaders as principal customers	We have some business with leaders but this is declining	We have some business with leaders and it is growing	Leaders form major part of our sales and also this is growing continuously	
			(a) (b)	(a) (b)	(a) (b)	(a) (b)	
B2. *Focus on strategic needs* Extent to which our business development investment is directed to meeting *known* customer strategic needs?			Have own independent (and private) view of market. Rarely discussed with customers	Have independent view but keep customers briefed on important new plans such as product launches	Policy based on mix of own and customers' views picked up by regular market intelligence	Regular reviews with main customers as basis of development planning for our business	
			(a) (b)	(a) (b)	(a) (b)	(a) (b)	

		Major customers losing market share in stagnant or declining markets		Major customers losing market share in growth markets		Major customers holding market share in growth markets		Major customers gaining market share in growth markets	
		(a)	(b)	(a)	(b)	(a)	(b)	(a)	(b)
B3.	*Growth customers* Extent to which our main customers' business is in developing growth markets *versus* declining markets?								
B4.	*Intelligence* Extent of our knowledge of main competitor SWOTs and actions taken based on this intelligence?	Information gathered for 'conventional' competitor analysis		Main emphasis on gaining competitor pricing and specification data		Prepared to 'outgun' competitors on product development/market share		Careful analysis of all competitor data. trends. etc.. as basis for validating customer support strategies	
		(a)	(b)	(a)	(b)	(a)	(b)	(a)	(b)

Instructions: Review each of the questions in turn. complete a key-point situation appraisal. assess which of the statements 1–4 best describes the current situation of the business. and tick the appropriate box (a). Indicate in box (b) the direction of the current trends. Lastly. plan appropriate action.

© Management of Technology Partnership 1992

Table 1.3 Basic audit questionnaire

Key Area C. Effective access and use of technology

Business: _____ Prepared by: _____ Date: _____

Issues and questions	Situation appraisal		Assessment/Description of our current situation								What action could we take to resolve identified problems?
	Current strengths and recent successes	Current weaknesses and recent failures	Poor 1		2		3		4 Excellent		
			(a)	(b)	(a)	(b)	(a)	(b)	(a)	(b)	
C1. *Management process* Do we have formal technology management processes that include needs analysis for products/ services/ processes/ systems, e.g., audits, trend mapping, action plans, sourcing charts and risk analysis?			Technology is created as part of R&D and/or IT programme in annual budgets		Technical board member decides on technology programmes based on new product/ service needs including IT		Company has separate and institutional-ized plans for new product, process and system enabling technology		We have a regular review of technology needs/appli-cations as part of strategic management process. An integral part of strategy reviews		
C2. *Replacement plans* Do we have replacement plans for our key tech-nologies based on 'business strategies'?			We rely on need being identified by product/ service R&D and IT programmes		We regularly review and update our investment in 'classical' technologies. Almost totally in-house		We maintain a competitive brief plus conventional product R&D in key areas. Sometimes buy in		We establish multiple sourcing insurance pro-grammes in key technologies to reduce risks		

24

	1		2		3		4	
C3. *Suppliers* Do we build and manage a network of strategic technologies?	We do not treat suppliers as a strategic issue		Supplier selection programme is based on product/service plans		We have started to integrate technology plans with overall strategy and source well from suppliers		Yes, we manage suppliers strategically with senior level reviews at regular intervals. Joint ventures in place	
	(a)	(b)	(a)	(b)	(a)	(b)	(a)	(b)
C4. *Technology time* How much time does our board of directors/management spend on 'management of use of technology'?	We have no specific technology reviews – only investment approval for R&D and IT		We have annual R&D/IT report plus approval of R&D/IT budget for coming year		Our board deals with plans for major spend on technology for specific products, plans and IT systems		We spend significant time visualizing and action planning for new products/services/processes/systems based on available technology	
	(a)	(b)	(a)	(b)	(a)	(b)	(a)	(b)

Instructions: Review each of the questions in turn, complete a key-point situation appraisal, assess which of the statements 1–4 best describes the current situation of the business, and tick the appropriate box (a). Indicate in box (b) the direction of the current trends. Lastly, plan appropriate action.

© Management of Technology Partnership 1992

Table 1.4 Basic audit questionnaire

Key Area D. Effective use and development of people

Business: _____ Prepared by: _____ Date: _____

Issues and questions	Situation appraisal		Assessment/Description of our current situation				What action could we take to resolve identified problems?
	Current strengths and recent successes	Current weaknesses and recent failures	Poor 1	2	3	4 Excellent	
D1. *Management development* Do you have a full management development activity involving all levels up to board members?			Basic induction training for junior supervisors/managers only on 'in-house' programmes	We also sponsor graduate trainees, use courses at management schools and sponsor distance learning programmes	Continuing 'in-house' programmes up to senior manager level. Variety of sources and styles used	Achievement learning concepts used widely	
			(a) (b)	(a) (b)	(a) (b)	(a) (b)	
D2. *Team emphasis* Do we approach management development on a multi-disciplined/ multi-functional team basis?			Largely a classical exposure by 'on the job' training both before and after appointment	Mainly management training in areas such as 'finance for non-financial managers' how to harness IT. Total Quality	'In-house MCi diploma' concepts for all subjects plus management school courses using multi-discipline case study concepts	Multi-discipline/modular courses at all levels with exposure to in-house live projects for individual and team development	
			(a) (b)	(a) (b)	(a) (b)	(a) (b)	

	1		2		3		4	
D3. *Strategy involvement* Are our professional staff at all levels involved in strategy formulation and implementation?	Generally a contribution to departmental submission of five-year-plan with no follow up discussion		Contribution to five-year-plan plus planning conference for senior staff run by planners with limited top management involvement		'Strategy briefing' for senior staff based on board/planning dept. strategy—action plans developed with participation and innovative ideas sought		Professional staff involved in business and functional strategy reviews. Action plans with senior staff involved in integration and regular review of progress	
	(a)	(b)	(a)	(b)	(a)	(b)	(a)	(b)
D4. *Management effectiveness* Do we have any measures of the effectiveness of our management development programme?	No objective measures but feel it is the right thing to do in a good year. No budget in poor years		Input measures only. e.g. number of apprentices staff on courses etc. Budgets cut drastically in tough years		Conventional business ratios in people areas used as final assessment. Essential programmes sustained		Formal and relevant output indicators in use and reviewed by board. Budget may even be increased in a tough year	
	(a)	(b)	(a)	(b)	(a)	(b)	(a)	(b)

© Management of Technology Partnership 1992

Instructions: Review each of the questions in turn, complete a key-point situation appraisal, assess which of the statements 1–4 best describes the current situation of the business, and tick the appropriate box (a). Indicate in box (b) the direction of the current trends. Lastly, plan appropriate action.

Table 1.5 Basic audit questionnaire

Key Area E. Management of company culture

Business: _____ Prepared by: _____ Date: _____

Issues and questions	Situation appraisal		Assessment/Description of our current situation								What action could we take to resolve identified problems?
	Current strengths and recent successes	Current weaknesses and recent failures	Poor 1		2		3		4 Excellent		
E. *Culture support* Is our culture derived from and in support of our strategy?			Only just recognizing importance of culture		Starting to develop from a personnel perspective		Now developing from a business perspective		Established culture achieving best practice. Reflected in behaviour and results		
			(a)	(b)	(a)	(b)	(a)	(b)	(a)	(b)	
E2. *Enables rapid response* Does our culture enable speedy changes to be planned and implemented successfully?			Bureaucracy stops creativity. Tend to be late followers		Organization and systems being slimmed, but slow to respond		Changes built into firm plans and budgets but not always flexible		Organized and funded to respond quickly to changes, new opportunities and risks		
			(a)	(b)	(a)	(b)	(a)	(b)	(a)	(b)	

		No real evidence of a common focus or corporate spirit		Mission written and communicated but lip service by senior management		Employees involved in development, action and commitment growing		Accepted and committed behaviour at all levels makes mission 'live'		
E3.	Mission focused Does our mission provide and achieve a clear focus and sense of purpose?									
		(a)	(b)	(a)	(b)	(a)	(b)	(a)	(b)	
E4.	Individual/team rewards Do rewards reflect contributions to corporate achievements?	Flat rates negotiated. Few personal variations		Individual packages possible but small differences in practice		Individual rewards motivate best performers but ignore team		Encourages innovation. Reflects individual and team achievements/ contributions		
		(a)	(b)	(a)	(b)	(a)	(b)	(a)	(b)	

Instructions: Review each of the questions in turn, complete a key-point situation appraisal, assess which of the statements 1–4 best describes the current situation of the business, and tick the appropriate box (a). Indicate in box (b) the direction of the current trends. Lastly, plan appropriate action.

© Management of Technology Partnership 1992

29

ANALYSIS OF THE RESULTS OF THE BASIC AUDIT

The results of the basic audit questionnaire analysis can be analysed in two ways. (Each approach will provide guidelines for future action by your management team.)

1. On the basis of the total scores in each area, as outlined in Table 1.6.

2. The profile of the scores on an area-by-area basis, as outlined in Fig. 1.7.

TOTAL SCORES

The total score will indicate the degree of readiness of the company/business to face tomorrow's business challenges with confidence. The following broad interpretations are suggested:

Overall score: 60–80 Generally well prepared, but will need to address specific areas of weakness

30–60 Likely to be deficient in two main areas from customer/technology/people

0–30 Major problems in all areas and need for urgent actions on a broad front.

ANALYSIS OF PROFILE OF SCORES

The transfer of the scores for each sub-section, Table 1.6, to the strategic profile chart presented in Table 1.7 will help highlight:

*   the relative strengths and weaknesses
*   the areas for action
*   the balance or imbalance of the company/business
*   areas of comparative competitive advantage if sufficient market intelligence is available to also plot a key competitor
*   areas of strategic match or mismatch if sufficient market intelligence is available to also plot a key customer or key supplier.

Closing the gap

The completed profile will provide a useful basis for 'personal' or top management 'team' decisions regarding priority actions.

When the initial scores have been entered and the profile has been discussed by the management team, it is possible to establish progressive improvement objectives by adding concentric profiles moving outwards towards the best practice score of four. Objectives can be set for six- or twelve-month periods.

In a multi-divisional company the plotting of the profiles for each division has proved to be of benefit.

For purposes of illustration, the profiles of two companies have been entered on the chart in Table 1.7.

Company A is a strong operations company.
  Its main characteristics are:

- a strong financial performance
- price competitive response to meet customers' short-term needs
- relies on traditional close personal social relationships with key customers, but losing market share
- technology looked at as short-term improvements to existing products and new 'me too' products.

Priority actions are likely to include:

- Consideration of appointment of new senior management or seek a merger
- A strengthing of marketing and distribution
- Improved market intelligence in order to better understand key customers' strategic v. operational needs
- Organization to access and maximize the use of competitive technology in products, production processes, services and systems in general.

Company B is strong in research and development.
  The main characteristics are:

- A good knowledge of the technological needs of customers
- Close working relationships with key customers
- Heavy dependence on the technology lead of the customers
- Financial results diluted by lack of direction and priorities
- Continuing investment in well-structured research and development
- Limited investment in manager and team development.

Priority actions are likely to include:

- A formalized thorough approach to strategy formulation and implementation which pays significantly more attention to the outside world than hitherto; in particular to customers' strategic needs, social/environmental issues, the use of available technology and business structural options. In this way, top management will be able to identify and evaluate a range of balanced strategic profiles as options.

Table 1.6 Total score analysis

Transfer the scores from Tables 1.1–1.5 to Table 1.6.

Key areas	Score for sub-section				Total section score	Priority for action
	Q1	Q2	Q3	Q4		
A. Business results						(H,M,L)
B. Customer strategy						
C. Access/use of technology						
D. Use/development of people						
E. Management company culture						

Total score A + B + C + D		Maximum score 64

The chart will indicate the broad areas for priority action by the organization analysed.

- The communication of a visionary but practical focus for the business
- Critical issue action plans steered and monitored by the chief executive
- Drive for improved results to finance the future development of the business
- Consideration of external technology as viable alternative to some in-house technology
- An acceptance by top management of the need to provide for ongoing organization development and individual employee development on a continuing career-long basis.

WIDER APPLICATIONS OF AUDIT

The application of the basic audit can be extended to key customers, competitors and suppliers.

- Customers to gain a deeper understanding of their capabilities, needs and culture as a basis from which to develop strategic relationships
- Suppliers to check possible match or mismatch and areas in which

Table 1.7 Self-audit company/business strategic profile

A. Own company

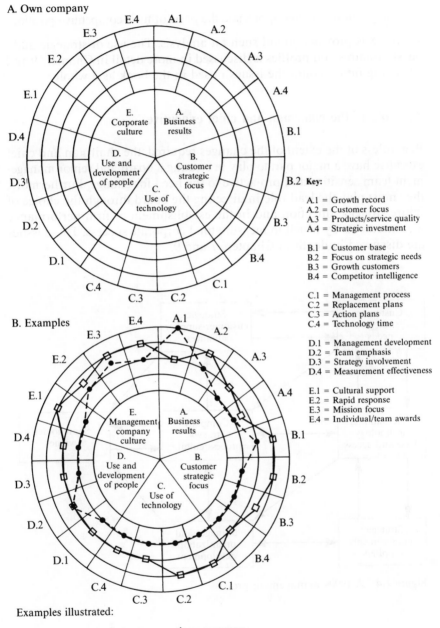

Key:

A.1 = Growth record
A.2 = Customer focus
A.3 = Products/service quality
A.4 = Strategic investment

B.1 = Customer base
B.2 = Focus on strategic needs
B.3 = Growth customers
B.4 = Competitor intelligence

C.1 = Management process
C.2 = Replacement plans
C.3 = Action plans
C.4 = Technology time

D.1 = Management development
D.2 = Team emphasis
D.3 = Strategy involvement
D.4 = Measurement effectiveness

E.1 = Cultural support
E.2 = Rapid response
E.3 = Mission focus
E.4 = Individual/team awards

B. Examples

Examples illustrated:

- - - - ● - - - - - A strong operations company

————□———— A company strong in research and development

they would require active support if a strategic relationship were considered

• Competition to better appreciate the basis of their competitive position.

Table 1.8 is provided to aid such an analysis. The use of strategic audit questionnaires and profiles is discussed in more detail in Chapters 9 and 10, taking into account the issues raised in the book as a whole.

The role of the chairman and chief executive

Regardless of the extent of the changes required, the chairman and chief executive have a major part to play in creating a board and senior management team sensitive and pro-active to the need for change. Furthermore, they must play the lead role in directing the board through the choice of future strategic direction and in the establishment of firm performance measurements by which to measure total corporate success. These issues are discussed in depth in Chapters 7 and 9.

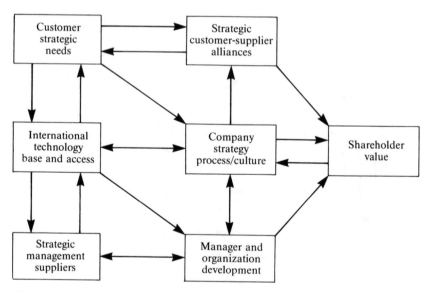

Figure 1.4 A 1990s management process

Table 1.8 Summary of basic audit questionnaire (Table 1.1). Scores for range of strategically important organizations — self, customers, competitors and suppliers

Key area	Sub-section		Company business	Key customer	Key competitor	Key supplier
A. Business results and overall strategic developments	A.1	Growth record				
	A.2	Customer focus				
	A.3	Product/service quality				
	A.4	Strategic investment				
B. Customer strategy and competitive situation	B.1	Customer base				
	B.2	Focus on strategic needs				
	B.3	Growth customers				
	B.4	Competitor intelligence				
C. Effective use of technology	C.1	Management process				
	C.2	Replacement plans				
	C.3	Action plans				
	C.4	Technology time				
D. Effective use and development of people	D.1	Management development				
	D.2	Team emphasis				
	D.3	Strategy involvement				
	D.4	Measurement effectiveness				
E. Effective management corporate culture	E.1	Support to strategy				
	E.2	Enables rapid change				
	E.3	Mission				
	E.4	Rewards				

Basic analysis   Optional analyses

© Management of Technology Partnership 1989

The next three chapters focus on the vital missing links in the strategic development of many companies:

1. The importance of strategic relationships with key customers — Chapter 2.

2. The strategic opportunities in the effective use of relevant technology — Chapter 3.

3. The strategic management of suppliers — Chapter 4.

If these links are not forged in the strategy process (see Chapter 5), the future competitiveness of even the best businesses will be undermined. This forging will require improvements in the total strategic management process.

The audits built into each chapter provide a practical starting point to taking today's first steps towards improved corporate effectiveness and shareholder value within the framework of a management process for the 1990s, as shown in Fig. 1.4.

Chapters 6–10 are concerned with the processes involved in implementing strategy and making things happen in a professional manner. Throughout the chapters the nature of and need for best practice business and management standards for success in the 1990s are highlighted.

ACHIEVING A CUSTOMER FOCUS FOR THE FUTURE

Future competitive success will depend more on an in-depth understanding and focus on customers' strategic needs and suppliers' strategic capabilities and less on a very detailed analysis of competitors' short-term actions. What are those needs? What are the practical implications? Where does your business stand? Are you prepared for tomorrow? Are you ready to manage both customers and suppliers strategically? Have effective strategic partnerships or alliances been established?

The challenge of supplier success factors

Successful suppliers of products and services in the future will most likely be those with the capability to create and sustain strategic relationships or alliances with key customers. Relationships in which customers feel they have a pro-active partner, sensitive to their future and changing needs, and providing genuine strategic support and guidance.

Successful suppliers are likely to be characterized by many of the following features:

1. Have an active strategy focused on the ongoing provision of timely high added-value products and services that are recognized by customers as value for money. A thorough analysis of customers' future needs being seen as an important input to the strategic decisions, as illustrated in Fig. 2.1.

2. The continuous design, development, and distribution of products and services which increasingly satisfy the medium- and long-term strategic needs of customers as opposed to only the satisfaction of short-term operational, problem-solving or occasional crisis needs.

3. A design, development and test market capability in a country and location, often in the 'home' country, that has the most demanding customer/supplier relationships, and close working relationships with the most demanding customer wherever he or she is in the world.

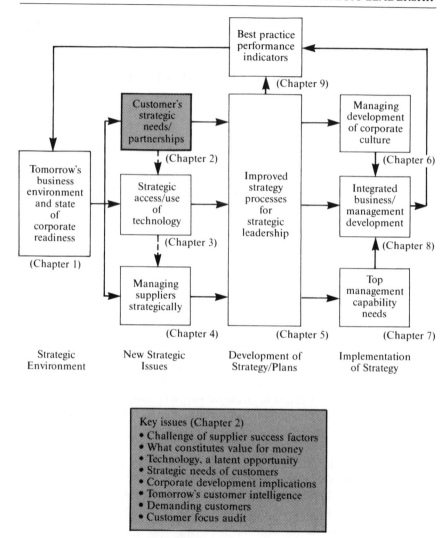

Figure 2.1 Analysis of customer's strategies — a key input to 1990s strategic management

4. The capability to support customers in accessing, evaluating and using relevant available innovations and technology to design, produce, distribute and support their products and services.

5. A constant search for new relevant technologies and applications of the available technology. A search that is focused, innovative and international in extent.

6. An ability to translate 'imported' ideas into competitive products, processes, services and systems, at least as speedily as the translation of the results of internal research and development programmes. This became a major strength of the leading Japanese companies *vis-à-vis* their US and EC competitors during the 1980s; the issue now scares many US managers as they plan for the 1990s. European managers need to pay heed in planning for 1993 and beyond.

7. Strategic collaboration with key customers and suppliers where beneficial for research and development rather than joint ventures with international competitors who may use the collaboration for parallel research to 'in-company' programmes.

8. A top management team that is both customer and technologically aware and willing to use that knowledge in an integrated manner.

9. A proven capability to help customers make significant step changes in the utilization of available technology as illustrated in Fig. 2.2, and helping key customers recognize the timely need to replace their existing technology.

10. A company culture which matches that of key customers in all 'strategic matters'.

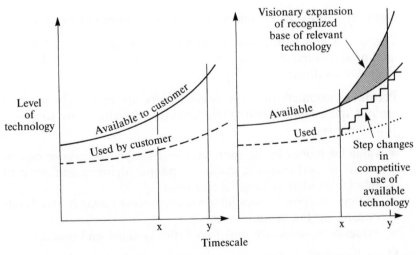

A. Position before establishing strategic supplier/customer relationship

B. Position after establishing successful strategic supplier/customer relationship

Figure 2.2 Exploiting a customer's technology gap

An effective strategic supplier will inspire the customer to: firstly, recognize a wide and deeper source of relevant technology, and second, to develop new or improved products/services and support processes/systems that utilize a higher percentage of the available technology than hitherto. The benefit will be improved results and an improved future competitive position for both customer and supplier.

Achieving this new corporate culture will be a tough task. It is a task that will require a heavy involvement of top management in leading the strategic development process and being personally aware of key customer needs and aspirations. This involves going beyond the majority of approaches to Total Quality Management. The strategic customer programme is about keeping ahead, not just catching up or keeping pace with competitors whether national, Japanese or others.

The acid test is whether the customer chooses to involve the supplier in a genuine approach to joint strategic developments, or not. It is a buyers' market, but unless suppliers take the initiative they will not even reach the auction room with competitive value-for-money offers.

What constitutes value for money?

Six messages about customers are increasingly demonstrated by research and practical experience. They are acted on by successful companies.

1. Customers buy satisfaction rather than the core product or service.

2. The satisfaction is inspired by the total experience achieved by the total product/service package offered and delivered by a supplier to a customer, as illustrated in Fig. 2.3.

3. Personal customers and corporate buyers are less likely to shop around and establish trading relationships with alternative suppliers if they receive:

    - value for money in the short-term — an experience above expectations in performance, quality standards, delivery and price in relation to lifetime benefits and costs
    - strategic support in supplier product/process research and development for the medium term
    - evidence of supportive business beliefs, culture and practices.

4. Many industrial and personal customers have become more willing, often forced by competitor quality, to replace a low-price component or sub-assembly, hotel room, computer system or appliance by one providing an attractive combination of enhanced performance,

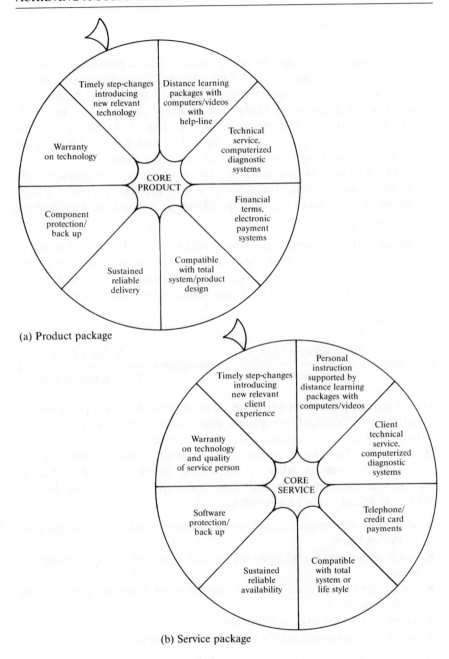

(a) Product package

(b) Service package

Figure 2.3 Typical product and service packages

image, quality, pre-sale and after-sale service at an incremental or, in some cases, significantly higher price.

5. Traditionally it has taken time and possibly several product generations to build up the confidence of the customer. For competitive reasons, this is expected to happen more quickly in the future. As a result, changes in alliances are likely to be reviewed unless strong, mutually beneficial strategic alliances are in place. Unless a real strategic relationship exists a simple slip-up or period of unfortunate lowering of standards can reverse years of good work in a month.

   In all industries and markets, including commodity markets, one supplier makes attractive rates of return through premium prices while another faces liquidity problems as a result of rock-bottom prices.

6. More and more long-term strong relationships between customers and suppliers are built on the capability of the supplier to provide the means of sustained added-value for the customer. Added-value is commonly expressed as added-value/unit total employee remuneration.

In practice:

$$\text{Customer} \left(\frac{\text{Value added}}{\text{Total remuneration}} \right) \propto \text{Supplier} \left(\frac{\text{Value added}}{\text{Total remuneration}} \right)$$

The relationship provides a conceptual but practical starting point for the identification of competitive options, which many competitors might find difficult to follow, and demonstrates the potential from an improved use of technology. The choice and scope of creative moves are extensive if a total business view is taken, as illustrated below. For the customer, incremental value-added benefit may come from two sources. Firstly, enhanced added value as a result of:

- increased sales from technologically enhanced reliable products sold to the end user
- stock reductions from improved product range and supplier performance
- component and material cost improvement from supplier quality improvement
- lower cost access to new technology
- lower cost environmentally compatible products.

Second, a reduced total remuneration bill as a result of:

- lower product management costs through improved systems and relationships

- reduced design and integration costs through better and simpler supplier designs increasingly achieved through direct CAD/computer links
- reduced labour costs through the productivity potential built into the supplier's products/services resulting in process and system simplifications.

For the supplier, strategic alliances offer several opportunities for incremental value-added improvements as well.

Firstly, enhanced added-value itself as a result of:

- increased sales and margins from a better match of customer needs by the total corporate team
- reduced marketing and sales costs by competing by the side of the customer and not against other suppliers
- stock reductions through improved design, demand management and manufacturing processes, planning and control
- component and material cost improvement from new materials and new design technology
- reduced sales costs as a consequence of more reliable repeat orders.

Secondly, a reduced total remuneration bill as a result of reductions in the cost of producing, distributing and servicing the product(s) through customer satisfaction and product simplification.

Technology: the latent competitive opportunity

There are many short- and long-term business opportunities implicit in the six statements and relationships outlined above. Once grasped, they can provide a productive route to securing the vital 70–80 per cent sustained repeat business and strategically selected new customers, year after year.

A multi-disciplined task-force or opportunity workshop are time effective ways of breaking into the process, and this is a low-risk exercise at any time in the corporate calendar.

Unfortunately, many customers and supplier managers remain competitively and technologically complacent, even inert. They see the opportunities as yet another source of problems or additional costs.

A strategic mismatch with such opportunities, not currency exchange rates, government industrial policy, or trade union policy is for many companies at the root of the following phenomena:

- the decline in the share of world markets for UK manufactured goods over two decades, parallel with a weakening pound

- the growth in the global share of purchases secured by Japanese products, designed with the customer in mind, at attractive prices, at a time when the yen has never been stronger
- the sustained international sales by Germany for products strong in life-time costs, if not initial cost, against the background of a strong Deutschmark
- the penetration of US-style food chains in the UK and Japan, in competition perhaps with complacent local convenience restaurants
- the impact of Japanese supplier philosophy on the quality management standards and union policies of suppliers and sub-contractors in the UK and US as well as in the Far East
- France being able to exert strategic leadership in trans-European projects such as the high speed train network, Channel Tunnel, commercial aircraft, and at the same time sustain a largely independent defence policy and industry.

The basic message is that management has to manage day-in and day-out and is ultimately responsible for shortfalls in national competitiveness. Problems with major customer product or process development projects tend to become public in the trade if not in the international business press. Enormous marketing budgets are often required to ensure that a market knows and believes the good news about new products and services.

However, bad news travels fast (and at no cost). The loss of one disappointed customer can establish a chain reaction through informal comment and conversation, resulting in a loss of repeat business and new customers becoming more and more difficult to attract and retain.

Buyers now shop globally for alternative suppliers and experiences, not because of professional buyers' pride and ambition, but of necessity because of their impression of declining product and service standards. In many cases, secure and reliable local suppliers would be much more acceptable and cost-effective, and would avoid the extra costs associated with seeking out, evaluating, quality auditing and policing new suppliers. The existence of strong and reliable local suppliers is a key issue in determining the competitive standards of major industries at international level. This is now a necessity and not an added luxury and is therefore discussed in some detail in Chapter 4.

However, in other cases, companies 'upstream and downstream' in the added-value 'chain' are waiting to grasp or pounce on the opportunity for a strategic 'leap-frog', as illustrated in Fig. 2.4.

Successful leap-frogs and a redistribution of competitive power can and will continue to occur in the following four situations:

1. The failure of the current agent or distributor/supplier to maintain a portfolio of products and services based on up-to-date technology,

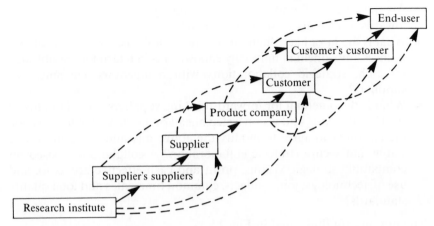

Figure 2.4 Potential and risk of strategic 'leap-frog'

leading to the establishment of direct trading links with original manufacturers.

2. The increased awareness of a supplier one or two steps removed from
    the customer in the supply chain, of key customers' emergent longer-
    term strategic needs and the potential for a timely approach with
    replacement technology.

3. The strategic decision by a customer to take over the supplier's role in
    integrating technologies in order to speed the use of tomorrow's tech-
    nology. The shift in the aerospace industry where prime contractors are
    absorbing the systems management role is a prime example.

4. The strategic decision by a customer to devolve complete sub-systems to
    supply 'associates' as in the automobile industry.

These four situations emphasize the need for suppliers to be more alert to
the trends in the source of significant new commercial innovations by
customers, and more pro-active in their attitudes.

The strategic information base needs to track and give answers to the
following questions:

- Which customers are, or are likely to be, most innovative in the use of
  technology?
- What have been their most recent successful innovations?
- What significant future innovations can be anticipated?
- What can we do to make our present key customers more innovative?
- What have been the traditional sources of innovation?

- Are the sources of innovation now changing, and is an emergent trend towards a new mix of sources evident?
- What is the most likely future mix between in-house ideas, acquisitions, licences, investment in university endowments in return for unpublished research, strategic collaborations with competitors' customers or suppliers?
- What is the potential for forward-thinking suppliers, with a quality of strategic thinking and vision a step ahead of the customer, to persuade the customer to agree to modify the above mix and move towards a stable and secure strategic collaboration? A collaboration based on compatible strategic visions, profit and cash-effective access to, and use of, technology, joint budgets, common timescales and total quality standards?

The options are illustrated in Fig. 2.5.

One thing is certain. Most customers would like to improve the management of technology process associated with the launch of new products, and find cash-effective means of reducing the number and timescales of the bottlenecks (Fig. 2.6) that sap competitive initiatives. The unexpected introduction of ready-to-use relevant technology, in the form of a substitute product, service or process, can change the fortunes of customers and, in some instances, industrial sectors. Examples include time and distance measurement and specialist retailing such as the Sock Shop and Body

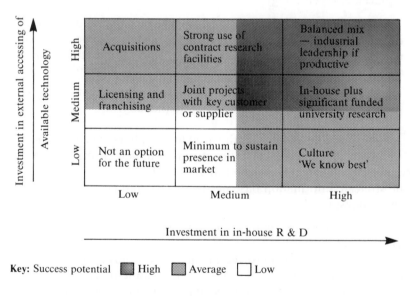

Key: Success potential ▓ High ▒ Average ☐ Low

Figure 2.5 Options for accessing technology

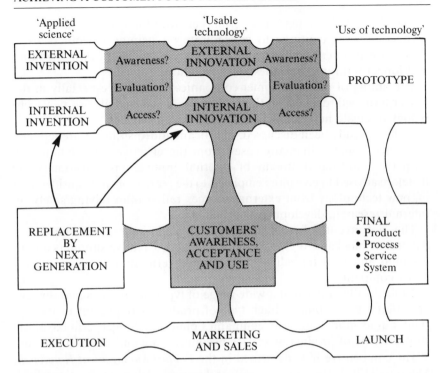

Figure 2.6 Critical competitive bottlenecks

Shop. The need to identify and evaluate such opportunities as part of the normal strategy process is discussed in Chapter 4. For many companies, strategic alliances with suppliers or customers will be preferred to alliances with competitors and those based on accessing technology will be as important in the 1990s as those designed to open up closed markets in the 1970s and 80s.

What are our most significant strengths and weaknesses? How vulnerable are we? What actions are required?

The strategic needs of customers

As discussed in a previous section, sustained customer/supplier relationships in both industrial and consumer markets depend to an increasing extent on value for money v. 'least price' products and services, except in true commodity markets.

Most supplier companies observe the phenomenon, but many continue to respond slowly, whether they be car manufacturers, local restaurants, banks, the railway system or supermarkets with their own brands. Often such companies continue to concentrate on helping customers solve short-term problems rather than aiding them to exploit *their* medium- and longer-term opportunities and aspirations.

The ability of many customer companies to survive, especially in the longer term, will depend on their ability to access and absorb new technology to create new competitive products and services.

As has already been discussed, significant added strategic strength can be gained, quickly in many cases, from the effective exploitation of a properly coordinated stream of external innovations. Customers are therefore advised to give more emphasis to the search for, and consideration of, new technology from external sources rather than relying solely on internal research, development and design.

The 'not invented here syndrome' and 'we know best' can become a dangerous blockage to global competitiveness. Creative suppliers are an essential and vital ingredient in the longer-term strategic planning for many companies.

Table 2.1 illustrates that a wide range of types of products and services are offered to customers. Each type of product is important in its own right, but as more and more companies plan on a longer-term basis, the strategic type of product or service becomes more and more important.

The competitive mix, described in the *Product Management Handbook*, McGraw-Hill (Handscombe, 1989) and several earlier articles since 1984, postulated that potential customers will respond increasingly to value-for-money products that are either market/customer-led or technology-led, provided they are promoted through appropriate marketing and sales techniques.

The concept recognizes that products have nine lives, the ninth for innovative, timely, products being price reductions through discounting. For basic 'me too' commodity products the only life may be discounted prices! Initially, the competitive mix was often only interpreted from an operational point of view. A more strategic interpretation is now required.

The extension of the concept to take account of the concept of strategic products and services is illustrated in Table 2.2.

During the 1980s, the competitive mix became important as more and more customers sought value for money as well as creative, economic life-time cost v. first cost products and services. During the 1990s, the concept is likely to be used even more extensively as more and more companies and hence customers establish effective strategic search and decision-making processes with three to five year (plus) time horizons.

Table 2.1 Typical range of products offered to customers

Type of product	Focus of product/service	Product examples
Strategic	Enables *customer* to initiate and achieve significant strategic change in the nature, direction and extent of business. Often associated with providing customer with a step-change in the use of technology.	IT — Numeric telephone Oil — Seabed, remote well-heads Travel — Concorde Architecture — CAD design option Leisure — Walkman Pharmaceuticals — Home diagnostics Toys — Computer games/home computers Clothing — Manmade fibres Banking — Merger and acquisition Insurance — Risk management Consulting — Strategy reviews
Operational	Enables *customer* to achieve annual objectives and budget in a productive manner. Generally associated with sustaining current technology with proven incremental improvements.	IT — PC networks Oil — Drilling mud Travel — Airbus, TGV Architecture — Modular units Leisure — Tennis rackets Pharmaceuticals — Aspirin Toys — New safe plastics/paints Clothing — NC machines Banking — Loan Insurance — Pension schemes Consulting — Product management
Security/ problem solving	Enables *customer* to speedily overcome 'regular' anticipated but unplanned operational risks. Generally associated with current technology.	IT — Back-up computer capacity Oil — Helicopter spares supply Travel — Car breakdown service Leisure — Ali Ross Ski Clinic Architecture — Window sealant Pharmaceuticals — Aspirin Toys — 'Wet day' puzzles Clothing — Plastic raincoat Banking — Overdraft facility Insurance — Motor insurance Consulting — Cash flow management
Crisis	Enables *customer* to tackle unexpected disasters in a professional manner. May involve novel application of technology for limited period of time.	IT — Back-up computer bureau Oil — Red Adair capping service Travel — Self-right lifeboat Architecture — Spray roof tile adhesive Leisure — Mountain Rescue Service Pharmaceuticals — Egg Test Service Toys — Teddy bear Clothing — Space envelope life-jacket Banking — Financial restructuring Insurance — Disaster insurance Consulting — Insolvency

Table 2.2 Evolution of the competitive mix

Dimensions of basic product competitive mix	Operational emphasis in 1980s	Additional strategic emphasis in customer relations for the 1990s
1. Product design/ specification	Fitness for purpose/styling	Step-change in integrated application of technologies — provides new strategic opportunities
2. Product quality and reliability	Right first time — up with the 'best'	Right each time — ahead of the 'best'
3. Product productivity potential	Performance/operational costs	Lifetime costs/economic access to new technology
4. Prompt delivery and dependability	5-star response to repeat orders	Matching customers' strategic milestones
5. Product package	Competitive extras	Timely use of relevant new technology
6. Product support in commissioning/ application	Speedy full use and benefits	Early competitive use of new technology
7. Product servicing and spares	Prompt customer support	Continuous customer support
8. Promotional follow-up and reality	Build up customer confidence	Build up customer strategic commitment
9. Price reduction through discounting	Less relevance with proven added-value	Less relevance with sharing strategic risk

The corporate development implications

There are six important implications arising from the trend in customer/ supplier relations that need to be taken into account in designing corporate development programmes for the 1990s.

1. Market research needs to be focused more on the emergent needs of important corporate and consumer clients and on related technological developments, and, as a consequence less on traditional competitor analysis which often searches hopefully for a convenient 'me too' copyist opportunity. The role of competitor analysis becomes one of benchmarking.

2. The development of deeper customer and technological awareness among top management, non-technologists and narrowly specialist technologists.

3. The involvement of directors and managers in participative strategy reviews on an ongoing basis: quarterly, six monthly or yearly depending on the nature of the business, market dynamics and the awareness and commitment of senior managers. In the 1990s, quarterly rather than yearly reviews are likely to lead to sustained success.

4. The extension of traditional strategy databases to include a more detailed assessment of the future, and the risks emanating from customers' strategic needs, and the potential for a more productive use of available technologies.

5. The need to develop the capability to manage high value-added products and services, and in particular the total quality dimension.

6. The organization of joint customer/supplier brainstorming sessions.

Such actions will establish a corporate team alert to the competitive dimension of the 1990s, and a culture in which customer-focused initiatives become the norm and not only the subject of one-off Messianic campaigns. This is discussed in detail in Chapter 6.

Building customer needs into corporate strategy

During the 1980s, much emphasis was given to the need for more comprehensive competitor analysis, which identified their apparent future strategy and likely response to anticipated market opportunities and threats, in addition to the more traditional analysis of strengths and weaknesses.

The emphasis of such market research has, therefore, slipped from the market research budget — which traditionally focused on recent and forecast customer demands — to the corporate planners' budget. As a result, many companies have become fanatical about attacking and matching competitors' short-term market initiatives and, at the same time, lost touch with significant changes in the corporate culture and core needs of customers.

All suppliers of products and services need to recognize that in the 1990s more customer management teams will think and plan strategically than in the 1980s. Thus, they will increasingly anticipate, adapt to, and take advantage of, fast-moving opportunities. There are a number of implications.

Firstly, the mix and extent of identifiable customer needs will expand, as illustrated in Fig. 2.7. Second, in many cases, the time-span of major buying decisions by customers is likely to be longer. This will be especially so in industrial markets if effective collaborations with suppliers are established. This will be effective in the sense that:

1. They establish joint programmes for the exploitation of new technology through shortening the life-cycle of consumer products, or extending the cost-effective lifetime of industrial products by a lifetime care philosophy, or product improvement on a continuous basis.

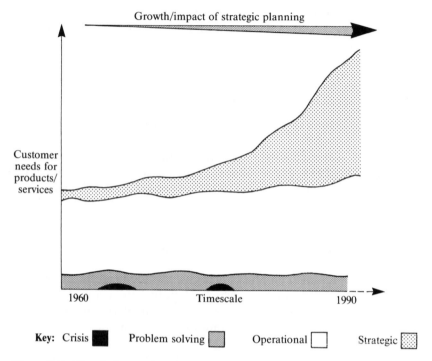

Figure 2.7   Trends in customer needs

2. Jointly, they re-educate both managers and the work-force in new technology to ensure that early competitive advantage can be achieved.

3. Leading suppliers will need to establish and sustain an informed analysis of the emergent strategic needs of customers. An analysis that takes account of the evident and likely long-term customer decisions, business directions and capability needs, and which requires regular access to informed customer executives to gain and test vital market intelligence.

4. The customer analysis must be developed alongside the competitive analysis that has become a norm as a result of the writing of Porter and others during the 1980s.

Tomorrow's customer intelligence base

The trends discussed to date have ramifications for the type and depth of customer intelligence required, and represent a danger area and risk if

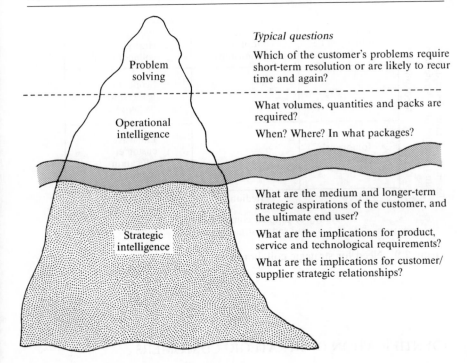

Typical questions

Problem solving

Which of the customer's problems require short-term resolution or are likely to recur time and again?

Operational intelligence

What volumes, quantities and packs are required?

When? Where? In what packages?

Strategic intelligence

What are the medium and longer-term strategic aspirations of the customer, and the ultimate end user?

What are the implications for product, service and technological requirements?

What are the implications for customer/supplier strategic relationships?

Figure 2.8 The intelligence iceberg

not gathered and interpreted early, as illustrated in Fig. 2.8. This is already the norm in some industries, such as pharmaceuticals, armaments, food and airlines. In the future, it needs to be a feature of all industries.

Success in the 1990s, particularly in high value-added high-tech markets, will require a deeper insight into the future direction and timing of customers' investments and product/market moves. Suppliers, therefore, require the ability to identify, interpret and respond to the quality of the customers' decision-making and planning as illustrated in Fig. 2.9.

The questions that need to be asked and answered on a real time basis include: Who will be our strategic customers? What will be their future strategies? How will the strategies be different to the past? What are their future product and service design needs? More detailed questions under each heading follow.

Extent of customers' strategic planning and recognition of strategic needs	Low	Medium	High
High	Supplier unlikely to be shortlisted	Customer in control of relationships	Potential strategic collaboration
Medium		?	Scope for leadership by supplier
Low	Tomorrow's losers		Extensive customer education required

Ability of supplier company to identify
and satisfy strategic needs

Figure 2.9 Need for strategic collaboration

IDENTIFICATION OF STRATEGIC CUSTOMERS

- Which customers think and plan strategically?
- Which end-users are likely to be the most demanding and innovative in the 1990s?
- Which current/potential customers are likely to be the most and least technologically aware?
- Which current/potential customers will be looking for step-changes in the extent and quality of externally accessed technology?
- Which customers are most adept at exploiting 'strategic windows'? The opportunities opened up by new market segments, changes in technology and distribution channels?
- Which current/potential customers are likely to be the largest purchasers for our type of products and technology in three to five years' time?
- Who are the market leaders today?
- Which current/potential customers are likely to be the fastest growing purchasers in three to five years' time?
- Which five important customers are the least likely to survive in their present form over the next five years? Why? What are the implications?
- Which five customers present the most attractive opportunities *now*, for the establishment of strategic collaborations for the future?
- How should we proceed speedily towards establishing strategic alliances?

ANTICIPATION OF EMERGENT STRATEGIES

- What is the current core mission and business strategy of each of the customers selected?
- In what ways is this strategy likely to be modified over the next three to five years, and why?
- What will be the customers' priorities in the need for technology to support strategic product design, process and systems development, and the achievement of total quality objectives?
- Where can the customer currently source priority technology such as components, sub-assemblies, materials or intellectual know-how or finished products on a national, regional or international basis?
- What changes in potential source can be anticipated?
- Has the customer the capability to search, access and use that technology productively?
- What are the future related technological strengths and weaknesses of the customer?
- Has the customer the strengths necessary for a strategic relationship?
- What management, specialist or work-force support will be essential?
- What can you do to the changing customer needs implicit in the previous questions?
- Will recent or anticipated changes in top management lead to changes in strategy?

DESIGN OF FUTURE PRODUCTS AND SERVICES

- What are the implications for the scope and extent of our future technology base?
- What are the implications for our products/service development plans?
- What needs to be accessed and used to ensure that our technology is correct and timely?
- What new sources for technology must be investigated and accessed? How? When?
- In what ways could existing product/service packages be modified to form the basis for a strategic v. operational/problem-solving relationship with key customers?
- What must be done to protect the intellectual property rights involved to reduce the possibility of leap-frog offers from competitors and suppliers?
- What scope is there for building in 'tied' standards to protect tomorrow's markets?

The market intelligence gathered will in total help answer the questions highlighted in Fig. 2.8 and will be important in three ways:

1. in providing a customer focus to the company's approach to the management and the use of technology (Chapter 3)

2. as a vital input to the total corporate and supportive business unit strategic planning process (Chapter 5)

3. as a vital input to identifying the development requirements for the commercial awareness and key capabilities of the board, senior managers and technologists (Chapters 7 and 8).

The questions listed in this section are fundamental and straightforward. However, finding answers presents probably a considerable logistic and intellectual challenge. Yet answers are essential if advantage is to be taken of the potential for enhanced customer/supplier relationships.

Supplier strategic intelligence

In practice, the answers also need to be considered downstream to evaluate the quality of the relationship with suppliers to ensure that they, in turn, are likely to give adequate support to the customer's attempts to establish a strategic relationship. In this respect, the following questions provide a useful starting point in ensuring that you understand the dynamics of the supply chain.

- To what extent are your key suppliers aware of your strategy?
- To what extent are your key suppliers technological leaders?
- To what extent are your strategic alliances with key suppliers stronger than those between your competitors and their suppliers?
- What strategic relationships are in place or likely to be considered between your key suppliers and your competitors? What are the security and competitive risks?
- What is the extent and quality of the emergent technology from your suppliers that could be used competitively over the next two to five years?
- Do any of your suppliers have the capability to leap-frog into the value-added supply chain?
- What suppliers of strategically important technology are vulnerable to acquisition?
- To what extent have suppliers established effective networks for identifying and accessing useful technologies, including universities and research institutes?

- To what extent are the directors of key suppliers strategically and technologically aware?
- Which suppliers represent the most attractive opportunities for the strengthening of relationships? What action should be taken now?

(This issue is discussed in detail in Chapter 4.)

The importance of demanding customer/supplier relationships

It is no accident that Paris is famous for perfumes, Japan for leisure electronics, Switzerland for foodstuffs and pharmaceuticals, Italy for summer clothes, Australia for lager, the US for military equipment and movies, Germany for cars, Scotland for whisky. This fame has resulted from designers and marketeers operating in, and having to respond to, a very demanding and critical clientele. Such markets comprise both personal and corporate buyers who have clear strategies, and expect a continued good experience each time they purchase and each time the product range is updated by improved design or technology. As a result, what started as niche markets expanded with the advent of speedy and cost-effective communication and distribution into global products based on a *national pride* and home market demand. The initial innovatory environment may not have been planned, but what can we learn that is relevant to the future?

The implications for the future are that whatever the global source of a new product or service idea and the source of enabling technology, the corporate base for product design, development and test marketing needs to be placed in a country, or indeed town, with a reputation for evaluating and using new products in a demanding way.

In the 1990s, the key strategic decision for many companies will be how to locate close to the source of demanding purchasers rather than raw material suppliers. Japanese consumer standards have had a major influence on the rise of Japanese industry. Japanese domestic customers and most importantly worker customers have been the first to criticize quality standards — not the Western export customer.

How effective is your current base for product development and initial market launch? Is the local market demanding? Can you recognize the impact on your business decisions? Is there market rivalry? Has a local, specific, reliable supplier network evolved? Have customer capabilities, skills and lifestyles been advanced? Is there scope for more?

In Europe, 1993 presents significant opportunities for both manufacturers and service organizations, provided they bring relevant technology close to the customer. For car manufacturers, this could involve the useful v. cosmetic application of computer diagnostics to assess road conditions, tyre pressures, vehicle balance when loaded, and so on. For banks, it could involve meeting exacting conditions for home banking and insurance v. automated branches and home or small business terminals. For the fashion designers, it will involve combining vision and flair in *haute couture* with knowledge of how to use fabric and production technology to translate new ranges to cost-effective high street models.

Two major organizational issues for all companies will be:

1. How to manage demanding strategic relationships or alliances with customers.

2. How to manage demanding strategic relationships with key suppliers.

In both cases, future relationships will go beyond the traditional salesman/ buyer relationship, and more towards and beyond OEM type arrangements requiring multi-level contacts and account management. The multi-level contacts will need to separate the processes concerned with gathering strategic intelligence and the process of supplying timely competitive products and services.

Chapter 3 will consider the management of technology related to this phenomenon. Chapter 4 will deal with the implications for the strategic decision-making process.

The following audit provides one input to the process.

Customer focus audit

This chapter has discussed the need to develop the capability and determination to identify and focus on the future strategic needs of key customers in considering future strategic options for your company.

The chapter also highlights the need for customers to explore in-depth the ability of current and potential suppliers to support them strategically.

Both sides of the analysis and action required will involve an appreciation of which management processes and behaviours need modification to achieve future competitive success.

The customer focus audit questionnaire (Table 2.3) is designed to aid an assessment of the current situation and the identification of priority action areas. Action planning as an activity is discussed in Chapter 5.

The customer focus audit questionnaire builds on and extends the second section of the audit questionnaire, included at the end of Chapter 1, as Table 1.2, i.e., Key area B: Customer strategy and competitive situation. The questionnaire includes both repeated and new questions to extend the depth of analyses.

The reason for including a number of repeat questions in this

Table 2.3   Customer focus audit questionnaire

Instructions: Consider each of the Issues/Questions in turn. Select the column best fits your current situation and tick the appropriate box 'a'. Consider the underlying trend and denote by ↑ → ↗ ↘ in box 'b'. Add score for all questions.

Issue and question	Assessment of (a) current situation and (b) trend							
	Poor		Fair		Good		Excellent	
	Score 1		Score 2		Score 3		Score 4	
1. Customer needs To what extent are emergent customer needs known?	Little useful market research for specific customers		Occasional review of operational/ problem solving needs		Regular review of operational/ problem solving needs for existing key customers		Regular review of emergent strategic needs for key customers	
	a.	b.	a.	b.	a.	b.	a.	b.
2. Customer contacts What is the quality of customer contacts as a source of market intelligence?	Field sales-force or branches only		Plus customer service/product specialists		Plus marketing/ product managers		Plus top management strategic dialogue	
	a.	b.	a.	b.	a.	b.	a.	b.
3. Focus of products/ services To what extent are products/ services focused?	*Ad hoc* — we respond to opportunities		Focused on problem solving needs of existing customers		Focused on operational and problem solving needs		Focused on strategic needs of selected key customers	
	a.	b.	a.	b.	a.	b.	a.	b.
4. Quality of technology To what extent do you provide technology leadership/ support to key customers?	Rarely. customer way ahead		On request only. tend to be a follower		Joint projects in hand		Continuous and pro-active strategic support	
	a.	b.	a.	b.	a.	b.	a.	b.

Table 2.3 *cont.*

Issue and question	Assessment of (a) current situation and (b) trend							
	Poor		Fair		Good		Excellent	
	Score 1		Score 2		Score 3		Score 4	
5. Customer base To what extent are major customers market leaders?	Limited business with leaders and declining		Some business and growing		Becoming significant and growing		Most business is with market leaders	
	a.	b.	a.	b.	a.	b.	a.	b.
6. Quality of relationships How stable are relationships with key customers?	Unstable, liable to be replaced		Among the preferred traditional suppliers		Increasingly involved in joint development projects		Established strategic alliances	
	a.	b.	a.	b.	a.	b.	a.	b.
7. Design/test location Where is design/test market capability located?	In low-demand, non-demanding territory		In stable, and increasingly demanding territory		In major growth territory		In most demanding territory	
	a.	b.	a.	b.	a.	b.	a.	b.
8. Competitive 'mix' To what extent is potential of strategic mix exploited?	Still sell largely on price		Increasingly exploit operational mix		Increasingly exploit strategic mix		Strategic and fully exploited	
	a.	b.	a.	b.	a.	b.	a.	b.
9. Quality of suppliers Do own suppliers provide strong support to strategic alliance with customers?	No. stronger links with competitors		Give us equal support to competitors		See us as a preferred customer		Strategic alliances in own right	
	a.	b.	a.	b.	a.	b.	a.	b.

Table 2.3 *cont.*

Issue and question	Assessment of (a) current situation and (b) trend							
	Poor		Fair		Good		Excellent	
	Score 1		Score 2		Score 3		Score 4	
10. Customer awareness To what extent are directors, technologists and work-force customers aware?	Know customer names but little more — meet when we have problems		Starting to become aware of competitive needs		Total customer care programme in place		Plus regular strategic reviews with customers involving all aspects of customer needs	
	a.	b.	a.	b.	a.	b.	a.	b.
Column scores								

Total score (sum columns 1–4) [ ]

questionnaire is that your perception of the current situation, related to the issue referred to, may have changed as a result of reading and thinking about the implications of Chapter 2. The cumulative score from the customer focus audit will be in the range 0–40.

The following broad interpretations are suggested:

31–40 Generally well prepared for effective relationships with only one or two weaknesses

21–30 Have a base from which to plan and establish strategic customer relationships provided weaknesses are tackled with urgency

11–20 Generally an operational relationship, much action required and need for major corporate development effort

0–10 Major problems in all areas.

If the customer focus audit creates a degree of discomfort, start to attack the concern by analysing existing and future customer-driven product and service opportunities along the lines of the following example. A complete example is provided in Chapter 8.

Products/services Customer needs	Today's products/ services	Planned products/ services	Possible new products/services
1. Strategic			
2. Operational			
3. Problem solving			
4. Crisis			

Further audit questionnaires are included in the remaining chapters of the book to enable you to complete a thorough audit of your company. Chapter 9 will explore the establishment of specific performance indicators for each key area to enable improvement actions to be monitored in a professional manner.

MANAGING THE USE OF TECHNOLOGY

Available technologies present a continuous stream of significant business opportunities.
They often remain under-recognized and under-utilized.
What does the effective management of the use of technology involve?
What are the dimensions, the issues, the skills and the risks?
How can technology be integrated into strategic thinking?
How can the technology gap be managed?

The strategic potential of technology

Chapters 1 and 2 highlighted *the management of the use of technology* as a vital missing link in the strategic thinking and actions of an uncomfortably large number of companies. Furthermore, crucial strategic actions were identified as the recognition, evaluation, access to and use of relevant available technology to secure strategic advantage for customers and the company. As such, technology is at the heart of future strategic and competitive success, and requires urgent consideration by most companies as an integral part of the strategic management process, as illustrated in Fig. 3.1.

In this context technology needs to be explored from three points of view.

1. The technology related to improving products, services and customer services.

2. The support technology important to achieving best practice standards of excellence in production processes, systems and procedures.

3. The support technology to manage and respond to environmental risks in a pro-active manner.

In this chapter, we explore this missing link from a pragmatic point of view. It is the experience of the authors that sufficient technology is already available (coupled with management processes, methodologies and skills) to achieve major improvements in the use of a wealth of under-utilized technology.

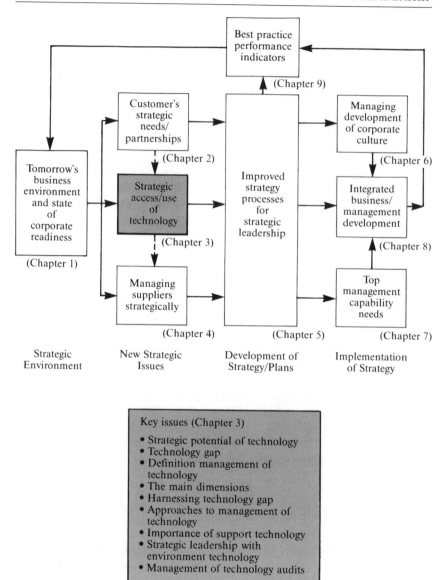

Figure 3.1 Use of technology — a key strategic issue

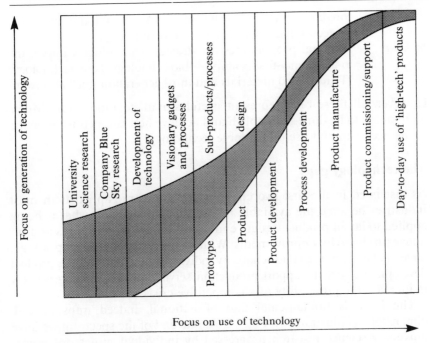

Figure 3.2 Use of technology — a key strategic issue

This stance does not deny the need for:

1. Improvement in the management of research and development. No doubt there is an urgent need, particularly in relation to the establishment of a strategic focus for R&D and within it priorities for investment and productivity inmprovement.

2. Research into the effective development and application of technology to meet both customer and community needs.

Research has commenced, but industry in the West does not have the time to wait for total answers. In this respect, we hope that our pragmatic ideas stimulate specific research programmes in addition to early practical application by top management teams.

Since the first edition was published, much has been initiated at international, national and company levels. For instance:

In Europe   The EC programmes entitled Esprit (IT), Eureka (General), Brite/Euram (materials), Europace and Comett (management of technology), and the UK DTI innovation initiative

In the US   The national programmes Semta (semiconductors), HDTV

(pre-competitive high definition TV), National Task Force
on technology (Managment of Technology)

In Japan   National programmes for strategic technologies important
to the twenty-first century — biotechnology, Nanotechnology,
IT, advanced materials and third generation nuclear power.

However, all these only represent useful stimuli to innovation. Much
more needs to be done to establish and achieve best competitive practice
in the access to and use of available technology.

The technology gap

As discussed in the first two chapters, a significant gap exists in most
industries between the available relevant technology and what is being
applied today in product design, end-user customer applications and in-
house productivity improvements. Without early actions, the gap will get
larger. A failure to integrate actions by individual functions such as product
development, systems support, production, servicing and marketing, is likely
to increase the probability of a competitive crisis.

The issue is fundamental and of national, indeed transnational,
dimension, as illustrated in Fig. 3.2. At one end of the spectrum we have
university science research progressed by individual professors. Sometimes, such research commences without a clear vision or end purpose.
Generally, it is not initiated within an integrated strategy for academic
research, contract research, academic teaching and timely communication
to industry via publications and continuing education programmes. At
the other end of the spectrum, we have customers using products
designed by their suppliers based on technology of five to ten or more
years ago.

Too often, the strength of the technology 'push' and user 'pull' is no
more than a Force 2 wind, an occasional squall or, at worst, a calm of
stability and status quo.

This statement may sound harsh and uncompromising but:

- Japanese car manufacturers have gained the edge for fully fitted high
technology economic cars and are now moving up market
- Japan's attack on US companies in the large market for powerful
computers is based on a mastery of novel materials
- US fast food products have sustained world market penetration using
new ingredients, new storage methods, new processing, new standard
dispensers and constant high quality, while many apparently preferred traditional approaches to convenience food appear bland, lack
appeal, are time consuming and are finding it difficult to achieve
stringent EC food regulations
- with the 'Walkman', Sony has been able to create an innovatory 'aura'

for a new product, and with it the ability to charge a premium price in spite of a wide range of 'me too' products

- British and French aerospace cooperation used novel technology to achieve supersonic civil aviation ahead of the US
- Korea and Taiwan have taken over much of the design manufacture of high-tech leisure shoes using novel materials, adhesives, component design, processes and attractive Western styles
- European textile processors have recaptured a significant share of high-tech yarn processing, previously lost to Asia
- leading food companies adapt process plant from other physical process industries.

In each case, success has been achieved by a focused approach. An approach based on the world-wide search for innovative technology and a dedication to the continuous speedy development of concepts, integration of science and engineering disciplines, and significant cumulative innovation through successive series of products. Moreover, success has not come from R&D alone, but from an integration of all the functions required for competitive success — the board, marketing, design, development, manufacture, quality management — often through a product management type structure. The aim has been to meet tomorrow's customer's needs with timely value for money products. As far back as 1982, one of the conclusions of the EC FAST programme was that as a result of the growing importance attached to the scientific and technology content of products, international trade negotiations might also focus on aspects such as technological exchanges. General Agreements on Technological Change (GATCH), on the lines of General Agreements on Trade and Tariffs (GATT), may not have had a major impact yet. However, at a company level, the trend has become very evident as companies attempt to search for and access under-utilized available and relevant technology on an international basis and influence the strategic path of key customers as discussed in Chapter 2.

Figure 3.3 illustrates the power of a strong opportunistic external and internal search for new relevant technologies; the exploration of integration possibilities and the resultant expansion of strategic vision. The combined search is important as few companies world-wide can fund and be sure of pre-eminence in the total field of relevant technology.

The quality of strategic thinking and customer/supplier relationships provides an essential ingredient for success.

As illustrated in Fig. 3.4, a focus on the strategic needs of customers is most likely to provide the greatest leverage in closing the gap between used and available technology.

Interestingly, in spite of the extent of international concern, there is no generally recognized definition of 'management of technology' and, to

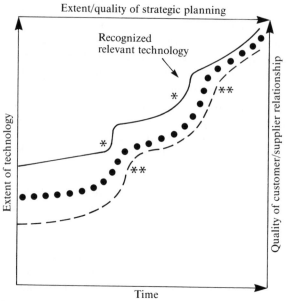

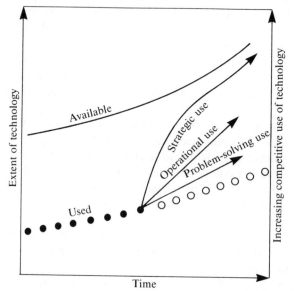

Key: * Expansion of strategic vision
       ** Step/series changes in offers to customer

       ● ● ● ● ● Customer
       − − − − Supplier

Figure 3.3   Progressive customer/supplier relationship

Figure 3.4   Competitive leverage from the use of technology

date, no generally applied framework of practical concepts and processes for effective analysis, access and application of technology in all aspects of the business.

The structure of this book is designed to start to fill this gap and present a number of usable methodologies related to the management of technology. These are methodologies that top management teams can identify with and use in a strategic and competitive manner.

The processes involved are not entirely new but, to our knowledge, have not yet been publicly codified for general discussion, debate and dedicated application. The management processes identified in this book are considered practical and conceptually sound, and have major implications for strategic decision-making and management development, as will be discussed in Chapters 5 and 8.

Inevitably, considerable academic research will emerge during the 1990s, but, unless there is a significant acceleration in the extent and speed of serious research programmes, the generic guidelines that will no doubt emerge for teaching purposes will be out-of-date and too late for many companies deserving to survive.

Practical definition of the management of technology

The management of the use of technology is defined as *'the management process by which organizations identify, access and use available international technology to achieve ongoing competitive advantage, profit growth and share-holder value through optimum customer and community benefits'*.

Optimum benefits imply that technology is made to work reliably at an early date and on time, all the time in relation to the development of today's and tomorrow's products, processes, systems and services. Ongoing competitive advantage implies a strategic management v. operational approach.

For the sake of precision, we would prefer the expression 'the strategic management of the use of available relevant technology'. For brevity, however, we will use the term 'management of technology'.

The above definition of the management of technology goes beyond many traditional definitions or perceptions of technology management. It is both more fundamental and far-reaching than the management of research and development, the management of information technology, or the management of advanced manufacturing technology.

In the next section, we outline the main dimensions of the concept of the management of technology. The dimensions proposed are both simple *and* complex. They take account of the following typical concerns of many top management teams all over the world.

- Today's world is changing rapidly. One of the principal motors of these changes is technology. Companies who do not develop or acquire the right technology will be left behind and fail to exploit a vital key asset of any business — the use of available technology.
- Our international competitors have now caught up with us, and are thoroughly accustomed to managing rapid technological change. We are not, and today the company is vulnerable to those competitors with the wisdom and foresight to invest in the access and use of tomorrow's technology.
- The important issue in technology is its rightness and timeliness, and not its source — and still our functional specialists are protective of internal innovative capability and intellect, and do not consider *using* what is generally available externally.
- Technology is not really understood or managed on an integrative long-term basis, i.e., not used strategically.
- The long-term prospects for wealth creation depend on the generation and commercial exploitation of intellectual craft and artistic skills. Unfortunately, the application of technology to products and manufacturing processes is still falling behind the performance of leading competitors.
- Unless business takes responsibility for chronic environmental problems, legislative demands, constraints and costs can only grow. In many cases the technology, but not the commitment, already exists.

The main dimensions

The effective management of the use of technology is characterized by the following eight dimensions:

1. Management of the use of technology (but not technology itself) is integrative and derives from, and contributes to, the other major management processes, as illustrated in Fig. 3.5. The management of technology needs therefore to be focused, driven and coordinated at chief executive level in parallel with the management of markets, productivity, finance and human resources. It is a top management business issue and not just a scientific issue to be managed at a functional level.

2. As a major corporate asset — alongside finance, people and property — the management of the use of technology needs to be closely integrated into the total corporate strategy process in a manner that satisfies the fundamental needs for success listed below:

   - focuses on enhancing strategic customer ties
   - establishes direction for development and investment

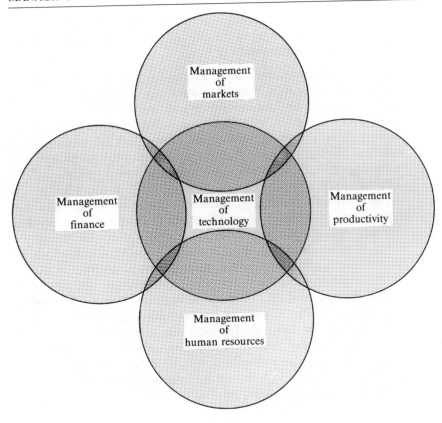

Figure 3.5 Interaction of strategic management processes

- achieves common multi-functional, multi-collaboration drive and thrust
- stimulates responsiveness to change
- sustains continuity of best concepts and process steps and absorption of new sub-processes in a predictive manner
- balances vision, creativity, pragmatism and 'hunches'
- ownership by the board
- provides umbrella framework for strategic and operational decision-making
- establishes basis for future financial and competitive success
- sustains equitable shareholder returns
- provides a cornerstone for a confident approach to change
- provides a basis for rapid and reliable response to opportunities.

This issue is discussed in detail in Chapter 5. Specific emphasis is given to the need for an ongoing technology opportunity search, and the organization of technology strategy sessions as occasional but vital inputs to the ongoing process of top management strategic awareness and decision-making.

3. In practice, the integrative use of technology will result in the development and application of new products, new services, new processes and new systems for both consumer and industrial markets, and in creative solutions to environmental and social problems. An essential starting point is, therefore, the establishment and maintenance of a visionary intelligence base that maps and tracks available relevant technologies — those technologies that one way or another might secure effective competitive advantage, as illustrated in Fig. 3.6.

The available technology inventory does not stand still but expands exponentially and, as discussed in Chapter 1, is a limitless resource. Successful applications of technology are increasingly a blend or integration of core technologies — technologies which, by chance, reach milestones in the development of traditional uses at similar points in time, thereby offering fresh synergistic opportunities for entirely new products, processes, services and systems. Technology route maps (see Fig. 3.7) are an essential management discipline.

A route map for diesel/electric suburban trains is shown. The technology milestones indicate the likely timescale. However, these could be advanced by accelerating the access, final development and proving of the new technology should the customer's strategic need for an earlier new product demand this.

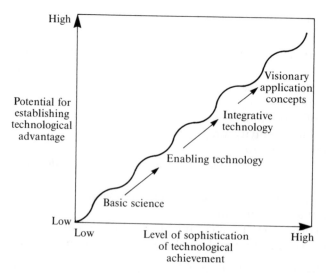

Figure 3.6 The impetus of 'vision'

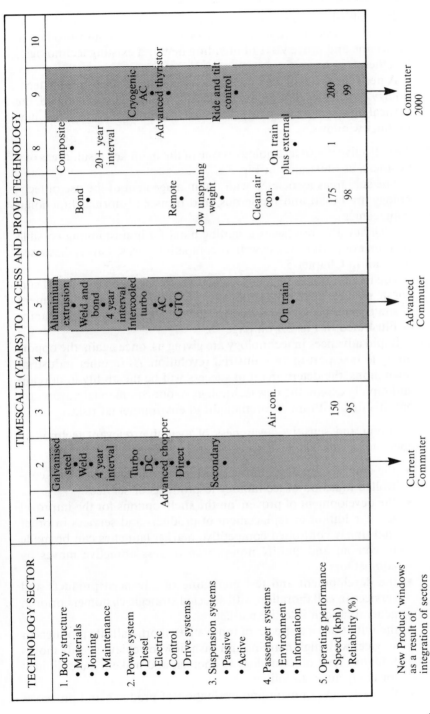

Figure 3.7 Outline technology route map: product group — suburban train

In establishing timescales, allowance must be made for the time required to produce either a prototype or a demonstrator product to determine and prove ways of blending new and existing technologies together.

A need for this will depend on the reliability of the available technology and the level of product reliability required. As illustrated, the vertical integration of newly accessed technology creates the new product windows.

4. The effective use of technology is one of the main key result areas of a business, as illustrated in Fig. 3.8.

   The sub-areas associated with the management of the use of technology are broad and numerous, and transcend normal functional management.

   Each key area represents a starting point for brainstorming possible customer opportunities as well as competitive risks. This is discussed in detail in Chapter 5.

   The issues need to be analysed and reacted to in an integrated corporate manner to secure significant contributions to the achievement of strategic results for the consumer, the company and the community, as illustrated in Fig. 3.9 on page 76.

   Rapid advances in technology are giving us, once again, the opportunity to take part in an industrial revolution. As in other industrial revolutions, the determinant of success will be the ability to develop and rapidly exploit the new technology to our commercial advantage, but this time with more forethought to environmental risks.

5. A strong and sensitive awareness of available relevant technology opens up a wide range of strategic options. These include:

   - the ability to manage product and market differentiation by controlled injection of technology to products or services
   - the development of proven 'on the shelf' options for the improvement, addition or replacement of products and services in order that timely controlled competitive market launches can be made to combat and stultify non-proven or less attractive moves by competitors
   - the development and test marketing of advanced products and services in collaboration with selected strategic customers prior to general launch into the market
   - the initiation of a stream of innovative, short, half-life products or services with high margins and cash flow to achieve speedy moves from one level of technology to another, and make it more difficult for competitors to follow
   - the early development and evaluation of products and processes

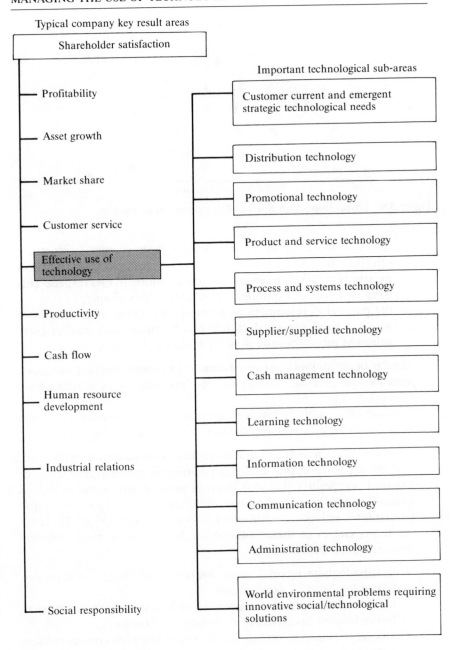

Figure 3.8 Dimensions of the key result area — technology

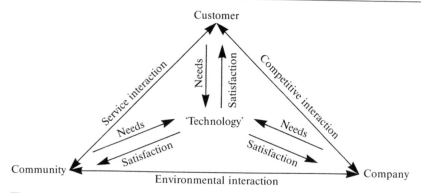

Figure 3.9   Direct impact on results of management technology

that are more environmentally safe than current competitive offerings. Both more perceptive customers and global government pressures are likely to ensure increased efforts in this respect. This issue is therefore expanded upon later in this chapter

- the parallel development and testing of a range of options from which a final preferred choice can be made and market entry achieved more speedily than by traditional means.

Similar opportunities exist in relation to improving internal processes, systems and premises to sustain total productivity as a competitive strength.

Above all a relatively low-cost competitive ability to sustain a stream of added-value products and services, as illustrated in Fig. 3.10.

6. Success requires a thorough understanding of the process of innovation, and the recognition that the major barrier to international levels of external competitiveness and internal productivity is not a lack of available science and technology, but often a series of awareness and perception barriers, or 'mind-blocks', as illustrated in Fig. 3.11. There are many causes of these bottlenecks. A number of more common ones are listed below:

- the inadequate technological awareness of boards of directors, hence low level of expectations
- the low management acumen of scientists and technologists, hence limited involvement in strategic decisions
- an over-dependence on functional experts and poor communication between functions
- the inability to move speedily into and out of changing technologies to achieve significant step-changes, as a result of fixations on currently used technologies

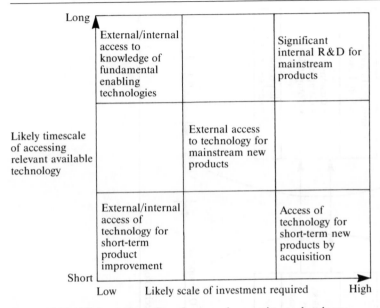

Figure 3.10 The cost benefits of external accessing technology

- the lack of a corporate technology profit and loss account and balance sheet
- a failure to understand technological success factors
- inadequate team creative skills at board and senior management levels
- the poor specification of technological initiatives related to products, process and IT systems, hence sub-optimal choice of projects
- a failure to recognize high added-value benefit of bought-in technology
- absence of specific management process for conceptualizing technological opportunities and risks.

The first series of barriers, illustrated in Fig. 3.11, are those which slow down the translation of basic scientific research into usable enabling technology. Typically, they represent the lack of strategic vision and direction of the marketing director and technical director, charged with identifying those areas of basic research that should be tracked and accessed to secure a competitive edge in the longer term.

The second series of barriers are those which block off or slow down the recognition by the entire board, functional directors and designers that new usable technology is available for independent or synergistic commercial application to produce new competitive products, services, processes and systems. The type of strategy processes described in Chapter 5 are designed to help remove these barriers.

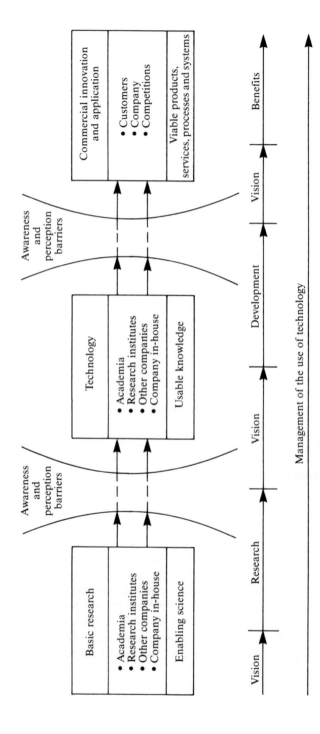

Figure 3.11 Perception barriers in the innovation process

7. Industrial history is not only full of cases of missed opportunities — late 'me too' followers — but also of companies 'jumping the gun' due to a narrow perception of the risks associated with new enabling technologies.

In many companies, the continued low productive use of information technology is a vivid example of the problem, even after 30 years of commercial computers. The banking industry is a prime example of a wide industrial concern.

Successful companies in the 1990s will be those who develop and implement a practical process for harnessing and responding to the power of all aspects of technology for the benefit of customers and end-users. This will be achieved through well-led programmes that define, strategically review, value analyse and develop competitive products, services, systems and processes.

A range of typical situations is illustrated in Fig. 3.12.

Case A represents the situation of a supplier whose top management team is technologically unaware. It has little to offer to support the corporate and competitive development of major customers. In such situations, the supplier is likely to be, at best, on the tender list for operational or problem-solving orders. In consumer markets such as home electronics the intending purchaser will know more about the products than the retailer.

Case B represents the situation of a technologically aware supplier who has yet to communicate the strategic benefits of a step-change in technology to a less aware customer. Without skilful marketing, the supplier could lose out in satisfying the customer's operational needs by being seen as too upmarket, too advanced, too risky and too expensive. In consumer markets organic and ecology products face this problem.

Case C represents a situation in which both the supplier and customer are awakening slowly to the latent potential of technology. Alternate incremental technological breakthroughs lead to vibrations between 'demands' and 'offers' which result in a state of nervous tension between customer and supplier and vice versa. Neither has yet started to grasp the real strategic opportunities.

Case D represents a situation where the supplier has made the strategic decision to invest in the capability required to manage the use of technology in an effective strategic manner. A progressive increase in the application of relevant available technology has established a firm credibility with a key customer. Major breakthroughs in the use of integrated technologies have been researched, planned and executed with a spirit of compatible collaboration. It is suggested that **Case D** should be the aim of many more companies. The challenge is illustrated in Fig. 3.12.

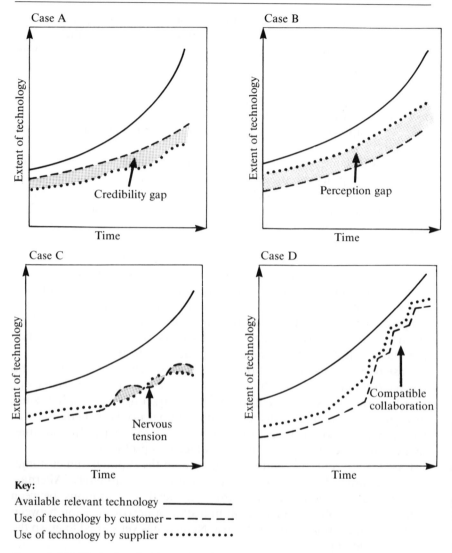

Figure 3.12 Typical technology situations

Harnessing the technology gap

The scale of the challenge involved in harnessing the strategic power inherent in available technology is illustrated in Fig. 3.13.

Area X represents the companies making use of technologies already widely used in industry; an area increasingly well researched, well taught and well applied. Yet IT has had a user-driven need since the late-1950s;

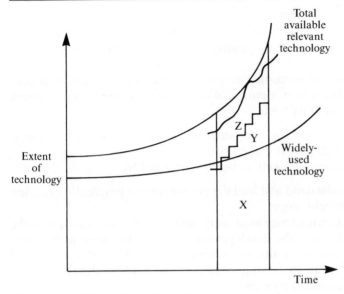

Figure 3.13 The scale of the challenge

robotic manufacturing devices have been in use since the mid-1960s. However, it is difficult to find full effective application of each of the technologies throughout British and European industry. There is clearly a need for management schools to train company personnel in how tested technology can be best identified, accessed and utilized.

Area Y represents those companies determined to take step-changes in the use of available technologies: steps required to achieve the strategic relationships with customers, as referred to in Chapter 2, and global competitiveness, as dealt with in Chapter 1. At this point in the learning curve, such companies are not aiming to be world leaders, but to be among the significant survivors with an even chance of developing the capabilities required to become global leaders. This is an area for urgent action by companies and it requires further research. In this book, we attempt to provide a realistic starting point by drawing together the available threads of practical knowledge. We provide a base from which to consider the management capabilities and processes required to control and influence the timing and integrated use of new technologies — a vital starting point for global leadership which is as important as a strong international distribution network.

Typical features of type Y companies would be:

- a recognition of the need for a more formal and thorough understanding of customers and appropriate technologies

- an increasing number of meetings at director level between supplier and key customers to understand and refine strategies
- an increasing interest in visiting research institutes and university campuses
- the emergence of sponsored contract research programmes with contracts placed on a firm commercial basis and no longer on a benevolent social responsibility basis.

Area Z represents the few companies in each industry who can claim to be moving towards global leadership.

These companies are likely to be characterized by:

- a desire to understand and lead the evaluation and practical application of emergent technology
- an emergent competence to identify, access, influence and control the timing and focus of the development of new/replacement technology
- the intellectual capability to harness the best external and internal brains to fuse the application of discrete scientific findings into integrated technological concepts
- a recognition of the importance of a high standard of support technology (e.g., manufacturing process technology) to fully exploit emerging product/service technology
- a planning process that continuously scans and evaluates a broad range of unrelated opportunities searching for a combination of extended and new business opportunities, i.e., practical lateral thinking
- a technologically and customer-aware top management team
- a determination to launch a sustained series of product/service improvements, innovation and replacements in time with the mood of the market, and not missing the market 'window' through over-kills in the area of marketing and/or technology
- a determination to manage total technology in a new and professional manner
- a significant investment in the continuous training of individual technologists and project teams.

Table 3.1 illustrates a range of possible situations within each of the three zones illustrated in Fig. 3.13. The example situations, objectives and competitive actions are illustrative only and do not attempt to examine all possible permutations of relative customer and supplier perceptions and positions. Exploration of such options will help identify who will be the most important customers in terms of providing routes to competitive advantage — the customers who will see advantage in technology-based collaborations as a safer route to accessing the step-change in technology required for global competitiveness rather than joint R&D programmes with latent or current competitors.

Original equipment manufacturers have used the concept for decades on an operational basis. There is now an opportunity to expand the concept to strategic relationships in all industries, and gain benefit from the full power of the strategic use of available relevant technology.

In reverse, the strategies will enable businesses to improve their definition of what they require from future suppliers, the profiling of a preferred supplier, the selection and management of suppliers to accelerate the implementation of the strategic customers. This will be discussed in more depth in Chapter 4. In an ideal strategic collaboration, the customer and selected supplier will work closely together to develop a common practical approach to the engineering and optimization of engineering systems.

Evaluation of typical approaches to 'the management of technology'

In compiling this text, the practices of a wide range of organizations affected by continual technological change were examined.

Four typical approaches to the management of technology were identified and the practical potential impact of each approach compared in an objective manner. We used six criteria to evaluate each approach as illustrated in Table 3.2 and below.

(a) *Customer orientation of company* — a dedicated focus on seeking out, developing and exploiting technology directly or ultimately of strategic benefit to key customers

(b) *Financial results from technology investments* — sustained investment in timely, evolutionary and controlled step-changes in technology for the design, manufacture, servicing and distribution of internationally competitive products and services

(c) *Evaluation of technology options* — evaluation of all corporate investment options on a common basis, whether investments in accessing technology, product/service development or Blue Sky research, university contract research, IT systems, distribution systems or manufacturing processes

(d) *Customer/user-focused IT systems* — a focus on the development of customer- and user-driven IT systems (rather than specialist/expert-driven) to support significant strategic objectives

(e) *Corporate technology awareness* — investment in a continuous process of technological re-education and updating from the board to junior employees, across all functions, to ensure a high level of strategic awareness

(f) *Facilitating Total Quality programme* — major investment to establish customer service driven culture, behaviour and practices for commercial benefit.

Table 3.1 Some situations and strategies

Zone	Possible situations	Possible objectives	Possible competitive initiatives
X	Customer in commodity markets	• Short-term survival by protecting market share • Upgrade technology base • Move from commodity market to niche speciality markets	• Continue to search for opportunities for low cost 'me too' products arising from deregulation, end of patents or weak patent protection • Thorough review of existing survivor strategy to determine a more attractive future strategy
	Supplier and customer breaking through Y Zone	• Strengthen emergent position in selected niche businesses • Introduction of new added-value products that clearly match customers' strategic needs	• Match/lead customers' move towards customer total quality/high tech. moves by upgrading products, processes and technology • Speed strengthening of capability by acquisition
Y	Customer in lead	• Respond flexibly to customers' competitive pressures for step-change improvements in technology • Become more competitive in the busy supplier/sub-contractor market	• Invest in technology capability • International sourcing technology, catch up with customer • Move towards strategic relationships with key customers in medium term

Supplier in lead

- Although not yet a world leader, aim to change key customers' perception of available technology and help them move from X to Y zone
- Become preferred supplier even in competitive bid situations
- Take advantage of added-value lead by exploring strategic alliances with global customers
- Watch for competitors' or suppliers' attempts to 'leap-frog' technology being used currently

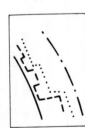

Supplier actively accessing

- Aim to establish market image as a global innovator in use of available technology
- Build market share with significant added value products
- Attempt to become controlling strategist in customer—supplier—sub-contractor chain
- Expand capability to rapidly convert accessed technology for products and services
- Promote company as a good licensor of technology

Supplier accessing and internal leading edge developments

- Maintain position as world leader in use, access and development of new enabling technologies
- Achievement of growing share of global markets for high added-value products
- Invest in constant strategic review of technology-based opportunities on international basis
- Ensure that customer intelligence network anticipates competitors' bids to catch up

Key:

——— Total available and relevant technology

—·— In general use

- - - - - Used by supplier

·········· Used by customer

Table 3.2 Comparison of potential impact of approaches to management of technology

Approach / Criteria for comparison	Customer orientation of company	Potential impact of approaches in terms of:				
		Financial results from technology investments	Evaluation of technology options	Customer/user focused IT systems	Corporate technology awareness	Facilitates Total Quality programme
(a) Independent technological innovations by a single function without overall strategic direction and coordination	Low/Medium	Low/Medium	Low/Medium	Low/Medium/High	Low/Medium	Low
(b) Multi-functional programme initiated by one specialist department from a functional productivity viewpoint with limited customer/user focus	Low/Medium	Medium	Medium	Low/Medium	Medium	Low
(c) Corporate operational approach to investment of technology to achieve short/medium-term reductions in head counts and overheads	Medium	Medium	Medium/High	Medium	Medium	Medium
(d) Corporate strategic planning approach with access and use of technology to achieve satisfaction of customer/end-user needs as basis for sustained competitive advantage	High	High	High	High	High	High

Approach (a) is typical of the initiatives taken by manufacturing, information technology or research and development departments to introduce new technology to improve the performance and productivity of the department but without supportive actions by other departments, and in the absence of a communicated corporate strategy. Such innovative and well-intentioned actions may spark off a more challenging corporate programme, but more often they lead to a mismatch of functional visions and subsequent frustrations.

Approach (b) describes the situation where a manufacturing manager launches a local Total Quality campaign and attempts, without corporate direction and support, to influence the supply department to be more stringent in their quality management of suppliers and sub-contractors; the design department to design for available machine technology; and the sales department to restrict the number of special orders.

Approach (c) is typical of the company that invests in a major integrated computer manufacturing system or refinery control system to improve the productivity of producing current products but without regard to new products, customer technology, and processes that can be anticipated within the next three to five years.

Approach (d) describes the well-managed company that sustains a regular cycle of corporate and business strategy reviews at all levels. These adjust the direction and investment priorities of the company, taking into account the emergent product and technology needs of key customers.

The comparative analysis in Table 3.2 highlights the potential power and benefit of a corporate and strategic approach to the management of technology. The basis for such an approach is discussed further in Chapters 5, 9 and 10.

The importance of support technology

Much of the chapter has concentrated on product and service technology. In practice, support technology can be as important and vital, and the concepts previously outlined apply. By support technology we refer to technology used within the business, particularly that related to processes and systems, IT and management practices to prepare for the future in addition to achieving short-term results.

Examples of important support technology include:

- manufacturing industry — automation and robotics and the systems to manage the processes
- processing industry — effluent controls and biological processes
- property development — project management and financing

- financial services — 'City' financial engineering and IT technology
- Eastern Europe — management technology associated with management of change.

The concept of the 'technology gap' discussed earlier is applicable in each of the above situations.

Strategic leadership with environmental technology

The use of technology to exploit business opportunities for environment and ecology-related products, services, processes and systems has never been greater. For most companies, from supermarkets to super tankers, from chemical manufacturers to car manufacturers, from paper mills to refuse disposal and recycling plants, and from the pharmaceutical industry to agriculture, the need to help customers, one's own company and suppliers anticipate and solve environmental and ecological problems and potential problems has become an important strategic issue.

In practice a wide range of mainstream opportunities exist in both the developed and developing world related to health safety, environment, natural resource conservancy, nature conservancy, ecology and pollution control. There may be opportunities for new, modified or replacement products, components, materials, processes, services and systems, and include the following:

1. Consumer products that have been produced and processed in an ecologically secure manner. Examples include: cosmetics, organic vegetables, free-range meat, recycled paper and card products, CFC-free products, returnable plastic bottles.

2. Consumer services that enable domestic health and the environment to be maintained in a hygienic, attractive and cost-effective manner. Examples include: solar refuse degenerators, bottle recycling, mobile sanitation and green investment trusts.

3. Consumer systems that enable use with reduced physical and mental hazards. Examples include: home diagnostic kits, low decibel home and car alarm systems, home banking systems with ease of operation and low eye strain screens, fire warning systems.

4. Industrial products or components that will enable customers to produce environmentally compatible or environment improving products, processes and systems. Examples include: biodegradable materials, substitute chemicals, energy efficient devices, dust/solvent extractors, recycled paper and board products.

5. Industrial services that assist customers to improve their awareness of the environmental dimension as well as cope with it. Examples include: intelligence/reports on likely changes in policy and legislation and their impact, market and competitive surveys, environmental test laboratories or on-site analysis and monitoring, waste disposal and recycling, ecological surveys and asbestos removal.

6. Industrial systems that assist customers to monitor and react to environmental problems. Examples include: process and effluent control systems in a wide range of industries, total quality approaches that embrace the environmental dimension, energy management systems. These opportunities are not new. Among other issues Dickens commented in the nineteenth century on the social conscience of industry and commerce. In the 1970s writers and speakers like Ralph Nader in the US and John Humble in Europe encouraged national and multi-national companies to become more socially aware as an issue of business self-interest and survival. The needs remain.

Responses have been and continue to be varied in viewpoint and impact. Typical socially responsible responses have included:

1. *Charitable*: corporate donations to worthy international, national or local causes such as the arts, conservation, environmental and health programmes.

2. *Corporate sponsorship*: corporate underwriting of awards, performances, exhibitions and events that might otherwise not be monitored.

3. *Community*: corporate funding of community facilities in the local area by an established business or in the property development world as planning gains.

4. *Corporate investment*: in new office and work environments by new building or refurbishing which engenders personal commitments, performance, team work, quality, safety and productivity.

5. *Crisis*: corporate donations of people, goods and funds to disaster aid programmes.

6. *Customer*: business response to needs of customers for new products, services and technology that will enable environmentally focused strategies and reduce the extent of operational problems.

7. *Changes in technology*: technology substitutes such as new processes, materials and substances.

8. *Chronic*: corporate investment in cleaning up major produced or

inherited environmental problems. Problems include radiation, contaminated earth, acid rain, dead rivers, suburban/industrial sanitation, CO and NO atmospheric levels, CFCs in refrigeration systems. A great success has been the noise reduction and emission control achieved by the aviation industry.

The latter three represent opportunities and risks for the 1990s and probably beyond. Farsighted companies recognize:

- added-value opportunities of environmentally friendly products, and profitable and cost-effective means of exploiting them ahead of competitors
- the benefit of being ahead of legislation in order to safeguard the possibility of continuing operations on a long-term basis.

Shortsighted companies often take the opposite viewpoint:

- customers are not yet ready for green products, would not pay for a premium and that, inevitably, such products would be more expensive to produce
- don't spend money on extra controls and clean-ups until competitors have to act to meet new legislative requirements.

The result of the latter position is that legislation becomes tougher and tougher based on evidence that some companies have found solutions and that others need regular fines, and perhaps the ultimate threat of closure, before they respond. The debate continues. However, more and more companies seem to recognize that a pro-active v. reactive corporate position is required and that effective use of technology has a major part to play. Making a change in approach will, for many companies, require a rethink of the culture of the businesses. This aspect is discussed in Chapter 6.

OPPORTUNITY SEARCH

The concept of 'opportunity search' is outlined in some detail in Chapter 5. The following questions need to be incorporated from an environmental technology point of view.

1. What opportunities exist for using currently available/accessible technology to help customers:

    - enhance and accelerate the development, launch and support of environmentally compatible or protective products, services, processes and systems from a strategic point of view?

- clean up aspects of their present day-to-day operations?
- solve specific one-off or recurring operational problems associated with contravention of environmental legislation and regulations?
- plan to prevent potential crisis such as plant closure or a product ban?

2. What opportunities exist for assisting suppliers to accelerate the availability of environmentally approved products, services, processes and systems?

3. If the technology is not readily available on a cost-effective basis, what in-house or sponsored research and development should be considered?

RISK MANAGEMENT

In parallel with the numerous opportunities, a large number of risks also exist. Increasingly, legislation lays down tighter environmental standards, and specifies in some detail the liability of operators and suppliers for environmental damage on a current and, in some instances, retrospective basis. It is, therefore, important that a risk analysis — similar in format to Table 5.7 and Fig. 10.8 — is prepared and maintained on a current basis. A failure to recognize risks at an early date and act upon them is resulting in more and more changes in the location of industrial plants or their effective closure. Planning applications for new property development and industrial projects are increasingly required to be supported by a thorough environmental impact analysis and resultant investment action plan.

HOW TO GET STARTED

The following practical options exist:

1. Include an environmental section in the pre-work questionnaire prior to the next strategy review session requesting views on opportunities and threats emergent from the company, customers and suppliers.

2. Establish a special environmental task-force to implement an initial survey as an input to the next strategy review. The task-force to identify impact currently or over the longer-term opportunities and risks.

3. Organize a technology strategy session along the lines of Table 5.3

with one stream of analysis, discussion and action planning related to environmental technology issues.

4. Allocate accountability for maintaining and communicating awareness of environmental opportunities and risks to an appropriate director.

5. Appoint a part-time strategically focused 'Environmental Business Development Manager'.

6. Join a national environmental initiative such as that actioned by the Confederation of British Industry in 1992. The Environmental Business Forum announced the aim was to 'show that a business-led voluntary action, rather than additional regulation, is the best way to protect and improve the environment'.

7. Commission an external survey. This could be broadly based on focused or specific priority issues identified through actions 1–5. The latter will achieve a deeper awareness and dedicated actions in many companies.

Such actions would enable companies to be in the position to comply with emergent eco-auditing requirements such as that proposed by the European Commission for European and national governments world-wide. When introduced, the 1990 UK Environmental Protection Act was claimed to initiate the most advanced system of integrated pollution control in the world. But the real crunch is that in the developed world there is a perceived trend in the courage of some companies to enforce the attitude that if companies cannot demonstrate a 'clean record' they will not buy, finance or insure. Inevitably, as the best improve, it will become tougher and tougher for the worst performers to stay in touch or catch up.

ENVIRONMENTAL MANAGEMENT AUDIT

How do you perform today? An audit questionnaire (Table 3.4) is provided at the end of this chapter to enable you to take an initial look as the trigger to more detailed analysis and action in critical areas. The audit questionaire is designed to be completed and discussed on an individual or group basis like earlier questionnaires.

The audit is in three parts:

Part A A broad view of the balance and synergy between managing customers and managing technology on a strategic basis

Part B An audit questionnaire covering a selection of the most important issues involved in managing the access to, and use of, technology

Part C An audit questionnaire related solely to the management of technology in relation to environmental issues.

As with previous audits, consider completing them individually or on a group basis as a one-off exercise, or as an integral part of ongoing strategic analysis and action planning.

Part A Synergy between customer and technology management

1. Review Table 3.3 and interpret to your particular situation if necessary.

2. Ask yourself *Where were we three years ago? Where were we a year ago? Where are we today? Where should we be in one and three years' time?*

A typical evolutionary path would be to follow the sequence 1, 2, 3, 4.

Table 3.3 Synergy between customer needs and technology availability

Present position	Emphasis of	
	Customer Management	Technology Management
1. At best marketing talks to R&D, and IT talks to product development but little integrated decision-making as yet	Functional	Functional
2. Board bases decisions on independent Annual R&D, IT and general market position reports	Corporate	Functional
3. Strong functional sales and market driven business supported by a corporate technology approach mainly focused on short/medium operational type products	Functional	Corporate
4. Commercial synergy through integration of customer-led and technology-driven leadership through integrated decision-making and regular joint strategic reviews between directors of supplier and customer	Corporate	Corporate

Part B Use of technology audit questionnaire

1. Complete the audit questionnaire presented in Table 3.4. The audit is based on issues raised throughout Chapter 3.

2. Add up the cumulative score which will be in the range of 0–40.

3. The following broad interpretations are suggested:

31–40 Generally well prepared and able to identify, access and use available relevant technology to help customers achieve competitive advantage

21–30 Have a base from which to plan and achieve early step-changes in the effective use of available technology

11–20 Generally a reactive stance, much action required to establish secure base for future competitive advantage

0–10 Major problems in all areas. Do not yet view technology as a strategic opportunity and resource.

Part C   Management of environmental technology audit

1. Complete the audit questionnaire presented in Table 3.5.

2. Add up the cumulative score which will be in the range of 0–40.

3. The following broad interpretations of total scores are suggested:

31–40 Among the environmental leaders. Influence national and international policy. Opportunity for public recognition and an Investor in Environment (IIE)

21–30 Becoming a responsible and responsive organization within industry, but unlikely to become one of leaders without major effort in several areas

11–20 Thinking about issues but urgent decisions and actions required in many areas. Vulnerable to further environmental legislation and controls

0–10 Serious risk of closure as result of action by customers or authorities.

Management of technology audit

This audit provides a practical basis for an initial evaluation of the current position and trend in the management of the use of technology in a specific company or business.

Table 3.4 Use of technology audit questionnaire

Instructions: Consider each of the issues/questions in turn. Select the column which best fits your current situation and tick the appropriate box 'a'. Consider the underlying trend and denote by ↑ → ↗ ↘ in box 'b'. Add score for all questions.

Issue and question	Assessment of (a) current situation and (b) trend							
	Poor		Fair		Good		Excellent	
	Score 1		Score 2		Score 3		Score 4	
1. Strategic resource Is the management of the use of technology recognized as a strategic resource?	Technology rarely discussed as an issue		Technology seen as R&D or IT only		Board starting to discuss as corporate issue on a strategic basis		Use of technology established as major source of opportunities	
	a.	b.	a.	b.	a.	b.	a.	b.
2. Management process Is the management of the use of technology recognized as requiring specific management?	Not as yet		Functional forecasting, mapping done		Specific budgeting and action planning		Specific sub-strategic processes used	
	a.	b.	a.	b.	a.	b.	a.	b.
3. Strategic inputs Are technological issues integrated to strategic analysis/ decisions?	Rarely		By function only		Increasingly at annual reviews		Yes, integrated ongoing processes	
	a.	b.	a.	b.	a.	b.	a.	b.
4. Technology awareness To what extent are directors and senior managers technologically aware?	Low level		Technical directors/ managers only		Improving with occasional updates		High level with regular updates	
	a.	b.	a.	b.	a.	b.	a.	b.

Table 3.4 *cont.*

Issue and question	Assessment of (a) current situation and (b) trend							
	Poor		Fair		Good		Excellent	
	Score 1		Score 2		Score 3		Score 4	
5. Technology gap Are active steps taken to improve perception and understanding of the technology gap?	No		Only on *ad hoc* project basis		Need recognized and being acted on		Yes, up-to-date emergent picture maintenance	
	a.	b.	a.	b.	a.	b.	a.	b.
6. Evaluation of technologies Are newly recognized technologies evaluated on a strategic basis?	*Ad hoc* only		On project-by-project basis		On strategic basis technology by technology		Integrated evaluation total technology	
	a.	b.	a.	b.	a.	b.	a.	b.
7. Access of technologies Is technology accessed internationally in an objective manner?	Invented here only		National universities visited		World-wide services now being examined		World-wide access of cost-effective sources	
	a.	b.	a.	b.	a.	b.	a.	b.
8. Focus of use Is the use of technology focused on key customer strategy needs?	Only by accident		Good focus on short/medium-term operating needs		Increasingly so		Yes, ongoing planned basis	
	a.	b.	a.	b.	a.	b.	a.	b.

Table 3.4 *cont.*

Issue and question	Assessment of (a) current situation and (b) trend			
	Poor	Fair	Good	Excellent
	Score 1	Score 2	Score 3	Score 4
9. Support technology Is support technology driven (by 8)	No, only *ad hoc* response if crisis	Recognize need and starting to adjust on *ad hoc* basis	Broad based audit and change pro-gramme in hand	Yes, regularly reassessed and fine-tuned
	a. b.	a. b.	a. b.	a. b.
10. Management approach Is the use of technology managed in a strategic, total and integrated manner?	Not really, only react to market crisis and environmental legislation	Beginning to approach in more dedicated manner. Audits when we have a crisis	Now beginning to benefit from a strategic approach, with regular audits programmed	As far as is possible today, constantly looking for new added-value ideas
	a. b.	a. b.	a. b.	a. b.
Column scores				

© Management of Technology Partnership 1989

Total score (sum columns 1–4) ☐

Profile summary

Issue and Question		1	2	3	4	5	6	7	8	9	10
Assessment of current level of performance	1										
	2										
	3										
	4										

Table 3.5   Management of Environmental Technology

Consider each of the above issues/questions in turn. Select the column which best fits your current situation and tick the appropriate box 'a'. Consider the underlying trend and denote by ↑ →↗ ↘ in box 'b'. Score all questions. Add up score.

Issue and question	Assessment/description of current situation							
	Poor		Fair		Good		Excellent	
	Score 1		Score 2		Score 3		Score 4	
1. Environmental responsibility What stance is taken?	Wait and see. React if affected by complaints or inspectors		Study newly published legislation and take actions necessary to delay complaints or inspections		Pro-active study of pending legislation or consultative documents and plan opportunistic action		Clear strategy. Attempt to influence legislation, regulations and standards. Attempt to maintain best practical position	
	a.	b.	a.	b.	a.	b.	a.	b.
2. Products Are products designed with environmental issues in mind?	*Ad hoc.* Tend to react to problems/ complaints as they arise		Increasingly prepare an environmental impact analysis to anticipate problems		. . . plus look for commercial opportunities for products and services using available technology		Full range of products designed to achieve environmentally friendly added-value	
	a.	b.	a.	b.	a.	b.	a.	b.
3. Services Are environmentally related services provided to customers?	Not seen as opportunity, particularly as our technology is largely out of date		Provide problem-solving support when essential to retain business		See as business opportunity, but constrained in fully exploiting by cash and lack of customer response		Range of strategically important services generate profit. Developed in cooperation with key customers	
	a.	b.	a.	b.	a.	b.	a.	b.
4. Processes Are processes used in-house or on customer premises environmentally clean?	Apprehensive that they are not, but analysis of processes incomplete		Know problems but have serious backlog of unsolved chronic/latent problems		Plans in hand to redesign, replace or close down all offending unit operations and equipment		International reputation for innovative clean processes and environmental clean-ups	
	a.	b.	a.	b.	a.	b.	a.	b.

Table 3.5   *cont.*

Issue and question	Assessment/description of current situation			
	Poor	Fair	Good	Excellent
	Score 1	Score 2	Score 3	Score 4
5. Systems Do systems use up-to-date technology to reduce health risks, stress, environmental impact and improve user-friendliness?	Now recognize problem, but little action to date	Task-force actively audit-ing situation and preparing recommend-ations	Active programmes to improve environment. Occupational health and safety	Have reputation and awards for safe, user-friendly, environmentally friendly systems and related facilities
	a. b.	a. b.	a. b.	a. b.
6. Replacements and substitutes Is leadership taken to find replacements for potentially sensitive materials and substances?	No, leave this to others	Respond if required to by legislation or customers	Now involved in industry task-force to determine and resolve replacement/ substitute needs	Have ongoing development programme to identify and develop environmentally compatible materials and substances
	a. b.	a. b.	a. b.	a. b.
7. Suppliers Do you rate vendors accord-ing to environ-mental history/ position in deciding on who will continue to supply?	No. Not an issue discussed with suppliers	No, but using pressure from our customers to cascade concern and need for action on to suppliers	Yes, actively dropping non-compliant suppliers	Yes, and have a number of joint environmental improvement projects in hand. Try to jointly design out the problems.
	a. b.	a. b.	a. b.	a. b.
8. Community projects Are management and/or technolo-gists seconded full- or part-time to local environ-mental projects/ initiatives?	No, prefer non-involvement, low profile and getting on with the business	Limited involvement by enthusiasts on voluntary personal basis	Will become officially involved if we see other local businesses or customers or competitors taking the lead	Often act in lead coordinating role. Raises profile as good corporate citizen. Provide personnel and technology.
	a. b.	a. b.	a. b.	a. b.

Table 3.5   *cont.*

Issue and question	Assessment/description of current situation							
	Poor		**Fair**		**Good**		**Excellent**	
	Score 1		Score 2		Score 3		Score 4	
9. National/ industry projects and studies **Is an active involvement sought?**	No, we don't want unexpected public relations, investigation or exposure		Not initially. Attend presentations and seminars. Would become involved to outmanoeuvre a competitor		Like to be fully informed at early stage. Nearly always consider an involvement if it looks important		Seek a public leadership role if within our management or technological competence. Seen as 'investor' in the environment	
	a.	b.	a.	b.	a.	b.	a.	b.
10. Environmental awareness **Are all staff fully informed and contributing pro-actively to environmental issues?**	No, assume our engineers keep themselves informed		Occasional teach-ins, particularly following complaints inspectors or to *post mortem* disasters		Becoming pro-active. Regular briefings for most staff on new problems, legislation, products, processes, etc.		Regular top-to-bottom briefings and workshops. Task-forces used to build commitment	
	a.	b.	a.	b.	a.	b.	a.	b.
Column Count								
Score weighted	(×1)		(×2)		(×3)		(×4)	

Total score

THE CHAPTERS THAT FOLLOW

The customer and technology missing links continue as core themes through Chapters 4–10 which follow. These chapters progressively build up a framework of actions that can be taken towards a more competitive position on a basis of continuous innovation.

MANAGING SUPPLIERS FOR STRATEGIC SUCCESS

Effective relationships with suppliers are critical to success. Success built on the satisfaction of your customer needs and access to essential enabling technology, either as a direct purchase or via joint design development projects. Improved selection, management motivation and support is therefore required. Excellent suppliers need to be treated as strategic partners. Others with promise need to be nurtured to accept new customer needs, higher levels of quality and reliability, investments in technology and a step-change in culture. The issue is important to industry, and also to government departments and agencies, seeking to contract out a wide range of current in-house services.

The supplier challenge

The management of suppliers has become a strategic issue, as indicated in Fig. 4.1. At the beginning of Chapter 2 we reviewed the characteristics of successful suppliers. In this chapter we review a number of important factors to be taken into account in building and using an effective supplier network. This network, in many cases, will include other member organizations of the same parent group, direct suppliers, original equipment manufacturers, distributors and agents.

In Chapter 2 we introduced the concepts of strategic, operational, problem solving and crisis products. The demands on suppliers for each of such products, and the obligations of the customer are illustrated in Table 4.1.

Looked at in this way, effective customer/supplier relations require that both customer and supplier act appropriately and ensure that relationships are monitored at an appropriate level. With a service contract for equipment such as the photostat copier, the order may well be placed by a relatively junior buyer with call-offs triggered by a phone call from a low ranking user.

The strategic relationship, however, will require two levels of contact, both well up the hierarchy from the first example. The establishment of the basis of the contract and performance criteria for both parties is likely to be a director's-to-director's level meeting or steering group with implementation and progress monitored by a joint management project group or task-force. This implies a modification in the buying process.

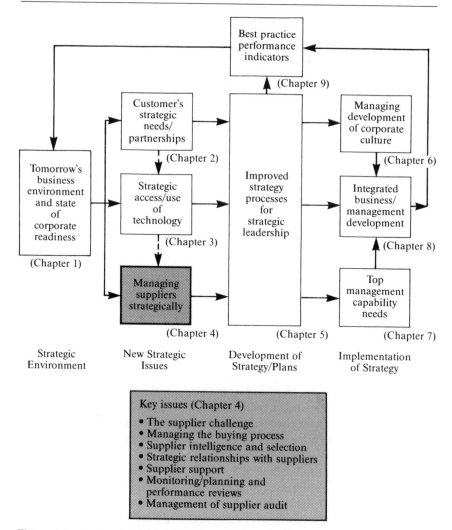

Figure 4.1 Framework for managing suppliers for strategic success

Modifying the buying process

The basic buying process is illustrated in Fig. 4.2. Some important differences between the operational and strategic situation are illustrated in the sections that follow.

Table 4.1 Demands on suppliers and obligations of customers

Type of product/ service supplied	Demands on supplier	Obligations of customers
Innovative strategic products and services to build tomorrow's business	• Continuous innovation • Security • Realistic prices • Speed/deadlines • Tell customer what is possible	• Strategy updates • Realistic programming • Sharing ideas/dreams • Active support • Medium-term security
Regular operational products and services to achieve annual plan	• Competitive price/terms • Consistent quality • Reliable delivery • Flexibility • Service level commitments	• Firm schedules • Minimum shocks • Knowledgeable contacts • Realistic quality needs • Service specifications
Problem-solving products/services to tackle recurring problems	• Speed of response/resolution • Professionalism/experience • Low price • Cleanliness	• Call off contract • Access • Maintenance • Recognition
Crisis product or service to meet occasional crisis	• Speed of response • Quick permanent fix • Realistic price • Low residual contamination	• Speedy call off • Leave to professionals • Good communications • Crisis containment

Supplier selection

The main differences will be

	Operational situation	*Strategic situation*
Who is involved?	Buyers/managers	Directors/managers
Frequency contacts?	Quarterly or annually	1–3 years
Typical selection criteria?	1. Product type? 2. Designs? 3. Quality 4. Cost? 5. Availability? 6. Financial security? 7. Operational controls? 8. Spares/service? 9. Effectiveness of scheduling?	1. Technology base? 2. Project management? 3. Innovation? 4. Profitability? 5. Capabilities? 6. Innovation funding? 7. Strategic vision? 8. Training/developing? 9. Effectiveness of CIDM?

A. Operational situation

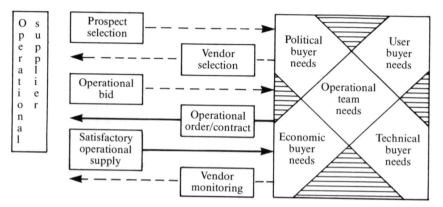

B. Strategic situation

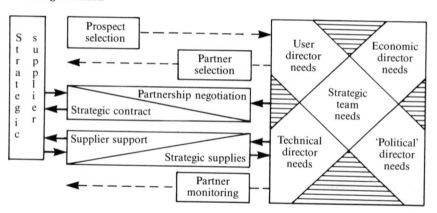

Figure 4.2   The buying process

The differences show up particularly strongly where major companies request trusted strategic suppliers to participate in new product design programmes from the pre-concept phase. In manufacturing, such concurrent engineering is becoming essential to achieve the reduction in lead times for new products required for survival.

Supplier intelligence

The market intelligence required to seek out possible operational suppliers will be fairly routine and often available from desk research in trade directories, catalogues and exhibitions.

Additional and deeper market intelligence is required in seeking out prospective strategic suppliers. The non-routine information will require carefully planned supplier research and face-to-face meetings at director level to establish the level of trust and openness necessary to collect the required up-to-date information first hand. Typical questions that need answering include:

- Which suppliers/potential suppliers are, or are likely to be, most innovative in the accessing and use of enabling technology?
- What have been their most recent successful innovations? Who have reduced development times by more than 50 per cent?
- What significant future innovations can be anticipated?
- How successful are they in the integrative application of different technologies?
- How effective is their project/programme planning and execution?
- How technologically aware are they in relation to used and available technologies in existing and related fields?
- What strategic alliances already exist?
- How active are national and international competitors in tying up key suppliers in strategic programmes?

Nature of strategic relationship with suppliers

An effective working relationship with suppliers is critical to all companies, but especially so for those with established or planned strategic dependence. Strategic dependence implies that the reality of the customer company's strategy and perhaps that of the customer's customer, is dependent on supplier support and performance. The supplier, therefore, needs to plan for a win–win relationship, whatever the starting point of the relationship.

Three starting points and possible trends in relationships, dependencies and win–win benefits are illustrated in Fig. 4.3. Such developments often require a change in the culture of both the customer and supplier.

The win–win relationship implies a relationship based on joint opportunity exploitation and problem solving. This is far removed from the often traditional relationship based on establishing a supply of quality products building to a level that is important to the supplier and then squeezing for low, lower and lowest prices.

Where strategic relationships are considered, it would be helpful if both parties completed the company culture audit described in Chapter 6, and compared the results to identify:

- probability for successful joint working
- risk areas

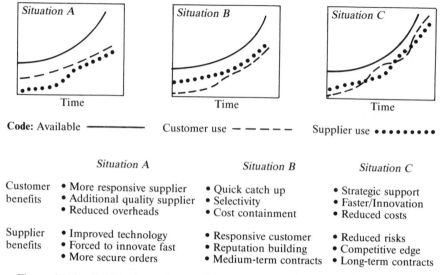

Figure 4.3 Availability/use of accessible relevant technology

- areas for joint change of culture
- areas for urgent support by customer to enable supplier to establish the capabilities and culture required for success.

This sharing approach is more likely to succeed in the longer term than merely an array of preferred quality awards and an IS9000 requirement for entry to bid lists.

Proven strategic suppliers will gain the advantage of single sourced contracts, but against strict quality cost and delivery performance and communication criteria. In such situations, it is to the customer's benefit also to lay down the basis for project management and joint problem solving, and be prepared to provide the supplier with the support to succeed.

Supplier support

By definition, strategic supplier success is crucial. Therefore, it is realistic to provide support to suppliers to supplement or accelerate the building up of their own technological or management capability. Typical areas of support include the following:

- joint programme of strategy reviews to improve quality of thinking and understanding
- advice on improvement in approaches to project management, systems integration, total quality management, cost management, culture development and environmental management

- technical and management training and achievement of Investors in People (IIP) award
- staff secondments or mutually agreed outplacements
- assistance in establishing test facilities, prototype testing, and in achieving registrations
- packaging advice
- design support
- establishment of dedicated CAD-machine tool on-line links
- computerized invoicing and payment systems
- provision or loans for special process equipment
- up front payment for joint sponsored research and development work to remove cash strain from supplier, and with performance bonus for superior performance
- equity stakes to demonstrate trust in a mutual future
- access to technology.

Monitoring suppliers

Customers need to monitor and track the emergent focus and quality of suppliers' management innovations, decisions and actions for a number of reasons, including the following:

- as part of routine vendor rating and evaluation activity
- to identify emergent weaknesses that require corrective action or consideration of a change of supplier
- to anticipate possible restructuring initiatives within the supplier chain that might be to competitive advantage or disadvantage
- to identify emergent strategic strengths that might prompt and facilitate a step-change in the supply chain by a supplier, as illustrated in Chapter 2, Fig. 2.4, alone or in partnership
- to identify opportunities for deeper strategic relationships and reinforced or new competitive advantage.

The strategic supplier scanning check-list may need strengthening to include such questions as:

- Which suppliers are recognized — or could in the future be recognized — as the most effective innovators in the supply chain?
- Which suppliers are — or are likely to become — the most innovative in the access and use of technology?
- What have been their most recent successful innovations? Have we, or their other customers, made best and total use of these innovations as business opportunities?
- What new innovations can probably be anticipated?

- What have been their traditional source of technology? Is this changing? Does this represent an opportunity or a threat?
- Is our company seen as the company best able to support the supplier's innovation process, and/or handle/use new innovations? Are we offered strategic innovations first, or are other customers — especially competitors — higher up their preferred customer list?

Supplier planning and performance reviews

Annual performance reviews with strategic suppliers are important to ensure that:

- an open constructive relationship is established and maintained
- both parties are achieving what they expect and want from the relationship
- the supplier understands the customer's strategy and newly emergent needs and demands
- both parties understand the current competitive situation and success criteria for cooperative efforts
- the supplier understands — and is realistic about — past and future performance standards
- the customer understands the strategy, critical issues and capability gaps of the supplier
- areas where supplier support would be of benefit are identified and actioned
- potential new/extended areas for innovative cooperation are identified at an early date
- ineffective partnerships are aborted at an early stage
- cost structure and quality standards are challenged, and means determined for improvements to realize mutual benefit
- the joint strategy and cultural initiatives required for 'the partnership' to be fully competitive are identified.

For both the customer and supplier to succeed symbiotic benefits need to be understood and managed on a pro-active basis.

Management of supplier's audit

1. The end-of-chapter audit questionnaire in Table 4.2 is provided to help you assess the effectiveness and trend in the management of your suppliers.

2. As with other audits included in the book, complete the questionnaire on an individual or group basis and add up the total score.

3. The following guidelines will help you identify the implications of the total score.

Total score	Typical implication
30–40	A customer in a strong position to succeed with innovative competitive moves, with the security that there is little risk of being let down by suppliers
21–30	Basis of partnerships being built, but much discipline and urgency required to tidy up and tie the knots
11–20	Problems and opportunities recognized, but a long way to go. Probably an uphill task, with competitors already well ahead.
0–10	Need to review overall strategy and take action fast. New supplier network required or do more in-house if capabilities exist. Probably low chance of strategic survival of company.

4. Examine the profile of your scores and identify action points for both short- and medium-term action.

In Chapter 5 we will consider the management processes involved in establishing and implementing strategy. As this chapter has identified, the effectiveness of key suppliers can have a major impact on the timely implementation of strategic change. At best, it often makes it just achievable; at worst, it demonstrates that the strategy is totally unrealistic in today's industrial climate. Therefore, spend time now starting to build up the strengths, capabilities, commitment and trust of your key suppliers. Exciting strategic opportunities are more likely to be achieved together than separately. Make your strategic partnerships with suppliers the winners.

Table 4.2 Management of supplier's audit

Instructions: Consider each of the issues/questions in turn. Select the column which best fits your current situation and tick the appropriate box 'a'. Consider the underlying trend and denote by ↑ → ↗ ↘ in box 'b'. Score all questions. Total up scores.

Issues and questions	Assessment of (a) current situation and (b) trend							
	Poor		Fair		Good		Excellent	
	Score 1		Score 2		Score 3		Score 4	
1. Business/ culture philosophy of key suppliers	Conflicting approaches to innovation, commercial relations and employees		Starting to identify suppliers with whom we can work best		Priorities understood and joint development programme in hand		Compatible and fully competitive	
	a.	b.	a.	b.	a.	b.	a.	b.
2. Number of key suppliers	Have large numbers of suppliers used on least cost, convenience basis		Starting to screen out and drop poor performers		Have decided what we need for future and putting in place		Reduced to small, reliable, committed core of value-for-money regulars	
	a.	b.	a.	b.	a.	b.	a.	b.
3. Supplier relations	Very *ad hoc*		Start made to establish control and consistent approach		Initial strategic relationships in place, others actively sought		Necessary long-term strategic relationships established and working well	
	a.	b.	a.	b.	a.	b.	a.	b.
4. Supplier support policy	None, let suppliers swim or sink		Occasionally help key suppliers out when in crisis		When requested, help solve problems through joint task-force approach		Major programme of strategic support established	
	a.	b.	a.	b.	a.	b.	a.	b.
5. New joint ventures	None, suppliers held at arm's length		Beginning to consider joint projects for specials on occasional basis		A few in place, generally for enabling technology versus new products		Increasingly in place for key unique new products/ services	
	a.	b.	a.	b.	a.	b.	a.	b.

Table 4.2 *cont.*

6. Acquisition of external technology	Don't rely on suppliers for any key technology		Generally not sought but had luck with unexpected windfalls		Major source of accessed technology — expect them to visit universities		Also have a number of joint search and development programmes	
	a.	b.	a.	b.	a.	b.	a.	b.
7. Innovation performance suppliers	Suppliers tend not to be the innovators — they follow or react		Innovative in some areas. improving rapidly		Can generally be relied on for new ideas		Regarded as leading innovators in their area	
	a.	b.	a.	b.	a.	b.	a.	b.
8. Supplier of management	Generally seems to be one crisis after another		Good problem-solvers, on road to getting house in order		Strong operational management and starting to act strategically		Strong strategic culture with total customer ethos	
	a.	b.	a.	b.	a.	b.	a.	b.
9. Relation-ships with competitors of suppliers to aid bench-making	Not evaluated systematically, pick up a few up things on on old boy grapevine		Have started to analyse systematically		Now have occasional meetings to fill gaps in information		Regular meetings/ analyses in order to benchmark current/ potential/ competitive suppliers	
	a.	b.	a.	b.	a.	b.	a.	b.
10. Board with suppliers	None, only contact normally through buyers		*Ad hoc* 'state' visits or crisis communications		Annual presentations of forward plans for next year or so		Regular joint strategy reviews	
	a.	b.	a.	b.	a.	b.	a.	b.
Column count								
Score weighted	(x1)		(x2)		(x3)		(x4)	

Total score

© Management of Technology Partnership 1992

STRATEGY PROCESSES FOR THE FUTURE

An effective strategic management process has become an essential norm for businesses. What are the main ingredients of process and content for success? How can they be managed for time-effective benefit at the corporate and business level? How can they become more flexible but more embracing? How can vision and analysis be balanced and integrated?

The challenge

Strategy concerns the nature, direction and focus of tomorrow's business. The management process of establishing, reviewing and updating a company's strategy should be one of the most stimulating and purposeful activities in which directors and senior managers are involved. Surprisingly, this is not the case in many organizations. The need for an improved approach is highlighted in paper after paper in management and academic journals and conference proceedings, and recently by government and trade association conferences concerned about member companies' competitive survival in the more open markets of the mid-1990s and beyond. Furthermore, the 1989/92 recession has highlighted the differences between the management practices of leading and average companies.

To date many companies have persevered with strategy processes led by corporate planners, with major investments in basic market analyses (largely historic) by external consultants, and with inputs from sub-business units and supportive functions obtained on a prescribed, piecemeal, and largely non-creative basis. Such a process tends to produce an inward looking and static vision of the future, and often an overly financially-oriented once-a-year prop for future actions — actions which will not be sufficiently challenging to stimulate the level of change required. In such companies, commitment to a forward strategy is shallow, progress reviews are essentially 'fire fighting', and management 'walkabouts' by the chief executive and board focused on short-term operational issues. For many executives, planning becomes a corporate intrusion into functional management issues. For others, strategy has become confused by the many academically-based generic strategies and profiling techniques published and taught by academic institutions. Fortunately, other companies recognize that the business world is in constant opportunistic turmoil and that strategic decisions need to provide the framework and guidelines for future investment and strategic development without attempting to dot all the i's and cross all the t's.

Strategy has a clear mission and purpose for these companies and is at the heart of the management processes, as illustrated in Fig. 5.1. In these companies, the chief executive is most likely to sponsor and drive the strategy process. Strategy reviews become visionary but realistic and occur on a quarterly and 'to need' basis. A process which is interactive and creative is established for the review of sub-unit strategies, the role of any consultants involved being that of a process leader or facilitator rather than an academic analyst. Executive walkabouts are organized as joint operational and strategic reviews with the emphasis on monitoring the progress and success of strategic development programmes against specific performance criteria. This aspect is discussed in detail in Chapter 9.

Mission of strategy process

There are nine aims to be considered and met in the strategy process:

1. To build a realistic dream or vision of the future that builds on today's strengths.

2. To commit the top management team to practical action plans towards the vision.

3. To develop the top management team and key support teams.

4. To watch, analyse and access customer and technological opportunities on a continuous basis.

5. To be commercially astute and adapt to significant changes in market and environmental trends and events.

6. To provide a sense of direction, a framework of reference and policy guidelines within which, and against which, to evaluate subsidiary, business unit and product group strategies.

7. To provide objective criteria against which to evaluate whether new opportunities should be pursued.

8. To create a common sense of mission to drive strategic performance.

9. To contribute to the development of an appropriate corporate culture.

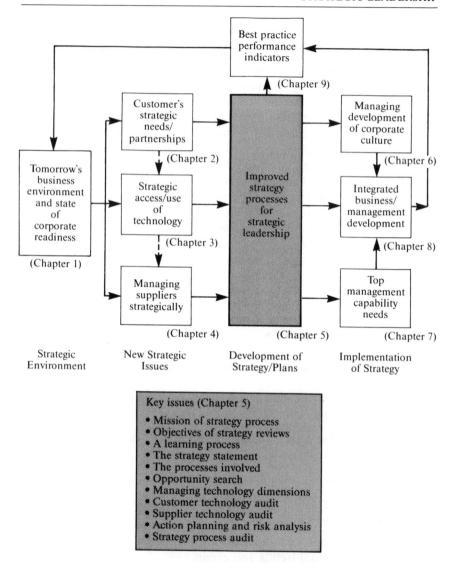

Figure 5.1 Framework of strategy-led management process

Where strategy reviews are held at subordinate levels, the nine facets of the mission apply as much as at corporate level and are essential in the development of a balanced corporate culture. This will be discussed in more detail in Chapter 6.

As discussed in previous chapters, the 1990s will be a different and more complex competitive environment than the 1980s. Success is likely to be based on unique strategies built on change and developed and implemented by exceptional top management teams rather than by generic strategies implemented by an enthusiastic average team, as illustrated in Fig. 5.2. This trend has significant implications for the design and implementation of the strategy process.

Unique strategies are only likely to emerge from a well-designed ongoing process of strategic analysis, decision-making and reviews. Reviews should both challenge and reinforce the competitive direction, nature and extent of the business. This requires that the core strategy process becomes a natural part of executive life. The process needs to be designed to be simple, flexible but rigorous. In this way, efforts can be concentrated on gathering and interpreting information as the content of the strategy process, rather than the process itself. The development of an effective strategy process is a key result area for all chairmen and chief executives in both the public and private sector.

Typical objectives for strategy reviews

There are 10 typical objectives for the establishment and design of a strategy review for a company or business:

1. To carry out an objective, open-minded reappraisal of the future opportunities, objectives and risks.

2. To update, refine and fine-tune an existing statement of strategy in the light of recent implementation successes and failures, trends in the business environment, and the deeper knowledge of the factors affecting competitiveness and shareholder value gained since the last strategy review. In particular, new insights into emergent customer strategies and related technology opportunities need to be considered.

3. To evaluate and test tentative strategic decisions in an objective and relatively unbiased manner and identify areas of disagreement within the top management team.

4. To establish commitment to the company or business by involving as participants those persons with most knowledge, experience and foresight in relation to the business environment and markets in which the company or business is likely to operate in the future, i.e.:

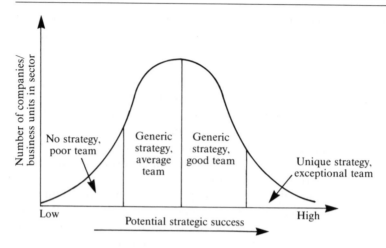

Figure 5.2   Distribution of strategic potential

- executive directors who have day-to-day accountability for improving results
- non-executive directors for breadth of vision and wisdom, if not about opportunities, then about corporate risks
- senior business, product group and functional managers with vision, information and vital implementation roles.

5. To establish priorities for seeking funds to improve the performance of core businesses by organic strategic development, acquisition and divestment.

6. To review, in a creative and integrative manner, the priorities for accessing and using available technology to satisfy the longer-term needs of important customer groups, as discussed in Chapter 2.

7. To establish a focus and strategic framework for the development of detailed marketing strategies and plans for priority business, product groups, markets and territories to ensure that optimum advantage is taken of strategic customer relationships and innovative products and services.

8. To establish the basis for ongoing series of discussions on strategically important issues between informed directors and senior executives.

9. To establish and initiate essential people and culture development priorities to support the strategic development of the business.

10. To refine strategic performance standards to reflect the intent to catch up with faster moving aggressive competitors such as Japan in

electronics, where companies come from nowhere to international prominence in a strategic time-frame of less than 10 years.

A learning process

Strategy reviews organized with these objectives in mind are likely to establish an innovative entrepreneurial and intrapreneurial climate, enable new issues to be incorporated, and accelerate the building of a cohesive top management team.

Companies that establish timely reviews which meet many of the above objectives are likely to see, and use, the strategic thinking involved as a learning process. The quality of decisions and plans will improve with practice and be in tune with a continuously enriched information base. This continuous learning process is illustrated in Figure 5.3

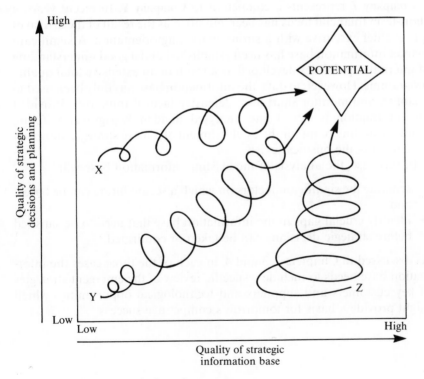

Figure 5.3   The strategic learning process

Company X represents an entrepreneurial start-up situation. A significant new business opportunity is recognized and visualized by a chief executive, business manager or new product manager. Initially only basic concept exists. Analysis and evaluation are required to give reality and dimensions to the visionary hunch. No significant resources have been allocated as yet to the embryo business. The sponsor of the business vision urgently needs information and a basic strategy process to establish speedily and explore options as a first step towards the preparation and agreement of an outline forward plan.

Company Y represents an established company with limited overt strategic thinking to date. The company has survived the competitive last decade by vigorous short-term operational planning and budgeting, but now has a drained management team and is starting to lose out to a number of competitors who are more strategically focused. The need is for an initial basic review of the inherent business mission followed by a progressively comprehensive definition of future strategy. A strategy focused on regaining competitive advantage is required. The process will be a learning process with visions and decisions becoming challenged and enriched as new information and insights emerge.

Company Z represents a competitor to **Company Y**. In recent years, a short-term financial focus has been modified as the result of the arrival of a new chief executive with a strong marketing orientation. A significant market information base has been established and a good understanding of internal capabilities developed as a result of an extensive total quality programme. However, to date, the information base has only been used to establish and monitor short-term defensive tactical initiatives. Provided the information is sieved and analysed to identify significant future trends, a starting point for the establishment of a more strategic approach to managing the business exists.

In this case, the analysis of the existing information base will:

- separate the significant factors on which a secure future can be based, and
- identify crucial gaps in the information base that need to be satisfied before strategic decisions can be taken or confirmed.

As discussed in Chapters 2, 3 and 4, in each of the three cases the information base needs to include a specific review of the emergent strategies of key customers and suppliers and technological opportunities which might provide a basis for tomorrow's competitive success.

The strategy statement

The contents of statements of strategy vary from company to company: some are practical, others too academic and an anathema to progress.

For practical purposes, a useful statement strategy needs to be:

- future oriented
- brief and to the point
- comprehensive in highlighting indications of all *significant* changes in the direction or extent of investing valuable resources
- easy to read and communicate
- readily fine-tuned in the light of as yet unexpected market developments.

A practical starting point is illustrated below. The framework integrates key decisions, including those related to the new dimensions of strategic customers and relevant technology.

TYPICAL FRAMEWORK FOR A 'BUSINESS' STRATEGY

1. Business title
2. Purpose of statement of business strategy (introduction)
3. Focus of strategy 1992–1996
   3.1 Business mission and vision of future market position
   3.2 Focus, priority strategic direction, initiatives and investment
   3.3 Focus of capability and culture development
4. Market priorities
   4.1 Strategic end-user customers
   4.2 Buyer groups/methods of distribution
   4.3 Industrial sectors/territories
5. Product/service priorities
   5.1 From existing technology
       5.1.1 Product/service improvements
       5.1.2 New products/services
   5.2 From newly accessed technology
       5.2.1 Product/service improvements
       5.2.2 New products/services
6. Acquisition plans
   6.1 Accessing technology
   6.2 Accessing products/services
   6.3 Accessing markets
   6.4 Accessing manufacturing and processing capability
7. Key capabilities that must be developed to support 1–6 e.g.
   7.1 Marketing
   7.2 Use of technology in products/services development

    7.3 Total customer management
    7.4 Accessing/evaluating/using new technology
    7.5 Customer intelligence
    7.6 Leader/manager development
    7.7 Project management
    7.8 Use of technology for internal process/systems productivity
    7.9 Use of management technology
    7.10 Management strategic suppliers
    7.11 Company culture development
8.   Financial objectives 1990–1994
    8.1 Growth in shareholder value
    8.2 £ profit
    8.3 £ turnover
    8.4 £ profit/turnover
    8.5 £ added-value per total employee costs
    8.6 Return on net assets
    8.7 Cash flow
    8.8 Investment flow, £ and timing
9.   Implementation plan
    9.1 Resolution of critical issues
    9.2 Implementation of timely strategic initiatives and change
    9.3 Maintaining opportunity search and strategy review process
    9.4 Initiation capability and culture building
10. Back-up analyses as addendum for reference and update as basis for subsequent strategy reviews.

At this point it is important to emphasize that a statement of strategy should highlight business activity that will be phased out as well as start-ups.

A continuous v. stop-start process

Strategic thinking adds value to the management processes within a business by nature of an integration of vision, direction and priorities within a time horizon typically two of five times that of detailed operational planning and budgeting. Strategic thinking incorporates the processes of strategic analysis, decision-making, mind-mapping and planning. Thus it provides a framework for the total decision-making of the company.

A statement of strategy provides:

- the focal point and thrust for investment and divestment decisions throughout the business
- the guidelines against which emergent and unexpected opportunities and risks can be evaluated for potential impact on growth and success at any time of the year
- the stimulus for a continuous and sustained search for market and technological opportunities
- through an annual review and update, a valuable starting point for the preparation of operating plans and budgets
- the basis for integrating management theory and practice
- the linking of today with tomorrow on a timely basis
- a firm base from which to tackle major changes in business direction
- a vehicle for communicating corporate intent to all levels of employee and gaining their commitment and contribution through the processes of fine-tuning and implementation
- focal point for commitment to invest in people development in line with the business. This is discussed in detail in Chapter 8, 9 and 10.

By nature, strategic thinking needs to be on a real time and flexible basis if significant competitive opportunities are to be identified and grasped before the competition. Many management teams are making considerable progress in this respect and recognize that the value of a learning process is that deeper insights and understanding are achieved the second, third and fourth time round. Unfortunately, in other companies, particularly large corporations, the standardization and institutionalization of the strategy process too often result in:

- lip-service v. enthusiastic participation
- matching of corporate systems requirements v. customers' strategic requirements at the sub-business level
- a once-a-year effort, at best done as the lead in the operating planning and budgeting for the following year v. a continuous search for opportunities and innovative ideas at all levels
- planning departments concerned with ownership and rigour of process v. opportunity stimulus and process support.

In practice, a statement of strategy is only as good as the quality of the intelligence base, vision, challenge and commitment achieved. Chief executives, therefore, need to motivate the board and senior management teams to accept and use the process as an essential part of good management practice. The regular update of a strength/weakness analysis, a visit

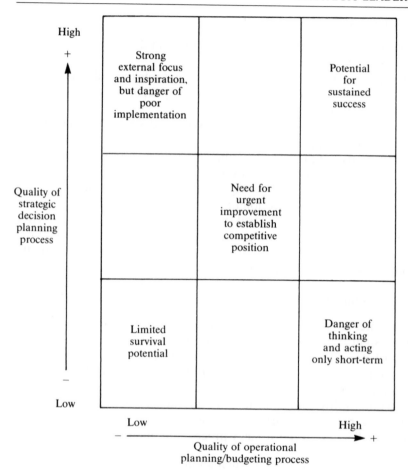

Figure 5.4 Quality dimensions of sustained success

to a strategic customer, a chance meeting with a competitor, a vacation vision of a new application for a product or enabling technology can at any time of the year, month, week, day or hour stimulate new strategic insights — the timely recognition of competitive opportunities and threats.

The process of strategic decision-making, therefore, needs to provide for and integrate informal and formal elements and link with the operational planning and control processes, as well as the venture fund part of the Budget.

At this point, it is probably timely to evaluate where the strengths and weaknesses of your company lie in this respect, as shown in Fig. 5.4.

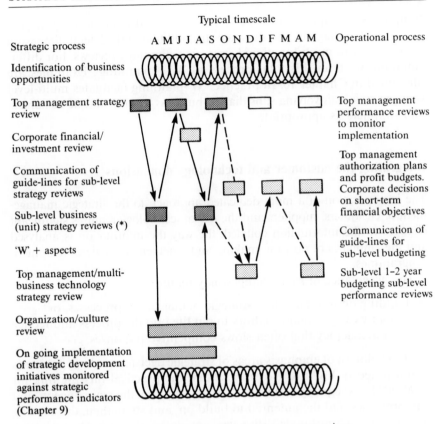

* Combination of business, territory and support function strategy reviews

Figure 5.5 The 'W-planning' process

The 'W'-planning option

What basic process is likely to stimulate and integrate vision, creativity, reality and commitment?

Historically, much planning has essentially been either 'top-down' (autocratic vision) or 'bottom-up' (participative ideas). Both approaches have been fashionable in the last 20 years, the style chosen depending often on the personal style of one person, the chief executive, rather than a conscious assessment by the top manegement team of what is best for the business at the time.

For many companies, a combination of the two extreme planning styles is found to be of most benefit. The resultant 'W'-planning approach is illustrated in Fig. 5.5, which additionally demonstrates how larger companies attempt to integrate 'W' strategic and operational planning processes. The diagram also illustrates the addition of the lateral dimension associated with multi-functional strategic technology reviews. For differentiation, we term this total process as 'W-+ planning'. Examples are illustrated in Chapter 10. In practice, 'W'-planning facilitates multi-level strategic reviews involving subsidiaries, business teams, strategic customers and suppliers as appropriate.

Integrating the customer and technology dimensions

The incorporation of a more dedicated approach to the strategic management of customers, suppliers and the use of technology requires significant changes in the information collated, the way the information is analysed and the emphasis of decision-making and emergent strategic development programmes.

The acceptance of such changes may require:

- building on to established strategic management processes, or
- in many cases, a major rethink to put life into the process and reduce the bureaucracy that often slows competitive responses.

The evolution of emphasis areas of strategic decision-making processes is illustrated in Fig. 5.6. We propose that the practical missing link for 1990–2000 is integration. At each stage of evolution, the new concepts and sub-processes had the potential to build on, and strengthen, the existing total process. Unfortunately, this was not always the case. Over-zealous, often academic changes, resulted in sub-processes swamping the basic core decision-making process, and often forgetting that the end result of strategy should be decisive innovative actions towards improved results, not an encyclopaedia of intellectual analysis. It should be a process which is owned by the chief executive and not by the planning department. In particular, the danger occurred with portfolio analysis, culture analysis and scenario planning. Each of these techniques has a place but as a means of improving the quality of strategic analysis and awareness in other key areas like technology, customers and competitors.

It is important to use a process that uncovers emergent opportunities and threats early, and to secure a dedicated drive to achieve significant step-changes in competitiveness, at the same time providing a flexible response to the unexpected. As already discussed in earlier chapters, the effective management of the use of technology is a vital opportunity for competitive success in the 1990s, and action is required now in response to the strategic needs of key customers and the demand for environment-friendly strategic investment.

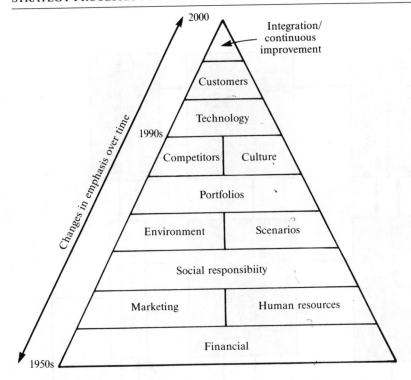

Figure 5.6 Changes in strategy process

For success, any process for the management of the use of technology needs to be:

- customer focused
- practical, but with an intellectual basis
- built on and strengthened by established concepts of strategic analysis, decision-making and implementation.

In particular, a usable process needs to strengthen the use of the well-established 'SWOT' or 'SOFT' approach and the portfolio analysis, popular during the 1980s, and at the same time incorporate new value-added features. An outline of one such process is illustrated in Fig. 5.7 overleaf. The process provides the flexibility to meet the range of top management objectives listed earlier.

The 'wedge' analysis

As illustrated in Fig. 5.8, the traditional 'SWOT' or 'SOFT' analysis needs to be extended to be a useful input to strategic decisions today. In practice,

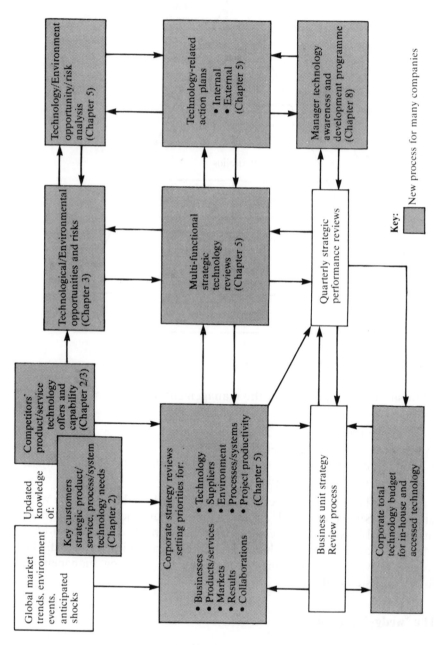

Figure 5.7 Outline of management process for managing the use of available technology

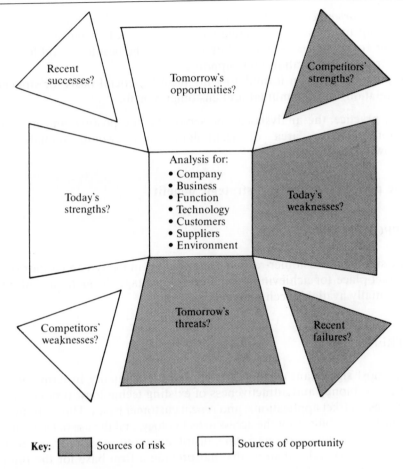

Figure 5.8 The strategic wedge analysis

the framework and basic questions are common to strategic analyses at the level of the total company, a division, a strategic business unit or product group and key support functions, as described below.

- *for the total company division and subsidiary* — in deciding on the most viable future strategy for the company as a total entity, including key decisions on organic growth, acquisition and divestment
- *for the business unit or product group* — in deciding on the most viable competitive strategy for specific priority product groups and territories within 'the umbrella' or framework of the strategy for the total company
- *for the functional department* — in deciding on the most productive strategy for the support of the business and competitive strategies described above

- *for a corporate-wide total technology strategy* — in deciding on the most competitively supportive strategy in support of the total business strategy
- *for key customers* — in deciding with them the best form and focus of strategic cooperation and support
- *for suppliers* — in formulating the most beneficial basis for strategic relationships for mutual and customer benefit.

In practice, the analysis can be separated into positive and negative factors. In the area of technology, these would include the following.

The positives — areas of strategic benefit

OPPORTUNITIES

The significant customer-related opportunities in today's and tomorrow's market-place for achieving competitive advantage through current and potentially available technology.

STRENGTHS

The most significant current strengths of the company in terms of the value for money and attractiveness of existing technology; products and services; market applications; and repeat customer bases. Those strengths related to capabilities for the access to technology, and the use of technology in design, manufacture, marketing, distribution and servicing. Essentially, the technology-related strengths that provide a firm base for the future competitiveness of the company.

SUCCESSES

The successes that indicate a significant current capability to innovate effectively. An indication of the ability to identify and exploit technological opportunities and strengths.

COMPETITORS' WEAKNESSES

The significant technological weaknesses of competitors that offer future opportunities and indicate areas in which competitors might be slow or unable to react to competitive moves, thus providing competitive 'windows'.

The negatives — areas of strategic risk

WEAKNESSES

The significant weakness which, if not corrected, will constrain the ability of the company to access new technology, innovate and implement competitive initiatives in products, services, processes or systems.

FAILURES

Significant indications that the company has recently been unsuccessful in overcoming weaknesses and in implementing new technological initiatives, and an analysis of the basic reasons for failure.

THREATS

Significant, anticipated, external trends or occurrences that threaten the competitive success of the company. The analysis will examine social, political, technological, economic, environmental, competitive and customer trends, and possible future shocks such as the technological supply chain 'leap-frogs' discussed in Chapter 2.

COMPETITORS' STRENGTHS

These are significant technological strengths of key competitors that will create difficulties for the company implementing new initiatives and responding to external threats.

The quality of the strategy and realism of the implementation plan developed will be directly related to the quality of the wedge analysis. Quality in terms of clarity of focus, concentration on the significant, the depth of insight, vision and lateral thinking, the multi-disciplined perspective and objective challenge rather than volume of information for intellectual curiosity.

Two essential needs are customer and technology audits. Such audits can no longer be delegated on a functional basis to marketing or research and development but need to be designed and implemented on a total business and multi-functional basis. The audit check-lists included at the end of each chapter are designed to provide inputs to the total corporate wedge analysis.

New dimensions for matrix analyses

Matrix analysis was a popular activity in the 1980s. Each of the four strategic matrices illustrated in Fig. 5.9 were timely and, in their own way, stimulated a deeper and wider understanding and application of strategic thinking. However, in practice, each matrix defined options and positions at specific points in time, and was narrow in concept and lacking detailed consideration of the customer and technology dimensions of strategy. Too often companies attempted to follow or match competitors' moves rather than think through and achieve a dynamic step-change to secure strategic leadership.

The four matrices illustrated in Fig. 5.10 attempt to provide for the missing dimensions that become increasingly important as markets become more demanding, faster moving, more complex and more global, and as the depth of the Pacific Basin's strategic intentions become more

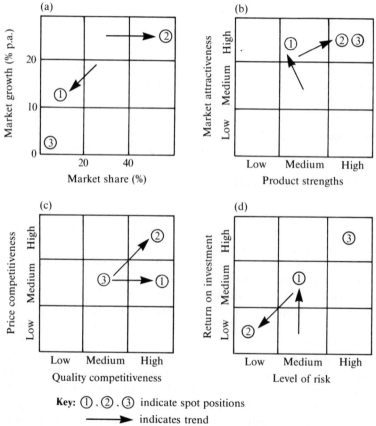

Key: ①, ②, ③ indicate spot positions
➤ indicates trend

Figure 5.9 Four strategic matrices from the 1970s–1980s

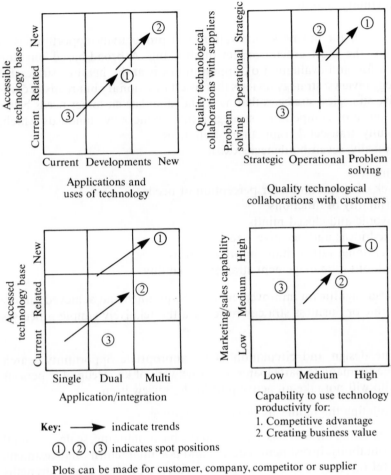

Figure 5.10 Strategic matrices for the 1990s

visible and understood. The matrices focus on key relationships between the customer, supplier, technology and capability dimensions.

However, matrices only help to illustrate, present and visualize today's position and tomorrow's options. Matrices do not establish an opportunity base from which to select competitive moves that competitors might find hard to match. Identifying opportunities requires a visionary rather than administrative search process and skills; a visionary process that searches for unique, and not generic, opportunities. As expressed in Fig. 5.2, a unique strategy steered and implemented by an exceptional team is required for total success.

Opportunity search

The search for business, innovation and productivity opportunities is perhaps the most crucial aspect of thinking. A broad-based ongoing search for, and evaluation of, opportunities is at the heart of successful strategy reviews: strategy reviews that result in visionary but realistic competitive strategies; strategies that meet and stimulate customer needs better than those of competitors; strategies that create new standards which, hopefully, transcend competitors' initiatives.

Typically, seven bottlenecks exist:

- time
- lack of vision and poor perception of needs
- insularity of functions
- myopic and closed minds
- fixed ideas and negative screening
- occasional rather than continuous work
- lack of top management strategic capability.

However, significant improvements can be planned and achieved for any corporate or business strategy review via the relatively simple processes of:

1. The design and circulation of an appropriate opportunity search questionnaire to participants and a network of knowledgeable persons who will not take an active part in the review itself.

2. Collating the replies as *silent brainstorming*.

3. Evaluating the ideas as a group on the basis of timing, scale, potential profitability, investment required and potential return on investment, level of competition, cost of entry, current product group strengths and capabilities as well as ease of exploitation.

4. Considering the base data in a creative manner; exploring individual and integrated ideas; applying logic and lateral thinking; searching for the simplification of ideas as well as synergy; asking the 'what if' questions. All with one question in mind . . . 'How can we discover tomorrow's world-beating idea *today*?'

5. Establishing an ongoing process for generating ideas for new and improved customers, products, processes, systems and services from all levels from the boardroom to shop-floor, from marketing to manufacturing, from the laboratory to the new product launch team.

6. Establishing product and technology champions with authority and influence.

7. Establishing a balance between informal and institutionalized analysis.

8. Experimenting with a variety of creativity methods such as brainstorming, brainwriting, lateral thinking and mind-mapping.

Table 5.1 provides a practical starting point to the process for a wide range of business.

Table 5.1 Framework for identification of opportunities for use of technology

What are the most significant opportunities arising from the use of technology for the profitable growth of the business over the next five years?

Type of opportunity	Current technology	For use of: Development of current technology	New or replacement technology
1. Application opportunities			
1.1 Current uses			
1.2 Related uses			
1.3 New uses			
1.4 Substitute uses			
1.5 Synergy/integration			
2. Product opportunities			
2.1 Sustain current performance			
2.2 Improvements			
2.3 Replacements			
2.4 New packages			
2.5 New/novel			
3. Service opportunities			
3.1 Sustain current performance			
3.2 Improvements			
3.3 Replacements			
3.4 New packages			
3.5 New/novel			
4. Process opportunities			
4.1 Sustain current performance			
4.2 Enhance performance			
4.3 Replacement processes			
4.4 Integration process			
4.5 New/novel			
5. Systems opportunities			
5.1 Sustain current performance			
5.2 Enhance performance			
5.3 Replacement systems			

Table 5.1 *cont.*

Type of opportunity	Current technology	For use of: Development of current technology	New or replacement technology
5.4 Integration systems			
5.5 New/novel systems			

6. Customer opportunities
   6.1 Current
   6.2 Related
   6.3 New
   6.4 Domestic
   6.5 International

7. Collaboration opportunities
   7.1 Licensing
   7.2 Pre-competitive development
   7.3 Joint venture
   7.4 Parallel development
   7.5 Integrated packages

8. Environmental opportunities
   8.1 Safety
   8.2 Pollution
   8.3 Environment control
   8.4 Quality working environment
   8.5 Reduction of health risks

9. Supplier opportunities
   9.1 Components
   9.2 Products
   9.3 Services
   9.4 Technological collaboration
   9.5 Systems support

etc . . . .

Final opportunities may be identified directly from the survey questionnaire, or result from subsequent evaluation and creative questioning. For instance:

- what opportunities could be grouped together?
- how can we re-shape the opportunity?
- where are the opportunities for synergy?
- what are the opportunities for integration?
- what if the technology could be accelerated?
- what could be the next development beyond the idea?
- what developments could replace the idea and be better ideas?

- in what other ways could the opportunity be interpreted or developed?
- how could the opportunity be simplified?
- how could the idea be appealing to customers, and match their strategic needs?
- where could the enabling technology be accessed and sourced?
- what strengths and weaknesses do we have in relation to the most significant emergent opportunities compared to our current and potential competitors?
- what actions are required next to evaluate or develop the opportunity?
- what opportunities are there for joint ventures with customers, suppliers or competitors?

MATCHING EMERGENT OPPORTUNITIES TO CUSTOMER NEEDS

The opportunity search will identify a wide range of possibilities; some easy to exploit, others considerably more difficult. But how will they be viewed by customers? How do they match their current, emergent and latent needs? Are they complementary to the existing product/service range? The completion of Table 5.2 can be a very helpful exercise as an initial analysis followed by discussion, lateral and cohesive thinking. The options identified can then be assessed in detail to determine the most attractive opportunities and the phasing of exploitation.

Table 5.2 Identification of product and service options

Type of opportunity / Type of needs	Continuation of existing products/ services				Possible improvements/ packaging of existing products and services				Possible infill products and services				Possible totally new products and services			
	Option	S	T	E	Option	S	T	E	Option	S	T	E	Option	S	T	E
Strategic													e.g.	H	94	M
Operational	e.g.	H	92	L												
Problem solving																
Crisis																

Code: S = Scale of opportunity (H, M, L)   T = Timing of opportunity (Year)
E = Ease of Exploiting opportunity

Managing the technological dimensions

The wide range of potentially important technological issues was high-lighted in Chapter 3. It is, therefore, important that the person responsible for the development of the strategic decision-making process develops a time-effective way of scanning, evaluating, and acting on critical techno-logical dimensions — those few issues that will be at the heart of future business success.

Such a process is outlined in Fig. 5.11. In concept it is not new, but it builds on similar processes conceived in the 1970s for social responsibility analyses and in the early 1980s for productivity gains analyses.

The most effective use of the process is as follows:

1. The development of a technology strategic impact questionnaire.

2. The completion of the questionnaire by a cross-section of informed persons, the board, key managers and technologists, retained academics and possibly an international advisory technology board.

3. The collation of the results as the basis for objective analysis of key issues, events, timings, and so on.

4. The consideration of the collated information at a specially convened technology strategy session.

TECHNOLOGY STRATEGY SESSION

The typical organization of a technology strategy session for a large com-pany is illustrated in Table 5.3. For a small company such a session can also be of benefit. External inputs should be retained but in less numbers and for a shorter duration in many situations.

Table 5.3 Technology strategy session

Objectives:

1.   To provide an enriched technological input to the strategic decision-making process

2.   To raise the level of technological awareness of senior managers involved in strategic decision-making

3.   To involve a balanced mix of internal and external persons with appropriate know-ledge and experience of markets, products, processes, systems and enabling services and technologies

4.   To share information, insights, views and visions in an objective non-competitive mutual learning environment.

Table 5.3 *cont.*

A typical participant group of 24 participants:
Internal participants
1.   Chief executive (1)

2.   Marketing director (1)

3.   Manufacturing director (1)

4.   Design and development director (1)

5.   Senior product managers (2)

6.   Advanced development managers (2)

7.   Market research manager (1)

8.   IT manager (1)

9.   Financial director (1)

External participants
1.   Research institute delegates (2)

2.   Supplier's technical directors (2)

3.   Strategic customers (2)

4.   Joint venture partners (2)

5.   University professors (2)

6.   Industrial economist or institutional investor (1)

7.   Process leader consultant (1)

8.   IT specialist (1)
      Total participants: 24

Basic Process
Month 1.   Pre-work questionnaire to participants

      2.   Collation of replies

      3.   Two or three day technology strategy session

      4.   Write up and issue results to all participants (with a confidentiality agreement)

      5/6. Company incorporates results into corporate strategy process.

Such a session can be a milestone in the development of strategic decision-making in a company if it is well organized, with a creative cross-section of informed, committed internal and external participants who are prepared to challenge. The benefits will include shared visions, values and commitment to a strategy founded on customers' strategic needs and available technological potential.

In addition to technology impact audits and formal technological strategy

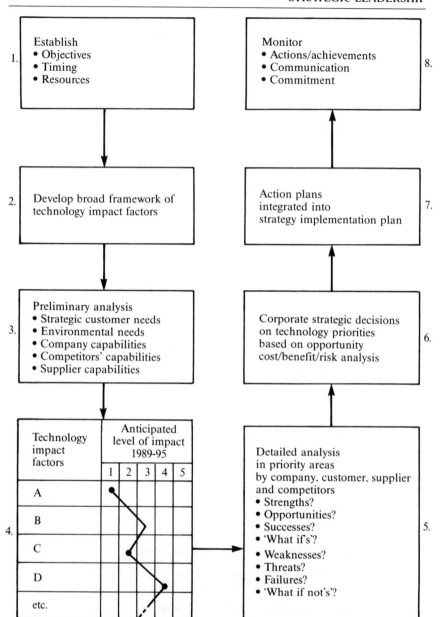

Figure 5.11 Framework for strategic technology survey

sessions, the following sources of technological opportunities and risks need to be considered. The most practical and time-effective need to be selected in each situation.

1. *Personal visits* to selected strategic customers as discussed in Chapter 2.

2. *Personal visits* to selected technological experts or organizations — the purpose being a general exploration or to seek information in a specific pre-defined area.

3. *External market or technological surveys* to a network of carefully selected individuals or organizations — the purpose being to explore patterns, trends and potential changes in needs and perceptions.

4. *Suggestion schemes* open to all staff, with perhaps a token reward for each idea and major awards for the idea of the quarter.

5. *Visit reports* from all directors, managers and sales engineers making visits to foreign territories.

6. *Exhibition reports* from all persons visiting trade exhibitions and shows.

7. *Conference/seminar* reports from persons attending marketing or technical events, including the graduates still keen to attend events of their respective professional institutes, to maintain personal professional development.

8. *Product strategy sessions* involving business or product group teams.

9. *Product circles* involving a selected mix of the manufacturing personnel concerned with the direct production, commissioning and servicing of engineering products, i.e., the skilled shop-floor and service technicians, who may have valuable ideas for improving both the current and next series of products.

10. *Innovation workshops* focused on the brainstorming and initial evaluation of technological opportunities and threats.

11. *Research collaborations* with industrial or university partners.

12. *Visionary listening posts* in relevant centres of innovation.

The time factor

In many industries new product lead times are shortening. The timing of key decisions and actions in the use of strategically important technologies is therefore critical and an issue that must be given sufficient prominence. In practice, there is a need to evaluate in detail the implications of the six time factors impacting the competitive use of technology:

1. *Recognition time* — the timing of evolution and awareness of the exploitation value of existing and emergent scientific knowledge and ideas.

2. *Response time* — the time delay between the initial recognition and the start to actively innovate and develop the idea into usable and useful technological innovation.

3. *Development time* — the time to develop an application of the idea to a marketable product or service.

4. *Launch timing* — the timing of the launch of the new idea or application: internally to the product group and company, and externally to the market-place and customers.

5. *Expansion time* — the time and timing required to develop and exploit additional applications by:

   - innovative marketing of a product or service to achieve expansion from the launch market niche to a broader market base
   - expanding a pilot application in a prototype or new product design or manufacturing process to other key areas.

6. *Obsolescence timing* — the critical timing of step-changes in product and process technology and design, to maximize the trends in product and process half-lives. (i.e., replacement technology).

7. *Patching time* — only relevant if (6) has been missed or overlooked.

The relationships between the seven time factors are illustrated in Fig. 5.12.

In many situations, today's technology represents an untapped source of competitive leverage:

- new business concepts
- new products and services
- productivity initiatives
- integration of multi-functional creativity
- new levels of quality and performance
- flexibility in response to customers' special needs
- choice of actions: today or tomorrow — leader or follower — initiator or 'me too' pioneer, or improver
- reduction of new product lead times by 50 to 90 per cent.

In practice, in order to grasp opportunities and be competent in this area, awareness needs to be stimulated and committed action is required.

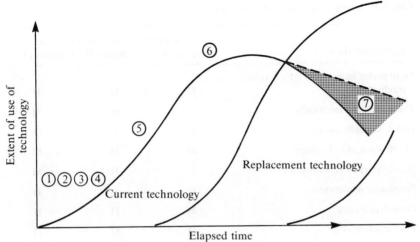

Figure 5.12   Relationships between technology time factors

Customer technology audits

Audits of the technology needs and capability of tomorrow's strategic customer base provide vital inputs to the strategy process for the 1990s, as outlined in Fig. 5.7.

The first step is to identify those customers most likely to be the important customers in three to five years for each of the planned core businesses. The criteria used to identify such customers are illustrated in Table 5.4.

The second step is to establish a reliable profile of the customer and the potential success of a strategic customer relationship. Inevitably, it will be difficult to obtain detailed and initially accurate answers to all essential questions. However, it should be possible to achieve an initial practical picture using the assessment charts illustrated in Table 5.5. The resultant charts can be used as the basis of an agenda for customer review meetings. Similar analyses of potential customers are required which can also be used in relation to pro-active discussions with customers.

The charts are designed to help identify the dynamics of potentially successful partnerships with customers.

The third step is to develop specific technology impact profiles. In practice, this step will most likely be iterative with the development of the customer–technology profiles. A basic format is illustrated in Table 5.6. Similar parallel analyses related to the technology of significant competitors should be built into the competitor analysis fed in to the strategy process.

SUPPLIER TECHNOLOGY AUDITS

Supplier technology audits play a major part in defining the potential contribution to strategic development of products and services and in the

Table 5.4 Identification of strategic customers

Selection criteria	Assessment of possible companies		
	Company A	Company B	Company C, etc.
Profit performance from added-value products/services	M	H	H
Think and act strategically	L	H	M
Technologically aware	L	H	M
Effective use of technology	M	M	M
Speedy/purposeful innovator	L	H	M
Position in market-place	H	H	H
Growth potential	M	H	H
Financially sound	H	H	H
No conflicting partnerships	M	H	H
Total quality management capability	L/M	H	M
Select for detailed investigation/audit	No	Yes	Perhaps

Key:
Level: H = High, M = Medium, L = Low

management of development risk. These issues, which are critical in the overview of existing suppliers and selection of new suppliers, include:

- the ability to add value to your operational and strategic development through their technological contribution
- the ability to think and act strategically
- track record in effective use of technology
- response to change situations
- growth potential
- financially sound
- understanding of joint relationships and no existing conflicts
- quality management
- quality of staff and training policies for the future

A similar analysis to that outlined in Table 5.5 is appropriate for this process, but with more emphasis on defining the most cost effective and minimum risk business interface. In addition, a conscious effort needs to be made to establish the overall impact of key suppliers' technology on potential product/service/process/system developments for your own business development investments.

Table 5.5   Extract from customer profile

Customer:		Date of first becoming a customer:		
Issue	Information available /(information required)	Trend ↑ ↓ ↗ ↙ →	Support to strategic relationship H M L	Risk to strategic relationship H M L
1. Proportion of sales to customer that result from customers': a. strategic needs b. operational needs c. problem-solving needs d. crisis needs				
2. Proportion of total orders placed by customer that result from awareness of: a. strategic needs b. operational needs c. problem-solving needs d. crisis needs				
3. Quality of customer strategic analysis and decision-making				
4. Extent and quality of customer strategic collaborations with: a. international competitors b. own customers c. OEM suppliers d. other suppliers e. universities				
5. Quality of customers': a. awareness of available technology b. perception of potential for competitive use c. in-house research and development d. international accessing technology				

Key: Level: H = High, M = Medium, L = Low

Action planning for technology

'Back to basics' has been a core message during the 1980s, not least in connection with the management process.

In the context of technology analysis (see Table 5.6), being thorough is meaningless without effective action planning to achieve strategic benefit and results in practice.

The following nine points provide guide-lines for the preparation of action plans emanating from technology strategy sessions or customer technology audits. They apply to all facets of strategy implementation.

1. Action cannot wait for a 100 per cent accurate quantification of objectives ... in many cases, current best — let alone worst — scenarios and estimates will highlight a need for urgency.

2. People at all levels need to see that something is happening at an early stage; something that secures a dedicated, if not tied, customer base.

3. Agreed action plans need to be both challenging and realistic in ambition ... planning for realistic technological breakthroughs and timescales that, with luck, can be beaten, will achieve more than planning for superhuman effort. In this context, technological breakthroughs may be based on newly accessed external technology or step-changes in the evolution of existing internal technology.

4. The actions planned need to achieve early results, for instance:

   - reinforcements of previous decisions which are, to date, loose in implementation or contain new risks
   - short-term initiatives which demonstrate to all levels that the board means business
   - medium-term actions to remove chronic bottlenecks
   - long-term focused actions related to customers' longer-term strategies.

5. The action plans need to achieve:

   - real accountability by committing specific senior managers to sponsor, control, coach, coordinate and drive specific actions
   - team commitment and peer appraisal by appropriate team technology audits and problem-solving.

6. Timescales for allocated actions that match the typical time perspective of the persons concerned. Typical examples are listed below:

Chief executive	12–60 months
Senior managers	6–30 months

Table 5.6 A technology impact profile

Company
Business area
Updated by: Date:

Technology impact factors	Anticipated impact level (H, M, L)						
	1992	93	94	95	96	97	98
External factors							
1.							
2.							
3.							
4.							
5.							
etc.							
Internal factors							
1.							
2.							
3.							
4.							
5.							
etc.							

Key:
Indicate impact level in two dimensions
Level: H = High. M = Medium. L = Low
Trend: ↑ ↓ ↗ → ↘

Middle managers   3–15 months
Foreperson   1–5 months

In some circumstances, these times may be too short, for example, where products are on a longer timescale, e.g., in the pharmaceutical industry and, in some cases, too long, for instance, in the fashion industry.

7. As many people as possible involved in implementation to achieve a committed critical mass, a wave of change, and acceleration and momentum in driving towards competitive technological superiority.

8. A recognition that progress reviews need to be tougher than the initial analysis . . . 20 per cent late, 20 per cent incomplete and 20 per cent

cost over-run may mean 'no tomorrow', regardless of quality of technology. Detailed risk and opportunity analyses will be essential in the management of strategically critical technologies. In practice, this leads to a creative rather than constrained approach to problem-solving.

9. The audits, analyses and actions essential to launching a manage-ment of technology renewal or culture are unlikely to be achieved within the standard 35-hour week and flexi-work framework. Special long-day, evening and weekend sessions are likely to be required which, in many cases, may break with customer traditions.

Table 5.7 illustrates a typical action planning format, and Table 5.8 a typical risk analysis. Although basic, they are, for many companies, management technology breakthroughs in themselves.

Technology risk management

The assessment of strategic risk is an essential part of an effective strategy process. The practical technology risk analysis illustrated can be of benefit:

- as a key input to a strategy review
- in preparing best/worst case scenarios for evaluating and fine-tuning emergent strategies
- in testing the robustness of preferred strategies
- in identifying and gaining understanding of the need for urgent actions.

As a broad guide to the interpretation of the impact and probability assessments, Fig. 5.13 shows the likely forms of action required to minimize or control risk. The actions shown are general and could vary subject to the form of potential problems, e.g., time delays may require different action over failures to meet technology targets.

As with other planning documents, a one-off analysis then discarded to the filing cabinet is of limited benefit. A rolling updated analysis is required to sustain competitive advantage. It is recommended that a parallel analysis of opportunities is also prepared.

A similar format can be used to define the scale and scope of opportunities and define exploitation actions.

Table 5.7 Format for technology action plans

Business:	Prepared by:
Technology area:	Date:
Mission 19 −19	Frequency review:

Specific objectives
1.
2.
3.

Action required	Priority (H M L)	By whom	Timescale 1993 A. M. J. J. A. S. O. N. D.	94 95 96 97
	I	I	I I I I I I I I	I I I
	I	I	I I I I I I I I	I I I
	I	I	I I I I I I I I	I I I
	I	I	I I I I I I I I	I I I
	I	I	I I I I I I I I	I I I
	I	I	I I I I I I I I	I I I
	I	I	I I I I I I I I	I I I
	I	I	I I I I I I I I	I I I
	I	I	I I I I I I I I	I I I
	I	I	I I I I I I I I	I I I
	I	I	I I I I I I I I	I I I
	I	I	I I I I I I I I	I I I

Key:
H = High, M = Medium, L = Low

Table 5.8 Technology risk analysis

Proposed action plan

Planned use of technology	Timing	Anticipated potential problems	Impact *	Probability *	Possible preventive actions	Success rating *	Cost rating *	Contingent action possible	Success rating *	Cost rating *
		Access?								
		Timing?								
		Reliability?								
		Cost?								
		Benefit?								
		Customer acceptance?								
		Customer readiness?								
		Competitor moves?								
		Technology leap-frogs?								
		Environmental compatability?								

Key:
* Assess. H = High. M = Medium. L = Low

		Look for insurance actions		Drop the idea
Negative impact of potential problems	H			
	M		Revise the strategy	
		Ignore for time being		Build preventive action into strategy
	L			
		L	M	H

Probability of occurrence
of problem

Figure 5.13   Risk management action areas

Management development implications

The extensions to the normally recognized strategic decision-making process are basic but considered essential to continued commercial success in the 1990s and beyond. Introducing the new dimensions requires a detailed review of existing practices, the timely incorporation of new or modified processes and, in many cases, investment in technological awareness programmes and reorientation of the management development process for directors and senior managers. These issues are discussed in detail in Chapter 8.

The audit questionnaire that follows is designed for a review of corporate practices prior to the next planning cycle and can be used as the basis for considering improved processes.

Strategy process audit

A basic audit questionnaire is shown in Table 5.9, along the lines of previous chapters.

It is suggested that this audit questionnaire be completed by a number of senior executives and the views pooled before reaching final conclusions on the specific areas for action.

The following broad interpretations are suggested:

31–40   In good position to identify and exploit strategic opportunities on a timely and profitable basis

21-30   Have firm base from which to build a stronger more resilient strategy process over the next 12-18 months

11-20   Urgent need to start to establish a more conscious process of strategic analysis and decision-making

0-10   Continued 'fire-fighting' a certainty.

The results of the audit provide the starting point for reading the remainder of the chapters which focus on three emergent critical issues:

Chapter 6   Balancing the development of corporate culture
Chapter 7   The impact of the new strategy process on top management
Chapter 8   Top management development
Chapter 9   Corporate performance/development indicators
Chapter 10 Making it happen.

Table 5.9 Strategy process audit questionnaire

Issue and question	Assessment of (a) current situation and (b) trend			
	Poor Score 1	Fair Score 2	Good Score 3	Excellent Score 4
1. Process audit To what extent is process audited and updated?	Outdated, no changes in hand	Occasionally when chief executive or planner changes	Changes considered annually	Process evolves on continuous basis to match needs/capability
	a. b.	a. b.	a. b.	a. b.
2. Continuity To what extent is strategic analysis/decision-making a continuous progress?	Only *ad hoc*	Annual planning sessions only	Six monthly or quarterly strategy reviews	Same, plus continuous scanning for opportunities/risks
	a. b.	a. b.	a. b.	a. b.
3. Strategic analyses What is depth/extent of strategic analysis?	Financial only	Traditional SWOT analysis	Extended wedge analysis	Extended wedge analysis with detailed customer and supplier analysis
	a. b.	a. b.	a. b.	a. b.
4. Strategic information base What is the quality of the decision support base?	Occasionally updated but mostly financial	Updated annually by functions	Updated quarterly by functions and freely available	Updated corporately on continuous basis
	a. b.	a. b.	a. b.	a. b.
5. Involvement What is the extent of involvement in the strategy process?	Planners only	Chief executive/selected directors only	Total board	Same plus business teams in 'W' process
	a. b.	a. b.	a. b.	a. b.

Table 5.9 *cont.*

6. Flexibility To what extent does the strategy process allow for flexibility of response?	Constant *ad hoc* changes initiated by board		Changes possible but constrained by annual budgets		Response possible at quarterly reviews		Speedy response to new opportunities within strategic vision	
	a.	b.	a.	b.	a.	b.	a.	b.
7. Opportunity risk analysis What is the effectiveness of these two two basic dimensions?	*Ad hoc,* narrowly based and subjective		Occasional bursts of enthusiasm		Broad-based integral with quarterly reviews		Continuous natural process	
	a.	b.	a.	b.	a.	b.	a.	b.
8. Technology dimension To what extent is technology considered?	Not normally		R&D functional input only and functional response		Broad corporate total technology analysis		Same, plus specific corporate responses	
	a.	b.	a.	b.	a.	b.	a.	b.
9. Customer dimension To what extent are customer strategies considered?	Short-term awareness only		Plus historic analysis only, including competition		Tracking and anticipation trends		Same, plus collaborative discussions	
	a.	b.	a.	b.	a.	b.	a.	b.
10. Quality of strategy What is the basis of the content of the statement of strategy?	*Ad hoc* short-term initiatives		Selection from generic strategies		Broad-based strategic initiatives		Same, plus unique visions and competitive initiatives	
	a.	b.	a.	b.	a.	b.	a.	b.
Column Scores								

© Management of Technology Partnership 1989

Total Score (sum columns 1–4) [   ]   Maximum 40

Instructions:
Consider each of the above issues/questions in turn. Select the column which best fits your current situation and tick the appropriate box 'a'. Consider the underlying trend and denote by ↑ → ↗ ↘ box 'b'. Add score for all questions.

BALANCING THE DEVELOPMENT OF CORPORATE CULTURE

Culture, the lifeblood of an organization, is the link between strategy and achieved results. The balanced development and management of culture can have a vital impact on the way in which a management team are led and involved in the strategy process, the strategy decisions they make, the manner of their implementation and the effectiveness of supportive management development. An effective 'good culture' will earn an external reputation with customers, suppliers, funders and society, and an internal reputation with employees for good leadership, growth opportunities and reward. An organization with a 'poor' culture is only likely to find favour with organizations on an asset stripping acquisition track or company doctors looking for a highly geared challenge and pay for success.

But what is culture? Why is it important?

Throughout the book reference is made to corporate culture and the importance of that culture being developed in support of, and to enable, the competitive development of the business and management team in an integrated manner. An effective culture will allow an appropriate response to emergent market conditions. A move into bottom gear in times of recession and overdrive in times of market boom will both be feasible if the culture is managed and not allowed to be purely the result of corporate heritage and history. We all observe cultures which, for a variety of reasons, we term 'good' or 'bad'. We all recognize that culture is both the facilitator and preventer of required change. The vital difference in many cases is the vision and mission of the chief executive and management team in unleashing talent within an agreed strategic framework. In this middle chapter of the book the culture issue is expanded on as a practical link between the first and second half of the book. The corporate culture audit included is designed to help directors and managers position themselves against a statement of good cultural practice and start the process of reform.

Much management literature refers to, but avoids defining, corporate culture. For practical purposes we find the following definition helpful: *Culture describes the civilization of the organization, the way in which a company and its key employees behave in preparation and in response to external*

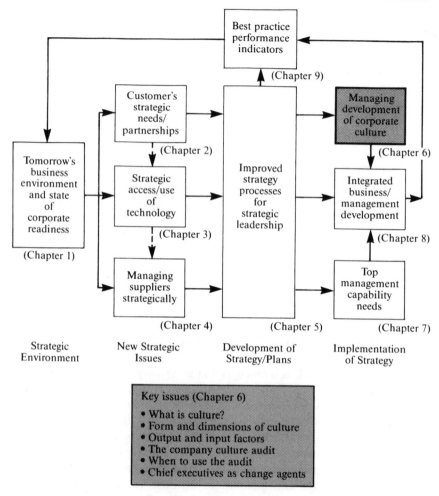

Figure 6.1   Culture is a vital link between strategy and results

and internal opportunities and threats. It integrates guide-lines for ethics and beliefs relating to *what* is to be achieved with *how* it is to be achieved. The guide-lines, spirit and success with which they are applied profile culture as the corporate dynamism of civilization. A good culture is synonymous with best management practice in relation to internal and external stakeholders. But even the leaders need to strive for continuous improvement. A company with an effective culture or 'corporate civilization' will have designed, developed, nurtured and managed a culture development programme over a number of years as an evolutionary process. The process will have balanced the external facets of culture with the internal behaviour required to set the external facets in place. At the heart will be the seed corn of a clear and realistic statement of mission.

The form of culture — the importance of mission

1. Commitment to a common goal can and does achieve above average, often exceptional, results.

2. Culture is worthless without a sense of purpose, but at the same time, certain aspects of culture must be in place to stimulate and enable the development and communication of mission throughout the organization.

3. The development, communication and commitment to a competitive mission is therefore proposed as the seed of an effective culture.

4. Culture formed around the mission of a company or business will accelerate the move towards management excellence in the same way that a cultured pearl is encouraged by seeding an oyster. Further, it can release and integrate individual talents and contributions. This is illustrated in Fig. 6.2 overleaf.

5. As discussed in earlier chapters, the capabilities of the various functions of a company or business need to be harnessed and coordinated within the framework of development programmes led by chief executives, business general managers or product managers. Also, Chapter 5 highlighted the statement of mission as a vital ingredient in the establishment of strategy.

6. Without such integration various things can happen to company culture.

    (a) *Confusion* — Employees at all levels become unsure about the intended direction and style of the business with different senior managers and departments going their own way with arrogance and abrasiveness.

    (b) *Bureaucracy* — Numerous policies, procedures and committees are introduced in an attempt to achieve coordination and adhesion to good practice by rigid control.

    (c) *In-fighting* — The different functions and business streams fail to cooperate and hence fight over priorities and resources. Much more energy is put into internal sniping and warfare than fighting the external battles in the market-place.

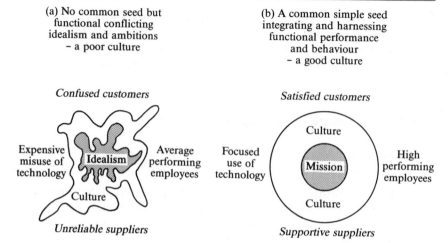

Figure 6.2 Mission as seed of company culture

(d) *Insecurity* — At all levels from directors to lowest level of employee the best people become unsure about the survival and growth of the business and the ability to fulfil career and reward ambitions, and start to leave.

(e) *Market bluff* — Extensive public relations, often led personally by the chairman or chief executive, build up an image of a forward thinking, quality-led productive business in good economic times when customers are hungry for supplies. With a downturn in the economy, customers are more critical, the euphoria of the chief executive's buoyant vision undergoes a melt-down; employees lose motivation or the company loses face with customers, bankers and investors — a frequent occurrence in the early 1990s.

7. Research indicates that two unhelpful (in our view) but popular schools of thought exist regarding culture — each often at a distance from reality. Since they represent opposing views they can cause confusion for many managers, particularly if both views are circulating in a company at the same time.

Firstly, there is the view that culture is a hard issue concerned with the visibility of external related outputs, with primary emphasis on bottom line results. Such a view often stimulates — or is founded on — a focus on short-term results and a relatively harsh approach to internal people-related issues.

Second, there is the opposite view that culture is a soft issue solely concerned with the comfort and creativity of the internal organizations. The proponents tend to be soft on people and often take a relaxed longer-term, charitable view of results. Proponents express the view that until the culture is 'correct' in behavioural terms, there is little point in involving people in reviewing the company mission and strategy.

Our experience supports neither of the above viewpoints. We see culture as an integrative issue. We take what we consider a balanced and practical point of view and believe strongly that:

- culture must be derived from, and driven by, the core mission and strategy of the organization
- culture development is a route which greatly helps the implementation of strategic initiatives
- both output and internal manifestations and dimensions of culture need to be recognized. The corporate culture audit that follows builds on this point of view and provides the pivot point between audits contained in earlier and later chapters.

The dimensions of culture — output and input factors

Successful companies have always been characterized by strong and identifiable elements of culture. In the past it has often been good enough to maintain the culture's main element, with little change over many years, without loss of competitive position or fall off in business results. For example: Rolls Royce, whose very name is synonymous with ultimate quality; Mars, synonymous with employee relations and product quality; Harrods, synonymous with customer service without equal; Sony, synonymous with innovation and novelty.

Look at your own industries. Which companies have had a special reputation? On what elements of culture was it based? Is that reputation still as strong? What elements of culture are now being strengthened?

Organizations are faced with two types of development, namely:

- output culture factors — those issues that have a direct impact on the business relations with external stakeholders in the business
- input culture factors — those issues that influence the ways in which the business operates internally, and which impact directly the internal stakeholders in the business: the employees.

Ten output factors and ten input factors are described in the next section. In combination, they provide a practical framework for auditing and reforming culture. A practical audit is provided in Table 6.1. It has evolved from our earlier well-used diagnostic audits such as the MBO (Management by Objectives) audit of the 1970s and the effectiveness audit of the 1980s. The use of the audit is described later in this chapter.

THE TEN OUTPUT FACTORS

The ten output factors selected are outlined below. They represent the externally observed manifestations of the culture of a range of well-run companies. As such they can be regarded as a framework of best practice.

Factor	Outline of best practice	Reason for importance
1. *Rapid change and response*	The company/organization is organized, led and funded in a manner that stimulates and allows timely and quick responses to significant changes in the external environment; where appropriate ahead of competition.	Critical in enabling company to catch up with best and, in some cases, be in control of events to competitive advantage.
2. *Strategic customer relations*	The company has, and continues to seek out customers which think strategically and has built strong relationships — even joint ventures — based on provision of products, services, processes, systems and enabling technology that enables customers to achieve significant step-changes in strategic posture or lifestyle.	Critical in securing excellent portfolio of customers with high probability of medium-term/ new business with low marketing investment.
3. *Strategic supplier relations*	The company has screened current and prospective suppliers, and contracted with, and invested in, the capability development of those best able to support future strategic ambitions.	Reduces chance of risk or shock in supplier chain or constraint on speed of strategic development.
4. *Strategic use of technology*	The company continuously seeks to identify, screen and access available technology on an international basis, and achieve optimum balance in the use of external and internal	Reduces risk of reliance solely on in-house ideas and chance of being leap-frogged in value-added supply chain.

Factor	Outline of best practice	Reason for importance
	innovation in product, service, process and system technology.	
5. *Value for money products and services*	Product and service 'packages' are specifically designed to meet the strategic needs of key customers, thus enabling customers to achieve strategic ambitions earlier with reduced risk and at lower cost.	Basis of long-term relationship/contract without regular competitive bidding.
6. *Continuous funding of innovation*	Company maintains an investment reserve fund for wide range of innovations under both good and poor economic conditions.	Stimulates continuous flow of competitive products/ services and evolution of productivity.
7. *Growing teams and individuals*	The capability and per-formance of key individuals and team is respected internally within and external to the industry. Key executives may well be regularly approached by head hunters but most stay because of culture, reward and continuous process of challenge and personal reward.	Continuous stream of capable people available for key positions, and confidence of being among the best.
8. *Environ-mentally compatible*	Company has visible history and reputation for keeping ahead of competitors in influencing and matching product, process, systems, and work-place environmental standards.	Unlikely to be handicapped by pending legislation and threat of major sapping investment to stay open.
9. *Socially responsible*	Company has reputation for watching and being aware of trends in society/ civilization, nationally and	Stream of supportive publicity. Less likely to be targeted by environmental/ ecology groups.

Factor	Outline of best practice	Reason for importance
	internationally, and as a good corporate citizen; contributing funds and people to worthy international, national, local community, social, cultural and ecological initiatives on a timely basis.	
10. *Achievement of business results*	The financial/business results are regularly in top three in industry or in comparative groups of companies on an international as well as national basis, in comparison with competitors.	Strong financial base in spite of significant investments in satisfying a full range of stakeholders; ongoing support from banks and institutions.

THE TEN INPUT FACTORS

The ten input factors selected are outlined below and represent the internal manifestations of the culture of a range of well-run companies. As with the output factors described previously, they represent a framework of good practice to be aimed for by the total organization and within subdivisions, subsidiaries and functions.

Factor	Outline of best practice	Reason for importance
1. *Mission*	There is a clear mission for the organization that stimulates a sense of direction and the spirit and behaviour of 'the team' makes the mission live. The mission is likely to be the focus of regular participative strategy reviews and communicated and discussed throughout the organization in a manner that achieves understanding and commitment.	A team with a realistic sense of purpose and direction.

Factor	*Outline of best practice*	*Reason for importance*
2. *Objectives*	Objectives and action plans are are developed and implemented around an integrated framework of up-to-date key result areas for key managers, teams and projects.	Realistic priorities, focus, integration of effort, commitment and challenge.
3. *Organiz- ation to handle new ideas*	The organization is led at all levels in a manner that generates a continuous stream of new innovative ideas which are screened objectively and the best implemented to secure contin- uous improvement in all aspects of the business including culture products, processes, systems and management processes.	Continuous competitive renewal and sustained product- ivity are the norm.
4. *Openness and effective- ness*	Upward, downward, lateral and and diagonal communication is effective, secured by a variety of means. Well-briefed individuals and terms operate in a supportive-trusting manner.	Ensures focus on key issues and responsiveness/ flexibility to change.
5. *Systems/ procedures*	Management, operational and IT systems and procedures are updated on a continuous basis to ensure continuing need, relevance, productivity and match to customer/user needs.	Sustained productivity and cost containment, things happen on time.
6. *Skills*	The development of capability in the key skills at all levels of staff is a permanent aspect of strategy, plans and budgets in bad and good economic times.	Capability to innovate. Reduced fear of executive/staff obsolescence.
7. *Spirit and motivation*	Observed behaviour demon- strates business/organization- wide sense of purpose and innovation, enabling strong corporate, department task-force and project group team spirit.	A deep desire to succeed.

Factor	Outline of best practice	Reason for importance
8. *Relation-ships*	Effective leadership and member-ship of teams accepted, understood and shows through day-to-day behaviour. Employees willingly accept and achieve challenges seen by competitors unobtainable. Inter-departmental conflict is not a problem.	Capability to tackle new step-change challenges.
9. *Risks*	Systematic procedures exist for identifying and managing risks. Managers are encouraged to take planned/controlled risks as a natural aspect of both business and personal development.	Deep understanding of tomorrow and capability to cope.
10. *Rewards*	Comprehensive approaches to reward for personal, team and company achievements balancing economic and social aspects of performance and productivity gain sharing.	Satisfied teams, individuals and shareholders.

The company culture audit

The company culture audit presented in Table 6.1 provides a basis for positioning a total company or different business streams against illustrations of best practice. The audit is designed for both individual and team use. The following procedure is suggested.

1. Complete the output factor audit by ticking the most appropriate box against each factor and indicating the score in the right hand column on a scale 1 to 4 where 4 represents best practice.

2. Add up the total score. Calculate the percentage score on a total possible score of 40.

3. Repeat (1) and (2) for the input factor audit.

4. For both output and input scores, a score of less than 20 points or 50 per cent will be an indication that there are 4 or 5 factors requiring urgent and detailed action. A score of 20 to 30 points or 50 to 75 per cent, indicates that two or three factors need to be attended to. Scores

Table 6.1 Company culture audit

COMPANY .... MANAGER .... DATE ....

OUTPUT CULTURE FACTORS	Level 1 Score 1	Level 2 Score 2	Level 3 Score 3	Level 4 Score 4	SCORE
1. RAPID CHANGE AND RESPONSE	Bureaucracy stops creativity. Tend to be late followers	Organization/ systems being slimmed but slow to respond	Change built into plans and budgets but not always flexible	Organized/ led and funded to respond quickly to changes in environment	3
2. STRATEGIC CUSTOMER RELATIONS	Company decides what customer wants	Product/ services developed against market research	Company listens to customers' views	Number of joint ventures with key customer	2
3. STRATEGIC SUPPLIER RELATIONSHIPS	Buy from lowest price supplier	Reducing number of suppliers	Regular review of future with suppliers	Joint ventures with key suppliers	4
4. STRATEGIC USE OF TECHNOLOGY	Only use in-house technology	Prepared to license occasionally	Regularly access outside technology	Make use of all available timely technology ahead of competitors	1
5. VALUE FOR MONEY PRODUCTS/ SERVICES	Aim to be lowest price supplier	Vary specifications at a price	Aim to have value-added products/ services	Products/ services support customer's strategy	3
6. CONTINUOUS FUNDING FOR INNOVATION	No money for innovation	Evaluate each idea on merit, and try to find money in budget	Pro-active ongoing funding from profits	Regular use of in-house 'venture' funding	1
7. GROWING TEAMS AND INDIVIDUALS	Not respected for competence	One or two key people respected	Key groups respected in industry	Company professionalism respected internationally	2
8. ENVIRON- MENTALLY COMPATIBLE	Threat of closure	Necessary actions in hand	Have matched legislation standards	Anticipate ahead of legislation	1
9. SOCIALLY RESPONSIBLE	Seen as 'cold' business	Random local involvement	Active social support programme	Exemplary company recognized as best practice	1
10. ACHIEVEMENT OF BUSINESS RESULTS	Poor	Sector average	In top three nationally	In top three inter- nationally	2
				TOTAL SCORE	
TOTAL OUTPUT SCORE		divided by 40 = 0.5	50%	20	

© Strategic Leadership Partnership 1991

Table 6.1 *cont.*

INPUT CULTURE FACTORS	Level 1 Score 1	Level 2 Score 2	Level 3 Score 3	Level 4 Score 4	Score
1. MISSION	Company plan available but has no real focal point	Directors have mission statement but not really actioned	Mission known to employees who were involved in development	Committed behaviour making mission live	4
2. OBJECTIVES	Company plan with no sharp objectives	Lip service paid to objectives by some departments	Senior managers have objectives for functions	Whole company committed to objectives co-ordinated by key result areas	4
3. ORGANIZATION TO HANDLE NEW IDEAS	Organization functional and entrenched; poor generation of new ideas	Generate ideas but poor at selecting best/ implementation	Productive processing of ideas for today's business	Organized for continuous implementation of ideas for to-morrow's business	3
4. OPENNESS AND EFFECTIVENESS IN COMMUNICATION	Functional fortresses exist	Regular briefings and good grapevine	Good two-way and inter-disciplinary exchange	Good total performance as a team who trust and support	1
5. SYSTEMS/ PROCEDURES	Only changed when they fail	Slow but sure updating	Review and update in line with strategy	Streamlined, productive and customer driven	1
6. SKILLS	No organized development programme	*Ad hoc* investment in skills development	Well structured 'classical' programme with operational	Development is a key issue in strategic investment programme	1
7. SPIRIT AND MOTIVATION	Bureaucracy bogs people down	Neutral style and not pro-active	Strong team and departmental spirit	Business-wide sense of purpose and innovation	3

Table 6.1 *cont.*

INPUT CULTURE FACTORS	Level 1 Score 1	Level 2 Score 2	Level 3 Score 3	Level 4 Score 4	Score
8. RELATIONSHIPS	Poor within and between functions	Good within but not between functions	Task-forces and internal customers accepted — the words are there	Effective leadership accepted and understood by all — behaviour shows	4
9. RISKS	Unexpected crises — no risk taking allowed	Experience and tight control keeps us out of trouble	Attention given to perceived high risk areas and people grow through risks	Systematic procedures exist for managing risk effectively	3
10. REWARDS	Graded job rates fixed by company-wide negotiation. Few personal variations	Individual package but little incentive as small differences	Individual rewards which motivate best performers but ignore team	Rewards reflect personal, team and company achievements	3
				TOTAL SCORE	
TOTAL OUTPUT SCORE		divided by 40 = 0·67	% 67·5	27	

of 34 or 58 per cent can be considered as excellent. A double score of 85 per cent for both input and output factors can be regarded as the ultimate objective rarely achieved in practice.

5. Plot the individual factor scores on the profile chart provided as Table 6.2. This will help highlight the factors requiring most urgent attention to achieve an effective balanced or rounded culture.

6. Plot both the output factor and input factor percentage scores on the culture output/input matrix presented as Fig. 6.3.

7. This will help highlight any imbalance in effort and achievement. The matrix also provides a convenient way of comparing a number of business divisions within a company, and comparing the company

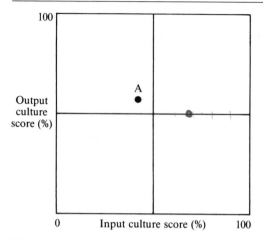

Figure 6.3   Culture output/input matrix — Company A

with customers and suppliers and selected competitors, if the information is available or an informed view possible.

The position of four typical companies within the matrix, together with the reasons and implications, are illustrated in the four examples in Figs 6.3–6.6.

In general, if output related development leads input related development there is a risk of the company or business becoming over-exposed and unable to sustain the initially excellent image when the company attempts to cope, often unsuccessfully, with hard times as experienced in the late 1980s and early 1990s.

Conversely, an over-emphasis on internal development — without an external mission-led focus and challenge — is often likely to lead to excessive bureaucracy with many nice soft culture words and features but without a vibrant competitive spirit and team.

Company A, in Fig. 6.3 represents a medium-sized subsidiary of a major manufacturing group, scoring 65 per cent for the output factors and 40 per cent for the input factors. The output score was helped by major group drives towards Total Quality Management; a new group image-building process; the international visibility and respect of a number of senior executives within the industry; the very visible social consciousness with significant investment in the arts, environmental and inner city initiatives.

Close relations with key suppliers and financial results regularly in the top ranks nationally, but not internationally, also helped achieve a reputation for trying to be a well run company in traditional terms. However, the input score was low for three reasons.

Table 6.2 Company culture profile chart

Output factors	Score				Input factors	Score			
	1	2	3	4		1	2	3	4

1. Rapid change and response
2. Strategic customer relations
3. Strategic supplier relations
4. Strategic use of technology
					1. Mission
					2. Objectives
					3. Organization
					4. Openness/
					   effectiveness
					   communication				

5. Value for money products/
   services
6. Continuous funding for
   innovation
7. Growing teams and
   individuals
8. Environmental compatibility
9. Socially responsible
10. Achievement business
    results
					5. Systems/procedures
					
					6. Skills
					
					7. Spirit and innovation
					
					8. Relationships
					9. Risks
					10. Rewards				

1. The emphasis on short-term cost containment imposed by the group, with minimum investment in developments aimed at securing improved medium- and long-term results.

2. The chief executive, although strong in marketing, did not have the experience and courage to introduce an integrated broad-based change programme. The easier things were done or tinkered with, such as introducing briefing groups through the personnel department, MCI competence based self-development distance learning by the training department, the update of systems led by the technical IT department with external consultant help which used up the total 'innovation' budget, and a more thorough completion of group budget returns by the new finance director.

3. There was no attempt to introduce an ongoing series of strategy reviews, or team and project based management development. Little was achieved in integrating inter-departmental efforts or establishing an effective process of management by objectives.

When times became tough with increased market competition, with resulting pressures on volumes, margins and product added-value, the company did not have the horsepower and gearing to respond speedily to the uphill demands. Banks, customers and competitors raised the veil of the external cover for internal ineffectiveness.

Survival was secured by a change of chief executive. The new chief executive scored highly in the chief executive self-capability audit included in Chapter 7 as Table 7.3.

Company B is typical of a bank that failed to keep pace with change. Financial results are poor; capital ratios difficult to achieve; AA credit rating lost; major customers changing the balance of business placed with a range of banks towards competitors. Typically, in-house IT systems have failed to keep up with the technology of leading banks, are internally developed, and still driven by the shape of management accounting v. customer profit profiles. Product packages are almost entirely based on what the bank would like to provide to match an outdated structure, staff training and systems.

Strategic development meetings with key customers are rarely held, but many take place with customers with insecure loans. Briefing groups lack the thrust of a clear strategic mission. Staff training concentrates on the graduate recruits, the capability of the solid core of branch customer care staff allowed to drift below that provided by new competitors such as leading building societies. Together with a bland reward system, Fig. 6.4 clearly indicates a 40 per cent : 60 per cent score.

A board-led corporate change programme on the scale of those stimulated by major 'management by objectives' programmes in the 1970s is clearly required again, but this time led by thorough strategic analysis v. basic operational mission statements.

Company C represents a medium-sized manufacturing company and subsidiary of a large group in both service and manufacturing sectors. It operates in a highly competitive sector of a global industry. The main drive in the market has changed from a traditional and largely domestic activity to one in which the company has now to interface with highly

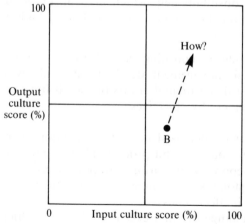

Figure 6.4 Culture output/input matrix — Company B

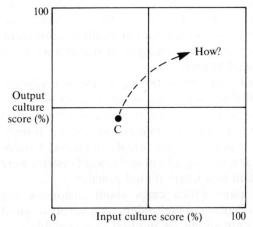

Figure 6.5   Culture output/input matrix — Company C

professional and technologically driven customers on an international basis.

The company has taken a number of steps to secure new overseas business of a strategic nature but has yet to establish other elements in output related areas to do with creation of effective suppliers, making full use of available technology and establishing adequate funding for necessary innovation.

Business in the domestic market did not impose pressures on the company to progress a number of internal issues which could today be of help in promoting the necessary rapid pace of change. In particular, the company has no mission, does not convert its long-range plans into objectives/action plans, is slow to generate and respond to new ideas and has no mechanisms for managing risk.

The company is now facing up to the development of its culture in a planned and prioritized fashion in a number of key areas, which can improve the stability of its future business. It is achieving positive results in the development of external issues with new clients and shareholders, but is under considerable pressure to update and upgrade a number of internal weaknesses perceived by external stakeholders.

Experience has also demonstrated that point C (see Fig. 6.5) represents those professional and trade organizations that have lost their way and where the lay board/council have not yet stimulated the full-time executives to apply strategic disciplines as a basic requirement, and no longer a luxury. **Company D** represents a leading food company which had focused on the management of culture continuously since its foundation more than 25 years ago.

The original mission of the founder stood the passage of time as the core of corporate strategy and ethos. The score of 85 per cent (see Fig. 6.6), for both input and output culture scores reflected the history of good leadership by a succession of managing directors under the governance of the family chairman. For several decades they were respected and indeed externally envied for a history of innovation, profit improvement, customer care, value for money, supplier development and as a source of well-rounded executives by head hunters.

Six-monthly strategy reviews had been the norm for many years, including an update on available technology — often from non-food industries — the spirit, sense of purpose and innovation were derived from involvement in the development and implementation of strategy. Jobs were designed to stimulate growth of individuals and teams. Coaching of subordinates was seen as a key ingredient and reward systems were continually evolved to maintain best international practice.

In balance, this is a company which cares about customers, the employee team, suppliers and other stakeholders as a result of good leadership. The company did not accept second best as acceptable.

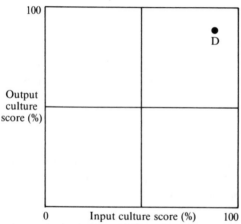

Figure 6.6   Culture output/input matrix — Company D

When to use the audit

The completion of the culture audit can be of benefit at a number of times in the corporate calendar:

1. As an integral part of annual strategy reviews.

2. As an integral part of manager/team development sessions to reinforce understanding of, and commitment to, the extent of change in culture required to commence, implement and/or sustain the company's strategic development programme.

3. As part of a communication/attitude survey designed to assess the degree of preparedness of the corporate team for today's and tomorrow's business environment.

4. As an essential part of acquisition or merger studies. A culture audit conducted before making a recommendation or final decision would help to identify at an early stage compatibilities, misfits, and the best way of combining the best of each organization to do things for real synergetic benefit. A strong culture can add much even to a strong balance sheet.

5. As an important issue in the selection of key suppliers and in the ongoing development of supplier relationships.

6. As a key issue in the identification of key customers for the development of close and joint relationships. In the first stages it may be necessary to form own judgements but better to gain advantage of discussing the issues with potential customers.

7. As part of the process of bringing in outside board members where their 'culture beliefs' should blend with what you are trying to build.

If the audit is used in these ways culture will not remain theory, but will become a live reality.

Chief executives as change agents

For many companies the culture audit will identify the need for considerable change and adjustment. In this no one can replace the chief executive as the principal agent of culture change with total accountability for ensuring that:

- the focal points for change selected and acted upon are those that have potentially maximum leverage, particularly in the early stages of the change programme
- the change programme is effectively resourced and managed
- money and time are not wasted on low pay-back cosmetic or flavour of the month change initiatives
- any changes considered are evaluated against the profile of culture and capabilities required to decide on and implement ongoing strategic change.

Effective chief executives will recognize the importance of:

- maintaining their own self-development as they move up through the ranks of company size and complexity, and face more onerous and demanding business conditions
- integrating the development of their management team with the development of the business on an ongoing continuous basis
- demonstrating good leadership through the effective behaviour and performance of their subordinate team.

These issues are the topics of Chapters 7 and 8.

7

THE NEW TOP MANAGEMENT CAPABILITIES

If the competitive benefits are to be realized from the processes outlined in earlier chapters, many companies will have to face a revolutionary change in the expansion of management capabilities, particularly at senior management level. Competitive pressures will also dictate that this expanded inventory of capabilities will need to be established quickly at best practice levels. What are these new capabilities, what is best practice and how does your management team match up to these requirements?

The top management capabilities challenge

Corporate capabilities and culture are the principal managed routes to successful implementation of strategy. As discussed in Chapter 5, day-to-day observations demonstrate that a capable team with a poor strategy, or a poor team with a good strategy, will find it difficult to sustain a market position and attractive financial results in competition with industry leaders. The competitive pressures of the next decade will sharpen the differences and contrast, and demand a combination of good team, good strategy and best practice performance.

There have been many publications over the past decades which have sought to define the critical 'people issues' in the management of change. They have rightly emphasized the importance of:

- leadership
- company management style and culture
- good internal communications
- well organized programme for personal development
- organizational structures for managing change.

This only covers one side of the balance, i.e., the good team, and does not emphasize either the need for sound strategy or indeed the people issues concerned with being a strategy-led business. The above capabilities are still important, but today cover a broader range of skills and must be developed to best practice standards. As an illustration, best practice in the above issues, which were recognized a decade ago, fall short in scope and standards for the 1990s in the following critical areas:

	1970s	1990s
1. *Leadership*	Strong capabilities in financial control and industrial relations. Disciplined approach to MBO, etc.	Strong team creative capabilities in strategic development, leadership in implementing strategy, drive for best practice standards, positive culture development and TQM
2. *Company management style and culture*	Open management, MBO, high fliers, functional professional standards encouraged	Heavy emphasis on encouraging change, best practice in all areas, strategy driven, informal exchanges
3. *Good communications*	Briefing groups, company news-sheets, no 'good news' barriers	All stakeholders are important in structured communications approach
4. *Programmes for personal development*	Well organized 'classical' company training programmes	Business driven team and individual development
5. *Organization for managing change*	Use of SBUs and task forces to promote change	Flexible approach to organization and promotion of innovation as a vehicle for change

The key vehicle for promoting and managing change has to be the implementation of a realistic corporate strategy, including the important new dimensions of response to customer strategies, strategic use of technology, and creating effective supplier strategies. These new dimensions focus and drive business priorities in products/services/processes/systems and further dictate the priorities in the development of company culture and for management development. Without the framework of strategy, it is extremely difficult for top management to be confident that their priorities and investment in management development are appropriate and, therefore, it is essential that the priorities in management development must be business needs as the norm and not just in isolated companies. This integration is illustrated in Fig. 7.1.

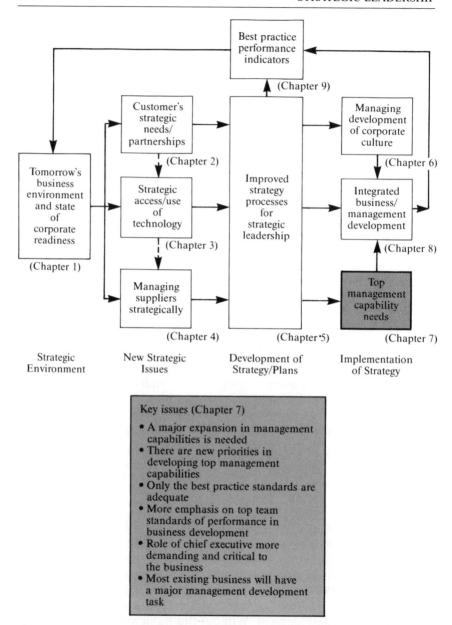

Figure 7.1   Top management development within the strategic process

The new capabilities needed for top management teams

The traditional organization and training approaches concerned with the management of change need to be adapted and expanded to achieve the full business impact from corporate strategic decisions. The following 12 key issues have been identified which require full attention from the future chief executive and top management team if the full benefits are to be realized for the business.

1. *Focus on corporate issues and not functional change* — top management teams must address the fundamental strategic issues for the business, however difficult the resolution may initially appear, and the early evaluation of current feasibility must not be allowed to kill an ambitious idea. This must be done on a team basis and not by accepting functionally developed proposals. Opportunity identification and evaluation must be ongoing and not inhibited by bureaucratic procedures.

2. *Creating a sense of mission* — the top management team must create a basis of agreement on the purpose, values, strategy and behavioural standards which are compatible with the values and aspirations of all stakeholders in the business. Above all, it must be recognized and accepted by all key employees.

3. *Participation in creating a realistic strategic vision* – the chairman and chief executive should initially work together to develop a strategic vision for the business. This should be challenged constructively and pragmatically by the top management team to achieve a realizable vision to which the whole top team is committed.

4. *Top management/board leadership in developing strategy* — the top management team should regularly review and update the core company strategy, including progress in achievement of key strategic action plans. They should also take the lead role in review and update of sub-strategies with a wide range of company managers and then use as guide-lines for strategic thinking at corporate level.

5. *Active involvement in strategic review of customer needs* — the board should lead in the activities to identify, secure and develop the key strategic customers for the business. A regular review of key customers' strategic needs, development of action plans and creation of workable long-term relationships with key customers is essential. A review of competitor SWOT analysis is needed on a regular basis to verify strategic decisions on key customers.

6. *Ensuring effective and strategic use of technology* — the top management team must ensure that the business has access to all relevant
technology and is not solely reliant on in-house development. Further systems are required for the regular review of use of technology
in products/services/processes/systems within the business and,
overall, the board must ensure that an active approach is used to
improve strategic development results by this route.

7. *Leading implementation of strategy* — the top management team,
including the chief executive, should be visible and active in the
implementation of business strategy. Such means as communication of
the strategic vision to all stakeholders, visible leadership in the execution of action plans and building strategic relationships with key
customers should be used. Significant individual time and board
discussion time should be devoted to this activity.

8. *Employ a pro-active approach to flexibility in board structure* — the
composition of the top management team should be flexible and
geared to the strategic development of the business. Short-term 'specialist' appointments to support development in specific areas should be
considered as a pro-active move. The appointment of outside directors
based on 'historic knowledge and experience' v. the capabilities
required for tomorrow needs to be questioned.

9. *Developing and monitoring stakeholder relationships* — a key issue for
the top management team is concerned with gaining commitment
and support for the strategic vision and action plans from all
stakeholders — shareholders, financial institutions, customers, and
all employees. This issue is gaining in importance and will be crucial in
the next 10 years.

10. *Growing teams and people* — the scope and scale of essential management development represents a major investment by businesses. For
effectiveness in integrating business and management development
the top management team must be heavily involved in both
planning and managing execution of management development,
which needs to be continuous through career timespan, at all levels,
and cover all processes and functions.

11. *Establishing and monitoring a decision-driven style of management* —
the top management team must ensure that a full range of management practices are used and supported by comprehensive business
databases and analytical tools. At all levels, particularly at board
level, businesses need to make and take development decisions and
establish risk management rules based on team analysis and not
solely based on proposals from functionally based reports.

12. *Ensuring rapid response and pro-active change* — the board/top management team should ensure that company culture is developed in a balanced fashion to create effectiveness in this area of business performance.

Top management capabilities audit

The above list of issues is extensive. However, it does constitute the necessary minimum top management reaction required to capitalize on the potential for development provided by the expansion of the strategic process. How does your business style, and top management team behaviour, relate to these key issues? Table 7.1 has been prepared to provide a basis for self audit, using the descriptions in the key issues as a basis for evaluation of present standards in relation to best practice.

The significance of the self audit is principally in two areas:

1. The total score which will indicate the extent and scale of development that is required.

2. The profile and trend information which provides a basis for setting priorities and outlining specific actions required.

The broad guide to interpretation of scores from the above profile audit should be as follows:

Total score 30–40   A well-structured approach requiring review and minor improvements in specific areas which are identified in the profile. Use strengths to expand the business.

20–30   This is indicative of a company that is either competent in 'conventional'/'traditional' board concepts or alternatively has some of the desired approach with weaknesses in a number of areas. The profile again will indicate which applies and areas for action which should aim for resolution in 12–18 months.

10–20   A potentially serious situation with very little recognition of future leadership needs, with likely downward trends being shown in a number of key areas. It is likely that significant top management development or restructuring will be required.

0–10   Substantial development for the future will be needed — this score does not mean necessarily that today's performance is poor but that the future is likely to be

Table 7.1 Board management capabilities audit

Issue and question	Assessment of (a) current situation and (b) trend							
	Poor		Fair		Good		Excellent	
	Score 1		Score 2		Score 3		Score 4	
1. Focus on issues of corporate development v. functional change	Functional managers advise board on plans for change		Board sub-committees advise board on five year plan		CEO takes lead with board on strategy		Board involved with strategy and culture development at company and unit level	
	a.	b.	a.	b.	a.	b.	a.	b.
2. Creating a sense of mission	No board involvement in mission		Board issues mission statement		CEO provides in-depth mission for board to approve		Board involved in drafting and 'negotia- ting' with all stakeholders	
	a.	b.	a.	b.	a.	b.	a.	b.
3. Board participation in developing realistic strategic vision	Strategic planning dept. produce vision		Functionally built up five year plan		Top-down and bottom-up five year plans		Board-led participative strategy programme	
	a.	b.	a.	b.	a.	b.	a.	b.
4. Active involvement in strategic review of customer needs	Board deals with serious customer complaints		Competitor section in five year plan		Top-down five year plan looks at key customers annually		Board spends substantial time on strategy to meet customer needs	
	a.	b.	a.	b.	a.	b.	a.	b.
5. Ensuring effective strategic use of technology	R&D director has *ad hoc* role		Annual R&D report to board		Regular review of new product spend in technology		Strategic review of use of technology in all activities in business	
	a.	b.	a.	b.	a.	b.	a.	b.

Table 7.1 *cont.*

6. Leading implementation of strategy	Functionally led plans (managers)		Limited board-led functional plans		Monitoring of key development plans		Directors/CEO lead key strategic action plans	
	a.	b.	a.	b.	a.	b.	a.	b.
7. Developing and maintaining stakeholder relations	Brief the employee representatives and read in the press		Strong company communication of good and bad news		Strategic briefings and walkabouts plus broker meetings		Strategic involvement and participation by all stakeholders	
	a.	b.	a.	b.	a.	b.	a.	b.
8. Growing teams and people	Board has policy on apprentice and staff training		Apprentice graduate and management training		Well-structured 'off-line' manager development		Board drives management development using company issues, IBMD	
	a.	b.	a.	b.	a.	b.	a.	b.
9. Practising and promoting decision v. data-driven style of management	Board has good accounting information		Board sees wide range of management information		Board uses sub-committee to advise on key decisions		Well-structured business information, modelling, etc., used by board	
	a.	b.	a.	b.	a.	b.	a.	b.
10. Ensuring rapid response and pro-active change	Dependent on efforts of a few individuals to respond		Chief executive has a 'Fire Brigade'		Chief executive has task-forces to react to and promote change		Structured programmes involving board to achieve this	
	a.	b.	a.	b.	a.	b.	a.	b.
Column Scores								

Instructions: Consider each of the above issues/questions in turn. Select the column which best fits your current situation and tick the appropriate box 'a'. Consider the underlying trend and denote by ↑ ↓ ↗ ↘ in box 'b'. Add score for all questions.

Total score (sum of columns 1–4) ☐

© Management of Technology Partnership 1989

bleak. It is likely that development action will be required in most key areas. Clearly, new direction is needed which may mean that there is a need to change the top management in some areas.

The profile and trend information is a useful starting point to define the actions required — based on the assessment of both trends and areas of weakness. It is most likely that action plans will need to cover the following six areas:

1. Development of new capabilities for senior managers in both individual and team activity — particular emphasis on customer strategic focus, use of technology, supplier strategic management and environmental strategies.

2. Changes and improvement of company in leadership style and performance — a recognition of the need to take a pro-active approach to culture development and the drive for best practice standards.

3. Developing a sense of mission throughout the business — top management must be pro-active in the development of the company mission and for its integration in a committed fashion into both strategic and operating activities.

4. Review of structure and composition of top management team — this should reflect strategic development needs, be clear in its responsibilities and make full use of short/medium-term outside appointments to the board to boost rate of strategic development.

5. Improved communication to all stakeholders — both outside and inside stakeholders need to be part of a structured approach covering the message and media concepts. This is an important area for development.

6. Future philosophy, commitment and scale of management development — the key issue is to recognize the need for a business needs driven approach which aims at best practice in all key areas. This is a key issue in developing the necessary corporate culture for the 1990s.

Experience shows that the process of creating a top management team which will respond to the challenges of the next 10 years will require individuals, and particularly the chief executive, who have proven skills in the following profile:

- strategic vision and skills in opportunity identification
- conscious competence in strategic development
- corporate consciousness, priorities and skills

- identification with strategic customers and their needs
- aware of importance and relevance of the use of available technology throughout all facets of the business
- vision to identify, access and introduce new technologies
- well practised in analytical management processes to achieve focus on business results
- acceptance and support of strategy-driven style of management
- effectiveness in planning and managing change
- a commitment to ongoing personal development, and involvement in top team development
- introduction of intellectual challenge in senior level decision-making and taking
- developing a sense of mission throughout the business
- active as a coach to managers.

The creation of management development programmes to respond to the above portfolio of skills is a strong challenge to most companies. A major shift from conventional off-line training to job-related/action learning is required, using the business development plans as a primary vehicle for management development.

The key role is that of the chief executive — chief executives have to meet most, if not all, of the above needs and also have personal skills which:

- bring vision for the future business
- have the ability to motivate all staff to support and achieve the vision
- are used to develop immediate senior colleagues to utilize these skills in an effective way
- integrate all of these to create a commitment to corporate mission at all levels.

Key capabilities required for chief executives

The role and required skills portfolio for chief executives has developed substantially over the past two decades with the growth of internationalism in key product and service markets and the recognition of the fundamental value of the inventory of available technology to strategic development. As the scope and scale of industrial development has accelerated, so has the breadth of the portfolio of skills required for successful business leadership. Figure 7.2 shows the rapid build up of new portfolio skills over the period since 1950, from which the following four key issues emerge:

1. The scale of industry is such that individual development alone is not effective — top teams and other senior groups are crucial — the day

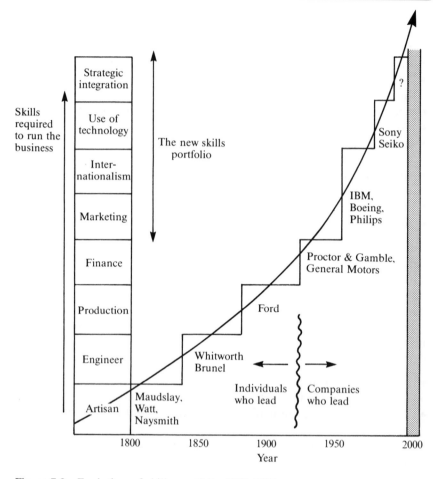

Figure 7.2 Evolution of skills portfolio 1800–2080

of the overall single leader's strategic control probably passed around 1920. Sadly, it continues in many companies.

2. The role of the chief executive has demanded, and will continue to demand new key capabilities — the chief executive is a prime candidate for development in the next decade.

3. Heavy emphasis is needed on integrative skills for top managers — to make full and effective use of the complete portfolio of skills — particularly important will be the skills to integrate business and management development aside from business development.

4. The chief executive must play a major role in establishing and directing management development of senior staff. The pace of development will almost certainly lead to short/medium-term board appointments with a development role via the routes of constructive challenge, catalysis and coaching of senior managers.

This general listing of skills needs to be converted into specific capability portfolios for chief executives and other members of the top management team. The following sections of this chapter will set out a broadly based approach to the identification of the skills portfolio for chief executives and chairman — it is recognized that, in practice, this will be specific to both businesses and individual skills and experience. However, it is essential that this issue is approached on a formal and analytical basis if strategic development is to be effective in tomorrow's business environment.

Expanding the skills portfolio for the next decade

In developing the definition of needs in key capabilities, it is necessary to expand on the extent of the skills portfolio demanded by business developments over the past decade. Figure 7.3 shows both the impact on strategic and operational management in graphic terms, and highlights the impact of:

*   market globalization in strategic and operations terms
*   the new dimensions of customer needs and use of technology
*   the increasing element of business-driven skills, particularly in strategic development.

The task of integration is also clearly demonstrated to encompass new dimensions in both strategic and operational terms.

Two trends emerge from Figure 7.2, namely:

1. The expansion of the scope of process-based skills, over the period shown, where senior managers need to evolve their skills portfolio to accommodate the additional process dimensions from the 'business-led' skills revolution.

2. The rapid growth in the portfolio of new 'business-led' skills which are driven by the strategic development needs of business.

Within the UK the Management Charter Initiative (MCI) has set out to define and create resources to respond to the progressive development of managers with the necessary process skills. The position with respect to providing resources for developing the business-led skills is at an earlier

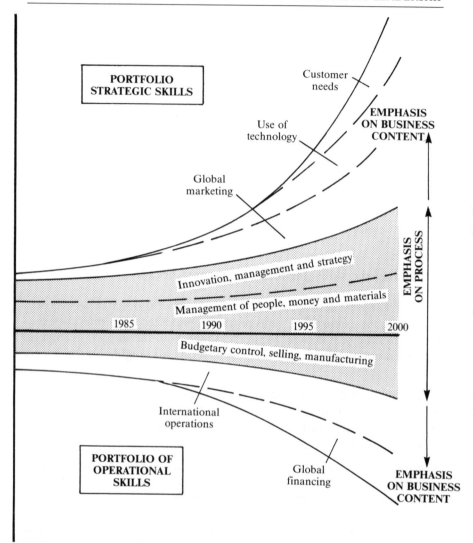

Figure 7.3 Expansion of chief executive and top management skills portfolio

stage of development but recognized by both government and industry/
commerce as an essential element for future competitiveness. The later
chapters of this book provide a framework to meet this challenge.

It is important to question what the impact of this generalized
approach is in terms of the specific skills development required for chief
executives. Table 7.2 sets out the development in the chief executive skills
portfolio over the period 1975–1995, at the level of specific areas of key

capabilities for both operational and strategic management. The trends required in key capabilities are clear, at least for UK managers, who have been required to face situations ranging from:

- managing growth in high inflation and difficult employee relations situations in the late 1970s
- recession, cutbacks with constructive moves in employee relations and inflation in the early 1980s
- capitalizing on international growth opportunities against fierce competition in the late 1980s to early 1990s.

Managing in the 1980s has been dominated in many companies by operational survival issues and therefore many chief executives have not built up experience in the key capabilities required for the next half decade — a serious issue which must be given priority if companies are to respond competitively.

As before, strategy remains the principal basis for starting to resolve this shortcoming in the capabilities of top management, and particularly chief executives. The development of strategic action plans as the basis for implementing strategy can be used through analysis to define the key capabilities required for implementation by the managers involved. This audit of key capabilities will provide the basis to define:

- the management style for strategic development and those areas requiring priority development of management capabilities
- the key capabilities required for implementation of strategy in terms of management practices and subject knowledge for individuals, top management teams and other managers
- the gaps between present capabilities and best practice.

The next chapter outlines one way in which the needs for strategic business development and management development can be integrated into an effective way ahead. The chief executive and chairman have a major part to play in setting up, directing and assisting in the process of development of senior managers, the corporate style of management and company culture. This issue should be treated as a major sub-strategy for the company and should have the chief executive as its project manager.

Chief executive capabilities — self audit

Where do you believe that you stand today in your personal capabilities to respond to the needs of the next decade? Table 7.3 provides a basis for developing a self-audit profile against the new and expanded management capabilities discussed in this and earlier chapters.

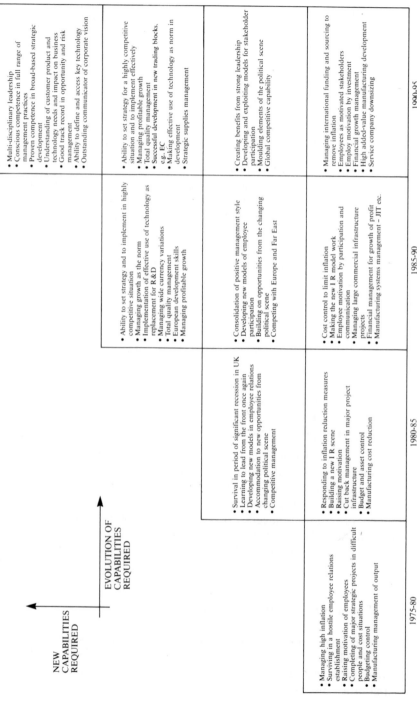

Table 7.2 Key capabilities required: 1975–1995

NEW CAPABILITIES REQUIRED

EVOLUTION OF CAPABILITIES REQUIRED

1975-80

- Managing high inflation
- Surviving in a hostile employee relations establishment
- Raising motivation of employees
- Completing of major strategic projects in difficult people and cost situations
- Budgeting control
- Manufacturing management of output

1980-85

- Survival in period of significant recession in UK
- Learning to lead from the front once again
- Developing new models in employee relations
- Accommodation to new opportunities from changing political scene
- Competitive management

- Responding to inflation reduction measures
- Building a new I R scene
- Raising motivation
- Cut back management in major project infrastructure
- Budget and asset control
- Manufacturing cost reduction

1985-90

- Ability to set strategy and to implement in highly competitive situation
- Managing growth as the norm
- Implementation of effective use of technology as replacement for R&D
- Managing wide currency variations
- Total quality management
- European development skills
- Managing profitable growth

- Consolidation of positive management style
- Developing new models of employee participation
- Building on opportunities from the changing political scene
- Competing with Europe and Far East

- Cost control to limit inflation
- Making the new I R model work
- Employee motivation by participation and communication
- Managing large commercial infrastructure projects
- Financial management for growth of profit
- Manufacturing systems management – JIT etc.

1990-95

- Multi-disciplinary leadership
- Conscious competence in full range of management practices
- Proven competence in broad-based strategic development
- Understanding of customer product and technology needs and impact on business
- Good track record in opportunity and risk management
- Ability to define and access key technology
- Outstanding communicator of corporate vision

- Ability to set strategy for a highly competitive situation and to implement effectively
- Managing profitable growth
- Total quality management
- Successful development in new trading blocks. e.g. EC
- Making effective use of technology as norm in development
- Strategic supplies management

- Creating benefits from strong leadership
- Developing and exploiting models for stakeholder participation
- Moulding elements of the political scene
- Global competitive capability

- Managing international funding and sourcing to remove inflation
- Employees as motivated stakeholders
- Employ motivation by investment
- Financial growth management
- High added-value manufacturing development
- Service company downsizing

186

Table 7.3 Chief executive capabilities: self audit

Capability	Score 1	Score 2	Score 3	Score 4	Score
1. Competence in all strategic and operations processes	Strong on operating systems	Strong on operations plus long-range plans	Have good operations and strategy but rely on functional specialists	Ability to integrate all facets of strategy	
2. Developing a strategic culture in the company	Business results must come before culture	Extensive input related training exists in company	Board has an *ad hoc* programme on specific culture issues	Active in leading a balanced programme for culture development	
3. Use of strategy-led managing change	Do not mix strategy with 'real' decisions	Some five year plan actions are followed up by board	Serious attempt by board to pursue key five year plan issues	Use of strategic action plans at all levels in business	
4. Management still in effective use of technology	We use our R&D function for advice	The board sees an annual R&D report and acts on it	Regular search plus in-house R&D against five year plan	Regular search acquisition and use in all areas of products/ processes and systems	
5. Definition of actions to meet key customers' strategic needs	Meet key customers regularly on a social basis	We respond to market research and competitor analysis	We hold planning presentations for major customers	Have joint strategic commitments with key customers	
6. Playing a leading role implementing strategy	We look at main developments as a board	Board oversees functional led development plans	Senior staff members lead main developments in five year plan	Chief executive and board members lead action plans and promote vision to stakeholders	
7. Skills in 'management' of business stakeholders	We use our annual report to communicate	Regular meetings with bank, brokers to talk about business	Structured approach on annual report to brokers, employees and shareholders	Committed to a regular programme of discussion with all strategic stakeholders	
8. Employing a decision driven management style	Board only gets involved in financial decisions	Board plays role in decisions from five year plan proposals	Board seeking to develop better support database	Have good business database and analytical systems for decision support	

Table 7.3 *cont.*

Capability	Score 1	Score 2	Score 3	Score 4	Score
9. Active in developing the top team	Top managers no longer need developing	The chief executive uses an outside consultant for board training	The board discusses annually and decides what training it needs	Strong open coaching style and personal involvement in team development	
10. Committed to continuous training and development of all employees	We have a training manager who looks after this	The company has a comprehensive conventional training plan	We use Total Quality Programme to define training	Involvement in strategic activity to ensure business-led comprehensive training	
				TOTAL	

Two forms of analysis emerge from this audit assessment, namely:

- an overall score from a maximum of 40 points
- a profile of strengths and weaknesses based on individual issues.

Earlier audits have provided guidance on the implications of level of audit scores but here it is probably sufficient to say that any score under 20 should be viewed as a clear indication for the chief executive of the need to take priority action. The chief executive must be able to lead the top team development.

The profile of scores is more important than the overall score, where the gaps in the profile identify the areas for planning by making initial judgements on:

- what could be the best routes to deal with the gaps which need to be closed urgently — outside consultant help, short-term director appointment in consultant/coaching role, management school programmes or a combination of these, with an in-house development project
- which capabilities require team versus individual development, i.e., which gaps should be closed by team programmes
- where personal needs match those of close colleagues
- how to build on personal strengths to the benefit of the business and one's colleagues.

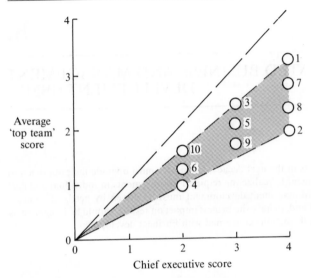

Figure 7.4   Chief executive audit analysis

The relationship between the chief executive and other members of the top team is probably the most critical element for managing change in an effective way. The members of the top team should also undertake the chief executive audit and indicate their perceptions of the way in which the CEO acts in each area. A useful basis for further analysis is shown in Fig. 7.4.

This analysis provides a basis for the top team to initiate discussion on both the role/performance of the chief executive and to introduce the audit results from Table 7.1 and, thereby, begin to review both the development needs for the CEO and the top team in an integrated fashion.

The routes to developing an understanding and action plans for major management development programmes are explored in the next chapter, which outlines a cost effective approach to integration of business and management development to maximize impact on strategic development.

8

INTEGRATED BUSINESS AND MANAGEMENT DEVELOPMENT (IBMD)

For competitive success in the next decade, businesses must upgrade their approach to management development to realize the required improvements in individual and corporate performance. Management development must be driven by needs of strategic business development and, to have the biggest impact on results, should be integrated as far as possible within the actions concerned with business development.

The challenge — integrating business and management development

Most businesses are faced with three forms of development during the next decade, namely:

1. Product, service, processes and technology development to achieve the business objectives derived from the company strategy.

2. People and systems development for new capabilities to support the implementation of strategy.

3. Progressive development of people and systems to achieve best practice standards of strategic management to realize the full strategic potential of the business.

It is clear, therefore, that programmes of management development are an integral and critical element of the overall business development process as illustrated in Fig. 8.1.

The previous chapter has already examined the impact on senior management in terms of the new capabilities that need to be acquired, but the dimensions of this issue go well beyond the important, but restricted, area of top management. In particular, the programmes will need to respond to:

- the total organization — all employees
- the full range of management processes — from crisis management to operations to strategic development
- all subjects concerned with the business content of the company activity

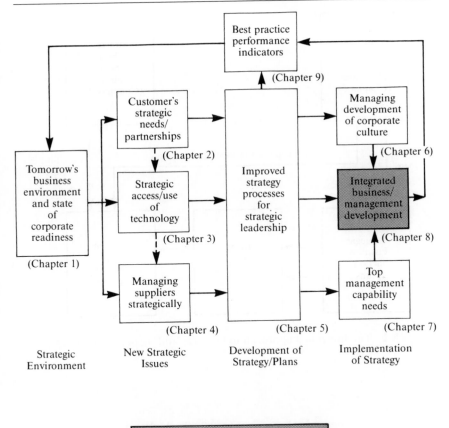

Figure 8.1 Integrating business and management development

- the full career span of all employees — it is important that this should be applied to all levels in the organization
- the priorities in business development.

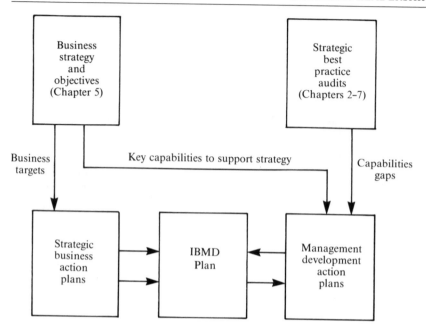

Figure 8.2 The integrated approach to business and management development

The above concept is shown in Fig. 8.2 which shows the interlinking of management/people development content with business development and builds upon the concepts shown in general form in Fig. 8.1. It is important to recognize the consequences on the content of the management development activity arising from the broadening of the dimensions referred to above in three areas, namely:

ORGANIZATION NEEDS

- Development of employees at all levels — it is particularly important that development should not be confined to management level — in today's dynamic business environment the continuing development of the chief executive is crucial as well as junior employees in their first job.
- Team development across functions must take place at all levels and in particular at board level, as it has to become much more influential in the direction of competitive strategic development.

- Multi-level development to foster better vertical understanding and relationships.
- Individual and self-managed development is to be encouraged at all levels.

CONTENT NEEDS

- Individual programmes aimed at the creation of literacy in all functions, e.g., emphasis on technology for accountants and marketing managers, etc., to produce multi-literate executives.
- Heavy emphasis in management processes as routine development, e.g., profit planning, strategy formulation, decision-making and action planning at all levels to ensure that business content, not the process, becomes the key issue in decision-making and business development.
- Creation of decision/data-driven style in both individual and team development.
- Use of business issues as the development vehicle for individual and particularly team development — formation of task-forces, to implement specific strategic action plans and new processes to enhance company culture.
- Use of specific organizational approaches to foster both business and manager development — product management, strategic business units, and quality circles, etc.
- A heavy emphasis on technology, processes and systems analysis for stimulating the effective use of technology.
- Regular review and update of both process and business information content, to ensure compatibility with IBMD needs.

TIMESCALE NEEDS

- A conscious commitment to individual development throughout the career timespan, irrespective of level in organization by both the company and individual.
- A conscious commitment of board and senior management time to management development and training at all levels.
- Anticipation of future management development needs as a key output from relevant parts of business strategy, e.g., new key capabilities in customer needs, technology, geographic scope, development of culture, etc.

Commitment to a programme of this magnitude requires significant senior management support in both time and cost to the business and therefore must be seen to yield positive business results. The programme must therefore be fully integrated into the business operations and development activity as a key sector of the strategic action plans. In short, what we are seeking is an *integrated business and management development* approach, which exists within the overall day-to-day business activity and uses business issues as the development vehicle for people and teams.

It is reasonable to question what might be the consequences of not accepting the IBMD concept. Some organizations have taken the approach which leads to priority in business development, looking to improved results to pay for people development and relying on the skills of senior managers to see them through this approach. It is accepted that this has worked in the past but it is highly risky and not advisable as a route in the highly competitive business scene of the 1990s. The opposite approach of creating the necessary management skills as a priority and then planning to use them in business development creates an organization with no challenge, and in the 1990s environment will lead to a progressive run-down of the activity if the business development challenges are not met. The likely outcome of a failure to adopt IBMD in the 1990s is summarized in Fig. 8.3. The best way to healthy corporate development is IBMD.

Exposure of the IBMD concept, described above, in a number of companies has led to the identification of a number of priorities for development, which illustrate the integrated nature of real development issues. There has been common ground in both business and management development in most businesses in the following six areas:

- developing strategic management programmes for key customers and suppliers
- making effective use of technology in all areas of the business
- fast track people development
- managing the development of company culture
- improving the management of innovation and change
- practical approaches to establish IBMD into present company operations.

These are practical issues which have arisen in companies who are looking to improve their strategic development performance at this time.

Routes to success

It is necessary to make use of the full spectrum of available management development resources and routes to respond with success to the highly

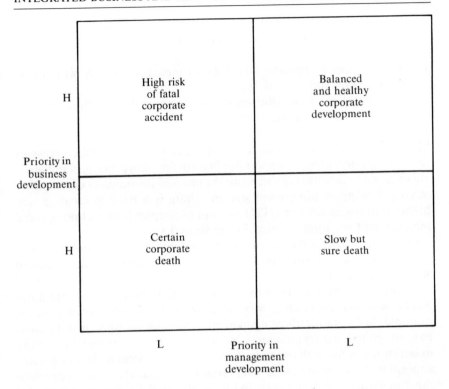

Figure 8.3   The IBMD corporate health indicator

competitive business scene of the next 10 years. In general, this means that the roles of

- modular cooperative programmes with non-competitive companies with similar needs
- higher education institutions/business schools/consultant trainers and coaches
- in-company training programmes and on-line business development training
- coaching and counselling by senior executives, non-executive directors or external consultants

need to be better coordinated and integrated in terms of planning and implementation of the teaching and training content involved. It will also be important to consider new institutions for both technology and management vocational training at all levels.

The analysis of future capabilities for senior managers in Chapter 7 illustrated two streams of development, namely:

The analysis of future capabilities for senior managers in Chapter 7 illustrated two streams of development, namely:

1. A management process based evolutionary approach with heavy emphasis on standard skills.
2. An expanding content/business based range of capabilities in both technology and management.

Much of the educational structure is in place to undertake the necessary research and teaching to support the first stream above, but new initiatives are required to develop both new institutions and in-company development activity to support the second stream. There is a need to create a new higher training institution (HTI) concept to support both technology and management vocation training in the second stream.

Figure 8.4 shows a typical range of development routes and how they focus on research, individual teaching and training, team development and business development.

A significant number of companies have well-structured programmes which define graduate entry standards and subsequently develop to, for example, MBA standards or equivalent. A smaller number of companies have structured and continuing training programmes to extend this activity to senior levels for both individual and team development. In Fig. 8.4 this concept is shown to include a wide range of individual and team development activities which are seen today as essential for future competitive performance.

The principal difference in the new module areas is in the 'hands on' aspects of the activity, generally associated with the areas of development related to the use of company issues for both management development and improvement of business results. Some examples from Fig. 8.4 illustrate this point as follows:

- *Company strategy review* — very specific to business and involving a team approach — identification of individual and team needs in development of key capabilities, identification of critical issues and development of strategic action plans.
- *Implementation of strategic action plans* — individual and team development, probably led by a board member, and concerned with a specific business related development issue.
- *Day-to-day experience* but backed by personal action plans and supportive development.
- *Organization as a route to development* — exploiting use of such organizational/team concepts as quality circles, *ad hoc* business units, skunk works, etc., as a basis for integrated business and management development.

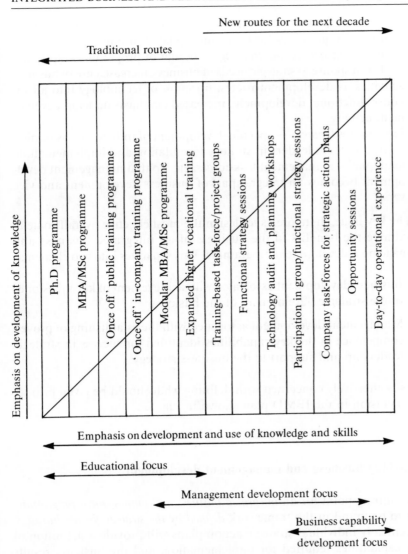

Figure 8.4 Routes to integrate management development

There are clearly ongoing roles for each of the routes for development, but with increased emphasis in specific areas as follows:

- *Higher education institutes* — technology updates, processes for effective use of technology, management of technology, modular higher degree programmes in technology and management and in-house company programmes for basic and update training.

- *In-company teaching and training* — design of programmes up to top level, as response to strategic needs of business, increased use of business activities as development routes, injection of technology into all in-house functional development, increased emphasis on team development activity.
- *Business development* — specific development of individuals as participants and team leaders in strategy formulation and implementation, total quality management task-forces, etc., so that management development becomes an integral part of business development and vice versa.

The key issue, therefore, is to design the most effective overall route to maximize the benefits to the business of an integrated business and management development programme. This separates into two elements:

1. Business development associated with achievement of key milestones in the strategic development of the business.

2. Management development associated with the establishing of proven competence in the key capabilities identified for success in strategic leadership and support to the business strategy.

This is effectively concerned with defining what should be given priority for inclusion in the IBMD plan shown in Fig. 8.2.

Matching business and management development

The starting point for an *integrated business and management programme* has to be found in the framework *defined by the strategy for the business.* Specifically individual strategic action plans will provide a definition of key capabilities required for implementation, and the business results projected from implementation. The following four principles are essential in the definition of an IBMD programme.

1. Business strategy and the likely results from this and moves to achieve strategic leadership drives the planning process. Any process, therefore, should focus on the five key areas defined initially in Chapter 1 and pursued in the structure of the subsequent chapter, namely:

   Area A: business results and overall strategic development
   Area B: customer strategy and competitive situation

Area C: effective use of technology
Area D: effective use and development of people
Area E: balancing the development of company culture.

2. The business strategic action plans emerging from the strategy processes of Chapter 5 define the key capabilities that are needed to support achievement of the plan targets. Some of these will already exist but others will require development to underpin achievement of plan objectives. The capabilities involved are likely to form part of the contents of Chapters 2–8 and, further, will be included in the audits of each chapter. In establishing management development support programmes in such areas, best practice levels defined in each of the relevant audits should be adopted wherever possible.

3. It is likely that the present strategy will contain strategic action plans which start the process of achieving strategic leadership — limited by either the absence of a clear view of what constitutes a leadership position or by the absence of specific key management capabilities. The audits of Chapters 2–8 provide an overall statement of the key capabilities required to support a business leadership position. Therefore, the IBMD process needs to be able to indicate which of these capabilities is most relevant to raising the 'strategic sights' of the business.

4. To create an IBMD programme in line with the above principles, will mean that full use will be made of all the audits contained in this book in that:

   • the capabilities required to support the implementation of strategy need to be screened against all audit points
   • a judgement needs to be made on which of the gaps in relation to best practice standards can contribute most to further improving strategic performance if they are removed by development.

   This is a lengthy and detailed process which has to be carried out initially by the top team, as it sets the framework and course for development of all people across the business.

Chapter 9 sets out a practical process for preparing an IBMD programme, taking into account all of the above principles. The next section of this chapter illustrates a section of the process for aligning action plans with the development of related management capabilities for the top management team.

Table 8.1 Key capabilities — linking company issues with strategic action plans

Strategic action plan (example)　　　　　　　Project leader:

Need to establish process for development and regular review of key customer strategy

Actions required / Key capabilities	Priority for action	Priority on corporate drive	Having realistic vision	Creating a sense of mission	Regular review of key customer strategies	Active in making more effective use of technology	Board members active in leading action plans	Active in developing relationships with shareholders	Dynamic approach to composition of top team	Growing teams and people	Ensuring board/company style is decision driven	
Identification of key strategy customers	H	√	×	√	×	×	×	×	0	×	×	2
Liaison with customer on technology and market strategy	H	×	×	×	×	×	√	×	×	×	×	1
Creation of technology route map for key customers	M/H	×	×	√	√	√	×	×	0	0	×	3
Understanding of features of key customers' markets	M/H	√	√	√	√	√	√	×	×	×	×	6
Organization to focus on customer needs	H	√	×	×	√	√	×	×	×	×	×	3
Prepare customer development plans		×	×	√	√	√	√	0	0	0	×	4
Establish regular review with customers	M	×	√	√	√	√	√	×	0	×	√	6
Tell shareholders and gain support	M/H	√	×	√	×	×	×	×	×	0	0	2
Establish understanding at all levels in business	H	×	×	×	×	×	√	×	0	√	×	2
Improving processes and systems to meet customer needs	M/H	×	×	×	√	×	×	×	×	×	×	1
Rating on 'Top Ten' board issues		4	2	6	6	5	5	–	–	1	1	

Key: √ Key capability relevant and available
     × Key capability relevant and not available
     0 Not relevant in this critical issue 'directly'

Process in practice

The key capabilities and best practice standards have been defined for board level in Table 8.1 and have been developed at individual level for the chief executive in Table 8.2. Assessed against individual experience and training, it is therefore possible to define development needs in key capabilities for, for example, individual members of the board/top management team against the background of desired management style and strategic business needs. This is an essential first step if an organized approach is to be made to strategic development and provides a clear indication of the strengths and weaknesses of the top management team against the needs of the strategic action plans. It therefore provides a basis to define a realistic approach and particularly to identify those capabilities which need to be acquired either by development, recruitment of new staff or appointment of outside directors or consultants. The role of suitably experienced outside directors is seen as an important issue in senior level management development, as this can be crucial in both a management and business development context.

In general, the development of key capabilities throughout the organization will largely be by a combination of teaching and training, with the emphasis on the latter. The definition of the organization development needs at team and individual level will be defined by strategic action plans and other individual group activity associated with operations and development of the business. After initial training exposure to the portfolio of skills, individuals/teams would be expected to refine and prove this by participation in implementation of strategic action plans, as part of a project team led by either an executive director/senior manager and, if appropriate, supported by consultants. The above process is complex, but straightforward, and can produce dramatic results in a short time. Involvement of staff in such activity provides a strong motivation for full participation and ongoing self development — leading to a high degree of individual and corporate dynamism.

What does this process look like in practice? In Table 8.1 the approach is illustrated for a top team IBMD assessment which integrates:

- the key issues for board capabilities and standards (as shown in Table 7.1)
- the key capabilities identified as required to implement a specimen strategic action plan.

The matrix presentation in Table 8.1 shows how capabilities needed for strategic action plan implementation can drive the development of overall corporate capabilities, and gives a good indication of the following:

- the extent to which specific plans call upon the key capabilities issues for the board
- the extent to which key capabilities exist in a relevant form in this group, i.e., strengths and weaknesses
- the areas for priority attention in the development of key capabilities at board level for both corporate capability and achievement of leadership in action plans (column scores)
- the elements of the action plan which are most at risk due to absence of relevant capabilities (row scores).

The detailed analysis of Table 8.1, while only illustrative, does provide some indication of the output of this analysis focused on a single group. In the example, the overall scores are poor, the indications from the above would be that the sales and marketing function is strong and influential but little else. The board capabilities score poorly on all of the high priority areas of the action plan. This analysis provides a clear basis for areas of development which have to be given priority for this action plan.

Relating business development needs to current management capabilities

The starting point of any business development is defined by the current management capabilities of the chief executive and top management team. It is therefore crucial to assess these capabilities as it may be necessary to establish specific programmes of basic management development at the outset and possibly look for some changes in individual manager's roles or portfolios of responsibilities.

Figure 8.5 shows a basis for management audit of the chief executive, top management team and the next layer of management. The audit analysis seeks to define three areas of capability which are important to strategic development:

1. Ability to achieve short-term results which define the extent to which the individual's performance can be relied upon for operational results.

2. Capability in managing change which is important in the selection of action plan project leaders for strategic development.

3. Ability to contribute to formulation, review and refinement of strategy which should be used as a measure of team contribution in strategic development.

The analysis, although subjective and limited in its detail, does provide

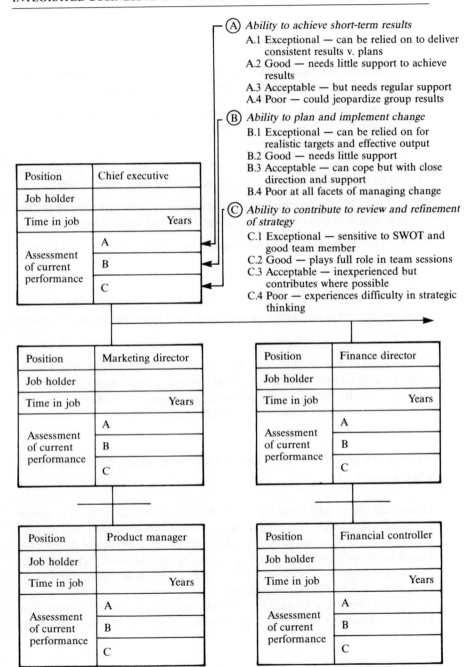

Figure 8.5 Company's current capability audit

a number of useful guidelines at the outset for a programme of business development. The following six issues are fundamental:

1. Are the current performance standards of the chief executive in line with development needs — if not what has to be done?

2. Do the members of the top management team meet the criteria for strategic development of the business — are there any individuals who might not respond to team activities?

3. Are there any obvious project leaders for strategic action plans at board level — if not, are there others at the next level down?

4. Is it possible to overcome shortcomings in the performance of the top management team by an outside appointment for coaching purposes?

5. Are there any obvious candidates at lower level who should become members of the top management team or its activity in strategic development?

6. Who are the likely members of project teams for specific strategic development action plans already identified from the corporate strategy review?

It is important that the top team should consider the output of this audit in detail and be prepared to act quickly in overcoming any shortcomings — this could be their first major strategic decision as a team!

Practical examples of what can be done are presented in Chapter 10.

Putting integrated business and management development into the organization

In general, there will be of the order of eight to ten critical issue action plans at board level. The preparation of the analysis shown in Table 8.1 for each action plan can provide a clear picture of priorities in developing board member/chief executive/top team capabilities and a clear picture of possible capability portfolios for outside directors as consultants to the board who could fill important gaps.

The following five guidelines are important in defining the management development strategies and programme in parallel with business development:

1. Define a management development sub-strategy with associated critical issue action plans and schedule of key capabilities required as an integral part of the business strategy.

2. Identify at the outset the obvious shortfalls in key capabilities where outside help is needed for either medium, long-term or short-term support. Appoint director or consultant, as appropriate.

3. Nominate one director to manage the implementation strategy for management development — probably a non-executive director.

4. Develop a broad definition of the board role in the integrated business and management development programme, i.e., what 'team' key capabilities need developing and what critical issue action plans rest with the board.

5. Lay down a 12-month action programme with regular peer review at the top executive team level on the integrated programme.

The above process and the integrated development activity is illustrated, in organizational terms, in Figure 8.6. The project direction of strategic action plans is assumed by nominated board members who are shown in this role for two areas of sub-strategy — customers and technology. They are concerned with the achievement of *business results* from these action plans. These plans are integrated on a function, team and individual basis with the action plans for the sub-strategy on management development which are concerned with the development of *key capabilities*.

The project directors ensure harmonization of their action plans to promote *integration* and should be visible and active in this role.

The development of the chief executive and chairman

This is the most important management development issue for any business — recent and proven competitive success must not be taken as a basis for complacency, but proof that the management team has strengths which can be built up for the future. On strategic development, the critical members of the top management team are the chairman of the board of directors and the chief executive. Together, they should create the future vision of the business which must include a description of the business management style and culture which plays a major part in defining the sub-strategy for management development.

Too often, the view is taken that the chairman and chief executive do not need to be part of the management development programme, but this has not been true in the past and is certainly not true for the next decade. They both have development needs and should be part of a tailored top level programme. They also have a role in the direction of the overall management development activity but probably the responsibility should

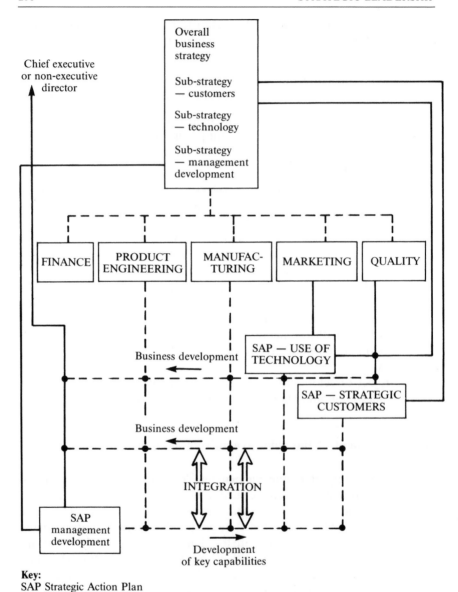

Figure 8.6   Integration of business and management

rest with a non-executive director, possibly the deputy chairman. Both the chairman and chief executive have a major role in overseeing progress in the IBMD programme as a whole.

As in earlier sections, the conclusion is that the business strategy has to define the development needs for the chairman and chief executive but with the difference that their development has to be established on a 'self-starter' basis — they have to define their own needs and in so doing set an example and thereby create the environment for development of their senior colleagues.

What then are the routes available for the chairman and chief executives to establish their own development needs and the ongoing support programme? The following six routes are available:

1. Make full use of the process described in Table 8.1 to define individual needs to support the business strategy and the audit results from Table 7.3 to identify ongoing best practice standards.

2. Involve an individual outside senior level adviser to assist in planning a programme and monitoring of progress in development. It is essential that this should be an independent individual who may come from a management school or consultancy — the key issue is to use someone who is forward thinking and does not rely on experience over the past 20 years!

3. Make use of short/medium-term outside board appointments to bring specific knowledge of either processes or subject matter to both individual discussions and board deliberation.

4. Establish basis for getting exposure to relevant processes for implementing strategy — too often, the processes and systems employed by businesses are defined at too low a level in the organization and are then accepted by top management. It is essential that the chief executive and executive directors should set standards in this area.

5. Take a positive approach to action learning and networking concepts. The chief executive needs to seek benefits from regular contact with other chief executives, if only to discuss mutual problems and specific development issues. This represents an extremely useful addition to discussion with inside 'generalists' such as the chairman and outside directors.

6. The business strategy will identify a range of new areas of activity for the future. A structured and pro-active approach to higher education institutes can provide an appropriate range of short (i.e., up to half-day) seminars on specific topics for either the board or for the action learning group/network of chief executives.

All of these development routes are concerned with providing the chairman and particularly the chief executive with an impetus which can contribute towards creating capabilities for leading the senior management team into the future. It must never be seen as a divisive activity which separates the treatment of the chairman and chief executive from the remainder of the board.

In practice, the moves towards organized development of the chairman and chief executives can have a substantial impact on both the effectiveness of board deliberations/decision-taking and on the way that the board has an impact on improving overall performance of the business. It is also likely to be welcomed by all managers in the business as a positive step for the future.

Practical issues involved in implementation

The previous paragraphs give an outline of the methodology/practice which should be followed to improve the planning of management development. These activities need to be integrated into practical business situations and existing internal organizations. One issue which concerns many businesses is that of short- and long-term actions for the improvement of existing staff.

SHORT-TERM V. LONG-TERM ROUTES

The routes for management development will differ for short-term improvement of existing individuals/groups and for the longer-term (and more integrated) approach for the future. A number of possibilities emerge for encouraging development for both of these two distinct routes:

1. Short-term actions for existing staff:
   - Use the key capabilities audit in relation to company strategy and critical issues — this may need to step back into process to create a provisional strategy for the business within the limits of existing capabilities stretch.
   - Set up individual and group programmes to remove shortcomings in process or systems knowledge and skills based on provisional/ initial strategy.
   - Establish definitions/specifications of 'key strategic' projects within the business and establish project teams or task-forces at a number of company levels.
   - Establish definitions of 'use specifications' for technology and set

up in-house programmes for non-technical staff — need to concentrate on *use* and not reproduce conventional research and development, e.g., technology for the non-technical executives (do not forget/overlook tomorrow's key technologies) and broadening of awareness base of specialists.

- Get the projects underway with outside *process and technology* help but on a planned basis — establish review points as part of the management development programme and accept commitment for two to three years.
- Make sure that programmes are both 'top down' and 'bottom up' to encourage integration of actions. The 'bottom-up' programmes can sometimes yield early and significant results at low cost and risk.
- A starting point for reviews and future action planning could be established in a short-term programme aimed at laying 'strategic foundations' and improving operating results.

2. Longer-term actions for existing and future staff:

The previous sections of this chapter have outlined a general approach, but it is important to recognize that any actions need to take account of the following specific issues:

- Most businesses will encounter at least two major shifts in their technologies during an average normal employee's working life. It is therefore critical that technology should be part of all employees' portfolio and should form a key part of ongoing individual and team development.
- The consequences of management development are far-reaching in time and cost terms and need to become institutionalized, i.e., part of the company culture.
- The company/business must accept the overall responsibility for management development and the consequential commitment of individual and group time and hence cost (which could be as high as 15–20 per cent of staff cost in lower age groups and 5–10 per cent in higher age groups).
- Management processes and system introduction should be taken as a priority basic module in early career development for all employees.
- Company processes need to be established which continuously involve as many staff as possible in the identification of new opportunities in the use of technology — it is essential to involve young staff in this process from the outset of their career.
- All programmes involved with the 'content' elements of develop-

ment will need regular review (over a two to three year period) to determine their relevance and priority in company strategy.

The main issues to emerge from the above are:

- the importance of a sound *process/system base* for all management and specialist professional staff
- the importance of *content* particularly in the use of technology and customer strategy
- the use of *in-company projects* (as distinct from case studies) at all levels as the route to successful individual and team management development
- the need to *accept a long-term and costly commitment* to management development
- the company culture and mission must recognize these issues.

It is recognized that the foregoing can only act to stimulate a more detailed review of individual corporate needs.

Management development audit

This chapter has highlighted some of the key issues in making changes happen in practice. The message of the chapter is that there needs to be a revolution in management development in terms of:

- much more emphasis on developing entrepreneurial capabilities
- a greater depth of understanding of a wider range of management processes by a wide range of managers
- the need to create multi-disciplined directors, with specific emphasis on skills in strategic use of technology in the business
- a management style that is decision driven and with strong strategic effectiveness
- a self-sustaining programme of change, generated at all levels, with emphasis on continual search to make better use of relevant technology
- a customer-driven strategic approach based on a sound input of key customer product/market strategies
- a key role for intellectual management processes
- a managed approach to the development of company culture.

A sustained approach over several years will be required to build a company and management team that is customer driven and technologically aware.

The audit shown in Table 8.2 is designed to assess the existing position and trends in a specific company or business in relation to management development needs for the future. The broad guide to interpretation of

Table 8.2 Management development audit

Issue and question	Assessment of (a) current situation and (b) trend							
	Poor		Fair		Good		Excellent	
	Score 1		Score 2		Score 3		Score 4	
1. Management development for chief executive	No visible evidence		Attends courses on *ad hoc* basis		Part of network of chief executives		Formally structured individual programme	
	a.	b.	a.	b.	a.	b.	a.	b.
2. Pro-active approach to culture development	No programmes directed at culture or mission		Internal training directed towards creating culture		Externally driven culture programmes with less emphasis on internal		Active programme to refine culture and create sense of mission	
	a.	b.	a.	b.	a.	b.	a.	b.
3. Development focus on creating multi-function managers	Development by *ad hoc* exposure		Finance for non-financial managers		Technology for technical managers		Conscious effort plus job rotation	
	a.	b.	a.	b.	a.	b.	a.	b.
4. Organized development at all levels up to company board	Training stops at staff training. No team skills training		Company has management training, plus team skills		Senior managers go on short courses — use made of task-forces		Board skill/ team develop-ment is integral part of development programme	
	a.	b.	a.	b.	a.	b.	a.	b.
5. Development of capabilities in defining customer strategic needs	Company has sales training		Company has sales, marketing and service training		Company involves customers in sales, support training		Organized training to senior level in this area	
	a.	b.	a.	b.	a.	b.	a.	b.
6. Development in effective use of technology	Training programmes in R&D management		Marketing/ product planning training		Total technology training		Organized training to board level in this area	
	a.	b.	a.	b.	a.	b.	a.	b.

Table 8.2 *cont.*

Issue and question	Assessment of (a) current situation and (b) trend			
	Poor	Fair	Good	Excellent
	Score 1	Score 2	Score 3	Score 4
7. Continuous development throughout full career	Stops after initial training	Stops at junior management level	Training to senior management	Through career training at all levels
	a.　　b.	a.　　b.	a.　　b.	a.　　b.
8. Manager participation in strategy projects	Task undertaken by planning group and board	All functions contribute to five-year-plan and are told what to do	Board reviews, five-year-plan and communicates decisions on actions	Company and sub-strategy developed by management and uses project teams to implement
	a.　　b.	a.　　b.	a.　　b.	a.　　b.
9. Manager's role in implementing strategic action plan	Only as part of normal operating role and *ad hoc*	Mainly functional tasks emerge from five-year-plan	Board define task-force for key development projects	Directors/top managers lead key action plans
	a.　　b.	a.　　b.	a.　　b.	a.　　b.
10. Conscious effort to develop broad based management 'process' skills	No training above initial training in specific functions	One-shot management training	Effort made to introduce relevant new skills to selected staff	Conscious effort to give all managers all relevant skills
	a.　　b.	a.　　b.	a.　　b.	a.　　b.
Column Scores				

Total score (sum columns 1–4)　　　　▭

Instructions: Consider each of the above issues/questions in turn. Select the column which best fits your current situation and tick the appropriate box 'a'. Consider the underlying trend and denote by ↑ → ↗↘ in box 'b'. Add score for all questions.

scores from the management development audit shown in Table 8.2 allows judgement in two areas:

1. The total score which will indicate the extent and scale of development that will be required.
2. The profile and trend information which provides a basis for setting priorities and outlining the specific actions which are required.

The following guide is offered to the interpretation of total scores:

Total score 30–40 A well-structured and forward-looking approach, requiring review and refinement in the specific areas identified in the profile. Use strengths to improve overall management capabilities.

20–30 An indication of competence in conventional areas of management development or alternatively a profile of extremes in strengths and weaknesses — both areas need to be acted upon.

10–20 A potentially serious situation with very little recognition of future needs in management development. The trend information is a useful guide to areas for priority action. It is likely that significant attention needs to be given to top level management development.

0–10 Substantial development for the future is required — this score does not necessarily mean that today's performance is poor but that the future is bleak. Management development will be required in all key areas.

A serious review of strategic performance standards along the lines outlined in Chapter 9 will be an essential first step.

PLANNING AND MONITORING OF STRATEGIC DEVELOPMENT — THE USE OF BEST PRACTICE PERFORMANCE INDICATORS

How can the processes of previous chapters be expressed in a practical programme for action? The final challenge is how to establish an integrated business and management development plan which supports an ambitious strategic development programme and, at the same time, introduces best practice management standards, essential for strategic leadership. This chapter outlines a practical approach to meeting this challenge with the capability to monitor business and management development on a quantified basis using performance indicators. The provision of overall visibility for top management is illustrated, coupled with examples of use of the process involved.

Putting the concepts into practice

Earlier chapters have identified the three principal building blocks for establishing a plan for achieving strategic leadership, namely:

1. Defining what constitutes best practice management standards for strategic leadership in the 1990s, in 100 key areas. These are summarized for convenience in Table 9.1 at the end of this chapter.

2. Providing an audit of present standards and, hence, areas of strength and weakness in management capabilities.

3. An updated strategy process which includes new issues for the 1990s and also provides a relevant approach to identifying strategic priorities, business objectives and supporting needs for developing management capabilities.

This chapter represents the end point of the process, as shown in Fig. 9.1 — the practical development of a plan to achieve strategic leadership.

The pace of change in the business scene is already fast and will continue to be. The integration of business and people development therefore will be the norm and an essential approach to retain competitiveness. If strategic leadership is to be achieved then best practice management standards also have to become the norm if the full potential of the business is to be realized in terms of overall results. The practical approach, outlined in

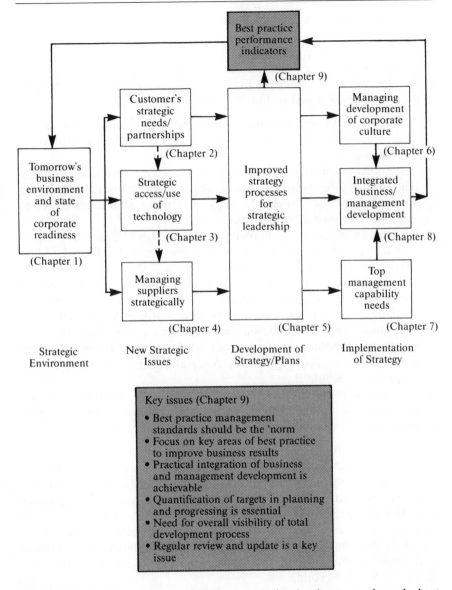

Figure 9.1 Planning and monitoring strategic development through best practice performance

this chapter, provides a basis for both planning and monitoring a strategic leadership development programme, using a quantified approach, based on the use of strategic performance indicators.

The concepts of the process outlined in this chapter, and the link to earlier chapters, are illustrated in Fig. 9.2. Six issues are important in relation to the processes outlined in Fig. 9.2, namely:

- Strategy is a dynamic statement within the strategic development process. The 'Present Strategy' is a stepping stone to strategic leadership in most businesses.
- The audits of Chapters 2–8 define best practice management standards. They also highlight those specific weaknesses which need to be resolved to implement the 'Present Strategy' and those additional issues to achieve best practice standards.
- The strategy statement (Chapter 5) and the audits of Chapters 2–8 provide a large volume of data. The process must provide a basis for identifying priorities and sharpening focus as quickly as possible.
- Developing beyond the 'Present Strategy' requires careful selection of those audit critical issues which can have the biggest impact in enhancing overall business performance — Route A in Fig. 9.2.
- A balanced approach to development towards best practice standards is essential. Emphasis on the output related culture issues from Chapter 6 will tend to encourage Route A development and input related emphasis — Route B.
- The management of the development of company culture is, therefore, an important issue in both the achievement of 'Present Strategy' and, particularly, in moving forward to a position of strategic leadership.

The process outlined in Fig. 9.2 and described above, provides a basis for the chief executive to resolve the traditional 'Catch 22' situation — here in the first instance the business drives the priorities for parallel programmes of individual and team development and the progressive moulding of company culture, all within the framework of the 'Present Strategy'. As development of company culture proceeds, it removes the 'Catch 22' dilemma by creating an atmosphere of balanced development — a capability found in today's strategic leaders and essential for success in the 1990s and beyond.

The essential need for best practice standards

Competitive pressures dictate that all businesses should aim for best practice standards in the relevant areas if strategic leadership is to be achieved.

The audits of Chapters 2–8 contain some 100 points/issues which

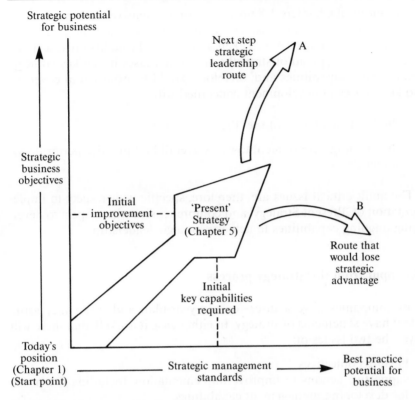

Figure 9.2 The route to strategic leadership

define these best practice standards. These represent the standards which all businesses should set out to achieve *in all areas.* Many senior managers will say that their business achieves these standards in a number of specific areas, *but the message for the 1990s is that all areas are important* and that a major effort should be made to meet all standards. The inventory of best practice issues which provide the portfolio or model set of stan-dards is given in Table 9.1 which lists the 'Excellent' standards from each audit. For convenience this will be found together with other tables at the end of the chapter.

The value of the individual audits

The audit of Chapter 1 provides an overview of the present position or starting point for strategic development and focuses on the five key areas for business development.

The audits of Chapters 2–8 provide a comprehensive assessment of the perceived position of the business in the new key areas concerned with strategic success in the 1990s. Taken as a whole, the audits provide a picture of the total spread of strengths and weaknesses in the key strategic management capabilities and, therefore, would be expected to cover the two key phases of development concerned with:

1. The implementation of the 'Present Strategy'.

2. The ongoing development towards overall best practice performance standards.

The audit critical issues are, therefore, specific with respect to implementation of 'Present Strategy' and comprehensive with respect to developing ongoing capabilities to achieve strategic leadership.

The input from the strategy process

Most companies have a three- or five-year-plan and to an increasing extent have statements of strategy. In either case it is likely that these will cover the two issues of:

- business objectives
- supportive actions to improve implementation, including the needs for developing management capabilities.

In many cases there will be a formal link between the business objectives/ action plans and the programmes to develop management competences or standards.

In developing strategic objectives there will be some constraints due to a recognition of the practical problems arising from weaknesses in management standards and the time required to overcome these. Further, it is therefore likely that the achievement of strategic objectives will not require best practice standards in all cases, e.g., it will be 'de-tuned' for reasons of shortfalls in management standards. This is a logical and pragmatic first step but is not acceptable for improvement in performance in the 1990s and certainly not for strategic leadership. 'Present Strategy' is, therefore, likely, in most cases, to be a starting point for development towards strategic leadership. The practical processes in this chapter recognize this issue.

A summary of the process described in the above paragraphs is given in Fig. 9.3.

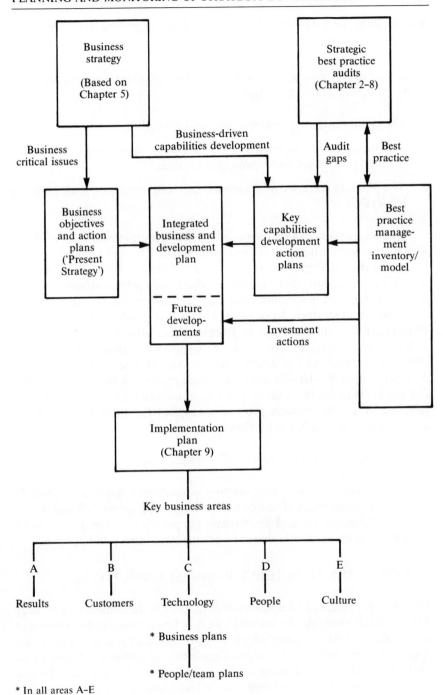

Figure 9.3 Strategic leadership development model

Establishing an integrated business and management development (IBMD) programme

Reference to Fig. 9.3 shows that the IBMD programme contains three key forms of action plans covering:

1. The achievement of strategic business objectives.

2. The focus for developments of management standards to support the achievement of present business objectives.

3. The plans to enhance management capabilities required for strategic leadership.

Practical approaches to create an IBMD programme in each of the above areas are outlined in the following pages. The text is written on the basis that the starting point is the 'Present Strategy', but it is quite clear that this could equally be based on a revised and updated strategy, i.e., the process is relevant through the full programme towards the achievement of a position of strategic leadership. This is discussed further in Chapter 10 in relation to the Investors in People (IIP) initiative.

A practical implementation plan will, therefore, contain action plans arising from each of the above sources. As outlined in Chapter 8 the development of the IBMD plan and programme will be in terms of the five key areas of business development outlined in Chapter 1. For ease of reference, the link between the five areas and the subject areas of the audits of Chapters 2–8 is as follows:

Area A: Business results and overall strategic development — Chapters 2, 5 and 6

Area B: Customer focus and supplier strategy — Chapters 2, 3 and 4

Area C: Effectiveness of use of technology — Chapters 2, 3 and 4

Area D: Effective use and development of people — Chapters 6, 7 and 8

Area E: Balanced development of company culture — Chapter 6.

ACTION PLANS TO ACHIEVE BUSINESS OBJECTIVES

The strategy process of Chapter 5 will lead to the development of a strategy statement following the format indicated. A key element of the statement is the implementation plan, which will identify the critical issues which need to be resolved to achieve the financial and business objectives, as well as providing a definition of the key management capabilities required to complete the related critical issue/strategic action plans. The resolution of each critical issue will, therefore, be covered by:

1. A statement of the critical issue.

2. The action areas for resolution.

3. The key capabilities required for resolution.

At senior level in the business, it is likely that the number of critical issues will be of the order of eight to twelve, being concerned with the key areas for development for which the top management team will assume project leadership.

The critical issues should be tabulated using a format which relates them to the key business areas — a suggested format for this is shown in Fig. 9.4. The action areas and key capabilities associated with business development now have to be related to the perceived strengths and weaknesses in relation to best practice, as assessed from the 10 audits contained in Chapters 2–8.

ACTION PLANS FOR ACHIEVING BEST PRACTICE STANDARDS

The audits of Chapters 2–8 provide a view of the perceived strengths and weaknesses of a business against some 100 issues of best practice in strategic development. It is not practical to introduce all issues into an IBMD programme and, therefore, two screening analyses are required:

1. To focus on below average and contentious audit areas.

2. To establish priorities in relation to the business.

In practice, it is most likely that these audits will be undertaken by the top management team initially, and that there will be a variation of views of strengths and weaknesses between participants. It is important that the reasons for such variations are understood before any analysis is undertaken and action plans committed — the variations in themselves may be based on differing interpretations, lack of information etc., or a result of genuine differences of view. The insignificant issues need to be erased so that the ongoing analysis can focus on the real and significant issues based on consensus, and therefore average team ratings should be used in subsequent analyses.

The emerging results of the audits will tend to fall into three categories of combinations of average group scores and spread of perceptions, as follows:

- low average ratings with low spread of perceptions, i.e., the agreed weaknesses for which action plans can be set without conflict on the causes — Zone A in Fig. 9.5

AREA	STRATEGIC CRITICAL ISSUE	ACTION ELEMENTS	KEY CAPABILITIES REQUIRED
A	• Expansion of programmes for internal innovation	• Identification of cost/benefit priorities • Defining links between customer needs and internal processes, systems, etc. • Defining priority areas	• Responding to change quickly and effectively • Dealing with employee suggestions • Ability to measure internal returns
B	• Need to establish process for development and review of key customer strategy	• Identification of key strategic customers • Creation of technology route maps for key customers • Prepare customer development plans	• Process for regular review of customer strategies • Making better use of technology in-house • Developing relationships with stakeholders
C	• Responding to the technology needs of market change	• Identifying what the customer needs strategically • Locating sources of external technology • Deciding on 'make v. create'	• Understanding customer technology needs • Ability to scan external sources • Open management of key suppliers
D	• Establishing business-led people development	• Translating business objectives into key capabilities required • Making the top team into the focus for developing people	• Using task-forces to develop business and people • Through career development • Using multi-disciplined management
E	• Establishing best practice as the norm	• Creating a sense of mission • Good communication of policies, values, strategies, etc. • Best Practice manuals	• Managing development of culture elements • 1990s leadership characteristics • Effective strategic management

Figure 9.4   Action plans to achieve business objectives

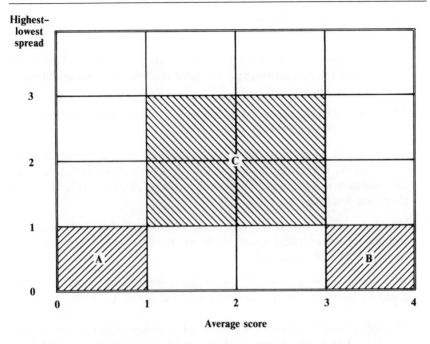

Figure 9.5 Top team audit overview: average ratings and spreads

- high average ratings with low spread of perceptions, i.e., the agreed areas of strength which should be used to support development in other areas if possible — Zone B in Fig. 9.5
- average and below ratings with considerable variation, i.e., those issues where performance is poor and where solutions could be difficult due to substantial variations of perception — Zone C in Fig. 9.5.

It is strongly recommended that all top team audit results should be plotted in the format of Fig. 9.5 as this provides a clear overview of the potential problems in establishing action plans in terms of overall average ratings, specific areas of weakness and degree of difference. Before analysis is undertaken to define areas for priority action, it is important to remove areas of difference which are not for significant reasons — this can be time consuming but is an essential first step.

Analysing the audit in this way would probably remove some 50 per cent of the total audit issues, which means that some form of screening analysis is needed to determine which should be given priority in action planning to support the business strategy and ongoing development towards best practice standards. In the latter case, the challenge is to follow Route A in Fig. 9.2 rather than Route B. This screening analysis needs to take into account six factors relating to each issue, namely:

1. *Impact* — would resolution of this issue have High (H), Medium (M) or Low (L) impact on the achievement of best practice standards?

2. *Ease of resolution* — a subjective judgement on the Ease (H) versus Difficulty (L) of resolution, e.g., are there attitude or financial barriers to overcome, etc.?

3. *Timescale for resolution* — timescale to achieve desired results: generally over three years (H) to one year or less (L).

4. *Downside risk* — the possible consequences on the business of failure to undertake or achieve resolution of the issue. If the failure causes the business not to meet a principal business objective it is H, but if there are few risks then it is L.

5. *Knock-on effect* — if the critical issue is resolved what is the positive impact on other audit areas? If there are two or three areas then impact is H with zero as L.

6. *Business results* — if resolution provides a direct and major improvement in business results, then this is H or, if not, L.

The profile which identifies the most relevant key issues on the above basis is HHLLHH, which means that it is of significant impact, easy to achieve in a short time, will not undermine the business if the action plan fails, impacts on other areas and should improve business results. In this approach there are other profiles which could be relevant, for example:

- HHHLHH — meets all the screening criteria but is of a long-term nature, which could be typical of Route A issues in Fig. 9.2.
- MHLLHM — not a major impact but easy to achieve with early results and big impact on business results.

The emerging list provides a clear definition of those areas to focus upon from the comprehensive listings of the audits of Chapters 2–8.

The key capabilities issues identified in developing strategy should be subjected to an initial check against the above audit critical issues to establish the extent to which the audit analysis has also exposed these issues. Any differences that are exposed by this analysis should be analysed before proceeding to establish causes for the variation. Any issues which remain after this validation, i.e., those identified by the strategy and not covered by the audits, should be analysed for priority as for the audit critical issues in Fig. 9.6 and, subsequently, added to the audit issues under the same audit headings as used in Fig. 9.6, i.e., a complete list of priority issues is now available.

Strategic area and audit chapter	Audit critical issue and reference	Rating		Analysis (H, M, L)						
		Score	Spread	Impact	Ease	Timescale	Downside	Knock-on	Business relevance
A. Business results and strategic development (Chapters 2, 5, 6)									
B. Customer/ supplier strategy and competitive development (Chapters 2, 3, 4)									
C. Effective use of technology (Chapters 2, 3, 4)									
D. Effective use and development of people (Chapters 6, 7, 8)									
E. Balancing development of company culture (Chapter 6)									

Figure 9.6 Identification of key capabilities development from strategy and capability audits

DESIGNING THE IBMD PROGRAMME

The analyses of business objectives and audit critical issues has yielded the principal input for the IMBD plan and programme. Designing and building the IBMD programme requires an analysis and understanding of four key areas as the basis for developing action plans, namely:

1. The extent to which business objectives are supported by strengths identified in the best practice audits shown in Zone B in Fig. 9.5.

2. The extent to which business objectives could be undermined by audit critical issues shown in Zones A and C in Fig. 9.5.

3. The additional critical issues identified from the strategy/planning process which could impact, in either direction, on achievement of business objectives.

4. The leadership issues which could improve business results beyond the objectives of the strategy — those concerned with following Route A in Fig. 9.2.

The careful selection of areas for business action plans, the double screening of results of the capabilities audits and limited linkages between strategic areas and audits does simplify the ongoing analysis.

A convenient summary format for developing an understanding of the relationships between business objectives, development of relevant key support capabilities and priority issues for achieving strategic leadership is shown in Fig. 9.7.

Each business objective needs to be reviewed to the extent to which both the strengths and weaknesses should be treated to ensure the best prospect of achievement of the objective's targets. It is particularly important to look for serious undermining of objectives from the audit results; in many cases these weaknesses are not highlighted by the analysis of key capabilities requiring development within the strategy process. The audit matching of Fig. 9.7 provides a basis of reviewing individual aspects of business development plans against the needs for developing capabilities in areas which have been shown to be weak and relevant to business success. As a result of this analysis it is possible to develop a detailed understanding of the integrated action plans required to achieve business objectives, and the ability to identify areas of opportunity and risk in these plans. This provides the essential basis for fine tuning of the action plans.

The issues concerned with getting on to the best track for achieving strategic leadership should also be subjected to the same analysis as that described above for matching to business objectives. It is important in this case to set out some targets for improvement in business results over and above those of the 'Present Strategy', i.e., adopt the concept of carefully selected investment in developing capabilities towards best practice management standards.

PRACTICAL ISSUES IN ESTABLISHING AN IBMD PLAN

There are two key issues which have been highlighted both in earlier chapters and earlier sections of this chapter, namely:

1. The need for a quantified approach to both planning and monitoring strategic development.

2. The need to provide overall visibility of progress towards strategic corporate business objectives and best practice management standards.

Strategic area and audit chapter	Business critical issues (from Fig. 9.4)	Screened audit issues (from Fig. 9.6)									
		Customer strategy	Technology	Environment	Supplier strategy	Strategy process	Output culture	Input culture	Top team capabilities	Chief executive	IBMD
A. Business results and strategic development (Chapters 2, 5, 6)		▓				▓	▓	▓			
B. Customer/supplier strategies and competitive development (Chapters 2, 3, 4)		▓	▓	▓	▓						
C. Effective use of technology (Chapters 2, 3, 4)		▓	▓		▓						
D. Effective use of development of people (Chapters 6, 7, 8)							▓	▓	▓	▓	▓
E. Balancing the development of company culture (Chapter 6)							▓	▓			

Key: ▓ Related audit/capabilities development

Figure 9.7 Integrating business critical issues and management development practice

227

The next sections of this chapter develop the concept of the definition and use of Strategic Performance Indicators (SPIs) as a basis for setting targets and monitoring progress in strategic development. In addition, a practical format is shown which can provide senior management with an overview of progress against plan, in a form which can be used to both manage and also communicate the key issues to the main stakeholders in the business.

Before moving into the next stages of detail planning, it is worth while to check that the main elements of the programme already identified meet the following criteria:

- Do the elements still recognize the already identified strategic focus for the business?
- Is there a mixture of key areas for business development associated with the 'Present Strategy' and future performance growth which confirms the strategic focus?
- Is there a clear statement of where management development needs to be focused?
- Is there sufficient information in terms of business databases, audit information, etc., to provide for developing sound action plans?

It is important that strategic development should be focused in those areas which are most significant to specific businesses. These will vary from business to business and will tend, therefore, to be very specific and relate to particular product/service areas, customers, areas of relevant technology, etc. It is believed that the majority of businesses, however, will find the choice in this book to be generally relevant and that it is worth reiterating here what the specific areas of focus consist of and why:

Area A: *Business results and overall strategic development* — a recognition of the need to establish better short- and long-term business results, coupled with an acceptance of the importance of a dedicated approach to strategy-led and focused business development.

Area B: *Customer focus and supplier strategy* — a recognition of the need to move from a generalized market and competitive style to an approach which focuses on the strategic needs of a few, but influential, customers. Also, the development of integrated and strategic relationships with a limited number of key suppliers.

Area C: *The effective use of technology* — acceptance of making maximum strategic use of available technology in all facets of the business — products/services/processes/procedures as a priority route to exploiting strategic opportunities. Using technology to gain competitive advantage in adopting 'green' policies in all areas of activity.

Area D: *The effective use and development of people* — the future demands on capabilities and performance for individual managers and, particularly, top management teams are growing exponentially. The establishment of best practice standards is an essential area of focus for all businesses.

Area E: *Developing company culture* — recognizing that a balanced approach to the development of output- and input-related culture issues is a key to achievement of strategic leadership.

The development of SPIs and action plans in subsequent sections of this chapter will follow the above areas of business focus.

The development and selection of strategic performance indicators

Business performance indicators (PIs) have been recognized for many decades, particularly in financial performance measures such as profit/sales, profit/capital employed and many other indicators tailored to specific revenue or capital activities. Manufacturing, sales, marketing and quality functions have also developed their own indicators. Indicators developed in this way are generally used to analyse historical data for the business, for establishing summaries of present plans and for setting targets/objectives associated with forward business plans. They also provide a valuable insight to inter-business performance comparisons.

Examples could be as follows, where the PI is in italics:

- to establish a *profit/sales* ratio of 0.10 on domestic product sales by 1993
- to reduce the ratio of *overhead costs/direct labour cost* to 1.0 by 1994
- to achieve a domestic *market penetration of 30 per cent by value* on new products by 1996.

The use of PIs has been principally geared to meeting business objectives, but within the context of an IBMD programme it is necessary to cover three main forms of activity, namely:

1. The progressive achievement of business results — for which PIs described above will do, supplemented by new ones covering the areas of customers, suppliers and technology — essentially based on currently available information.

2. Measuring progress on a specific management development programme — where new PIs will need to be created for specific programmes.

3. Measuring progress towards best practice standards — where new approaches to PIs are needed.

The consequence of this is that databases and information systems will need to be tailored to corporate development needs in each of the above areas — in many cases today development is not adequately monitored, due to lack of suitable information. This need not mean that a major new activity has to be created — *those responsible for action plans should be encouraged to propose indicators and data needs at the time of establishing these plans, and for ensuring that such data is created and collected.*

There is likely to be a period of development over the coming few years during which SPIs and their required back-up databases will be established. It is possible, however, to establish SPIs at this time within specific businesses which can be refined and developed as a broader base of experience in IBMD programmes become available. For the five key strategic areas it is possible to produce broad-based SPIs which can be used, or adapted with minimum change, for a range of businesses.

BUSINESS RESULTS AND OVERALL STRATEGY

This strategic area is concerned with the quality of business results and issues concerned with the ability to follow the principal strategic focus for the business. The following five areas are suggested for consideration of SPIs in any action planning:

1. *Financial performance* — concerned with year-by-year profit performance, the ability to finance growth and the achievement of capital value growth for the business. It is appropriate here to consider indicators which deal with the classic measures of profit, cash flow performance, dividend levels and growth in market valuation. There could also be a requirement to developing SPIs concerned with investment profile, projections and milestones, particularly if an above-average level of profit is to be reinvested in the business over a period of some years, to support growth and development at the expense of investor return.

2. *Product improvement/financial return on internal investments in manufacturing processes, quality, operating systems, etc.* — an important area of corporate performance for the development and use of SPIs, as it can have a major impact on the effective management of market share, cash flow, growth and investor confidence during strategic development.

3. *Customer profile* — although there is a separate strategic area concerned with the issue of customer focus and strategy, it is important to monitor this issue as it is likely that it will be part of the main strategic

driving force for the business. The issues which are likely to merit consideration of SPIs in this area are the fraction of business with market leaders, the extent to which new products/services development is a joint venture with customers and the extent to which 'strategy sharing' forms part of key customer relationships.

4. *Total quality of products/services* — an important issue in a strategic development towards the high added-value products/services usually associated with market leadership. It is likely that many businesses would seek to develop SPIs to reflect their progress towards target levels of added-value, sales mix of products/services and competitive standards.

5. *Developing a strategically driven business* — it is important to monitor progress in this key business area. This can be done in either absolute terms via milestones in development plans or by the use of SPIs. The most valuable source of SPI design here is to use the best practice issues from the company culture audits of Chapter 6, e.g., such issues as the number of new products/services/processes that emerge from the strategy process, or that fraction of total investment in people or business emerging from that source.

Indicators, based on the above concept, are shown in Table 9.2 (included at the end of this chapter) for illustrative purposes for issues concerned with both business and management standards development. All businesses will have different and specific needs and the important point is to define SPIs which are relevant to the immediate strategic development needs and the ongoing developments towards a leadership position associated with the main strategic focus.

CUSTOMER FOCUS AND SUPPLIER STRATEGY

In this area of strategic development there are a number of traditional PIs which deal with such issues as sales performance, market share, competitive status, etc. However, most of those in regular use refer to a current situation and do not provide an appropriate measure for monitoring strategic development. There are five key areas for considering SPIs:

1. *The extent to which specific customers match your business strategic ambitions* — generally this means that there are particular areas of customer performance and culture which are critical, such as growth record of the customer's business, market position/leadership, extent to which product/service policies are based on total quality, and the extent to

which the customer's culture is consistent with your own development. This gives rise to forms of SPI which seek to develop customer profiles for a range of potential customers covering market share, fraction of business in 'new' products, profitability of new products, fraction of customer business which is driven by formal strategy process, added-value on new products and extent to which customer has formal relationships for development with suppliers. Developing such indicators has to be done with customers and can provide the right starting point for developing strategic customer relationships.

2. *The extent to which your investment in products/services/systems is led by customer strategic needs* — most companies say that their product/service development is market-led but not generally customer-led. There are examples where product/service development is heavily influenced by a leading customer whose choices have a big influence on the remaining customers, e.g., leading airlines who act as launching customers for new aircraft. It is also extremely important that internal investment in new manufacturing processes, systems and procedures should be customer-requirements-led. In both of these areas it is important that investments should be customer-led to a large degree. It is important, therefore, to create SPIs which monitor the extent to which all investment has been subjected to customer needs evaluation and, further, that the return to the business should be monitored — this applies to both incremental improvements on existing and for new business, e.g., the fraction of your approved investment projects by both number and value which have been customer 'screened', and an isolation of the returns from this in terms of increase in added-value, market share, etc.

3. *Competitive success in gaining market leaders as customers* — the published analyses on development of competitive performance highlight the key issue of gaining market leaders as key customers. This analysis complements that in 2. above but does require some simple ratios as either number of key customers/product or service or percentage of total sales to market leaders, etc. There are other indicators which are important and concerned with the extent to which investment is linked to market leaders and the extent of jointly agreed strategic activity as referred to in earlier sections.

4. *Supplier strategies* — many businesses have traditionally neglected the potential for support in strategic development, which can come from careful strategic management of suppliers. There has been a progressive acceptance that a constructive and deeper relationship with fewer suppliers is better than the former 'cut-throat' scramble by large numbers of suppliers. The SPIs which are important in customer relation-

ships have a mirror in suppliers and it is important to monitor issues such as market leadership of suppliers, extent of suppliers' investment which is dedicated to your business, the extent of your investment which is linked to joint ventures with key suppliers, the trend in numbers of suppliers per product/service activity, quality performance ratios, etc.

5. *Customer and supplier relations at senior management level* — the top management team should spend a substantial amount of their time on securing and building upon sound strategic customer and supplier relationships. Indicators concerned with allocation of top management time to decision-making on customer and supplier issues, visits to key customers and suppliers, strategic content of discussions with key customers and suppliers, extent of board time spent on these issues, etc. These indicators link into those which deal with such issues as the percentage of customers with high level strategic arrangements such as those referred to above.

An example is included as Table 9.3 at the end of this chapter.

EFFECTIVE USE OF TECHNOLOGY

There are traditional indicators in this area which deal with such issues as investment in new product/service development as a percentage of sales, and many variations on this somewhat narrow concept. Few indicators exist which consider the impact of the use of technology in all facets of the business and, in particular, the more recent issue of the environmental integrity of the business as a whole. There are four areas which can provide a basis for planning and monitoring the impact of the effective use of technology across your business.

1. *Reduction in time-cycle for product/service development* — this is a critical competitive issue as the pace of introducing new products/services quickens and as the specification between successive product generations/service standards is likely to widen. There are a number of areas concerned with monitoring the issues involved, such as the cost of conceptual design as a percentage of total product/service development cost, total new product/service investment, including supplies, as a percentage of sales on specific activities, extent of review, use and cost of outside technology as a percentage of total spent on project and reductions of launch time.

2. *Influence of technology on business effectiveness* — the key issue is to achieve balanced investment in products/services/processes/proce-

dures and to establish ratios to make both 'investment' decisions and to monitor progress — these are likely to be very specific to particular businesses as investments may be made to reduce costs, improve quality, reduce time, expand market share, etc. Two levels of SPIs could be required in many businesses, one dealing with specific, and often major programmes, and the other dealing with the search for continuing incremental improvements through many day-to-day projects.

3. *Management of technology upgrading, improvement and replacement* — part of the business strategy should focus on having a good balance across all areas of programmes to upgrade existing technologies by introducing available improvements and full replacement. The management of this process is closely linked to both customer and supplier relationships. It is possible to construct 'primary' SPIs which cover such issues as remaining life of upgraded/improved key technologies versus replacement time (probably 150–200 per cent), number of options available to replace key technologies (probably two in most cases), and the extent to which replacement technology is to be sourced externally. At a 'lower' level, there will be SPIs which focus on the monitoring of the process to follow the primary SPIs above.

4. *Board of directors/top team contribution* — this issue is concerned with the extent to which senior management fosters a comprehensive approach to both accessing and applying technology to all facets of the business. It is also concerned with the amount of time spent by the board/top management team on issues concerned with the use of technology. In terms of involvement, all senior managers should carry a percentage of the total action plans, and top team meetings should average some 15–25 per cent of their time on such matters, the level depending on the nature of the business. The indicators should not be about research and development but about the performance of the business in its full exploitation of technology.

Indicators, based on the above concepts, are shown in Table 9.4 included at the end of this chapter for illustrative purposes.

EFFECTIVE USE AND DEVELOPMENT OF PEOPLE

This area for establishing action plans and SPIs is not about the content of management development programmes. It is concerned with the actions taken by management to ensure that the right steps are being taken to develop capabilities to the right standards to achieve both busi-

ness objectives and strategic leadership. There are four key issues which
need to be monitored:

1. *Making business-led people development work as the normal approach* —
   a significant part of individual development should be by participation in the development and management of programmes for
   change, e.g., strategy formulation, action plan development, project
   task-forces, etc. Specific targets can be set for percentages of time
   planned for such development in relation to attendance time and,
   also, to project success levels. In addition, there are indicators which
   can be used to indicate the extent of involvement of senior managers
   in terms of percentage of time and numbers of 'projects' — probably
   six to eight is a good number.

2. *Creating conditions to foster development through innovation* — programmes need to recognize that individuals and teams have to be
   developed to practise constructive innovation on a continuous basis.
   In particular, innovation which is focused on smaller internal innovation projects can provide a basis for rapid returns on investment of
   training time and money. The areas in which SPIs could be formu-
   lated here are those which monitor the effectiveness of company suggestion schemes, the percentage of such ideas which are adopted, the
   time to appraise proposals for change, etc. Clearly, another measure
   of effectiveness is the success rate in such innovation activity.

3. *Driving for best practice standards* — all people and team development
   should aim to produce best practice performance and results. It is
   important that there should be a review of what constitutes best
   standards in key areas, as well as the achievements demonstrated
   from business performance. It is recognized that much individual
   and team development is aimed at 'bread and butter' skills but some
   percentage, perhaps 25–35 per cent, should focus on the drive for best
   practice in priority areas of business development. The development
   of an understanding of those elements of capability which are
   required for development of best practice (beyond immediate strategy
   needs) will provide a basis for developing relevant SPIs.

4. *Creating multi-disciplinary management* — this is a key issue in achieving leadership. Again, the quantification of SPIs to achieve relevant
   targets will be dependent on developing the IBMD programme. As a
   guide here, there are two areas which represent a good starting point,
   firstly, the amount of development time spent in creating multi-
   disciplinary managers (65–75 per cent) and the percentage of professional staff involved in multi-disciplinary action plan projects
   (100 per cent).

Indicators, based on the above concepts, are shown in Table 9.5 included at the end of this chapter for illustrative purposes.

DEVELOPMENT OF COMPANY CULTURE

Successful companies have always been characterized as having a strong and identifiable culture which, in many cases, has been sustained over many years without significant downward impact on business results. Most people can provide examples of businesses that are known for best practice standards in quality, people development, customer service, etc., and these businesses represent the ultimate standards quoted by many works on the subject. Today, culture has to be developed consciously and it is one of the key elements in the achievement of a strategic leadership situation. There are five key issues which need to be monitored:

1. *Effectiveness in managing change* — probably the key issue in the culture of leading companies is their ability to plan and execute change in a trouble free and successful fashion. Monitoring of this issue is about business change and the continuing review, update and pursuit of best practice. The areas for consideration of SPIs will, therefore, include such factors as total numbers of change programmes, the percentage accomplished on time (internal delivery) and to target (quality), and the extent to which the company supports development of best practice, in terms of cost, as a percentage of total development investment or rolling totals of relevant programmes.

2. *Growing teams and people* — the exposure of individuals and groups to continuous development, multi-disciplinary projects, job rotation and assessment of change proposals, are all key issues in developing company culture. It is important to develop indicators which monitor the extent to which these activities are taking place in the business. Typically, SPIs could be created in the form of time allocation profiles for all key/professional staff and a major effort made to adhere to such arrangements, i.e., a percentage time allocation to development within total time, further subdivided on an individual needs basis into each of the above categories.

3. *Developing a sense of mission* — there are differences of opinion on the value of this concept but in our experience the balance is in favour of the approach. The issue here is identifying values and standards for individual fulfilment with those for the business as a whole. The business will have defined the purpose of its endeavours, strategy and cor-

porate value and behaviour standards (if it has not, it should do as a priority) and these need to be reconciled with the values and standards of all key employees. Whilst strategy will change by review and update, there should be less change in the elements concerned with purpose, values and behaviour — *except during the initial key period of cultural development.* There are some SPIs which can be developed which set out to recognize the extent to which these elements are agreed, the percentage of staff who have been consulted, the percentage who have had changes accepted and 'polling' result indicators to check knowledge, acceptance and adherence.

4. *Openness and effectiveness in stakeholder communication* — many leading companies recognize the value of open and effective communication with all stakeholders, i.e., customers, suppliers, employees, shareholders, funding institutions and the community. The stakeholders all have the power to either support or reject business development, particularly those developments which will mature over a period of some years. It is important to develop programmes for effective and positive communication, and the key elements might be subject to ongoing monitoring. It is possible to construct SPIs which demonstrate regularity of communication, its effectiveness in terms of accuracy of reception, the reliability of meeting standards for timing of communication, etc.

5. *Riding the storms* — strong culture is usually the basis for a resilient business. Developing company culture in a balanced way is one way to create strengths and avoid exposure to either excessive 'market' expectations or too much bureaucracy. Probably the most significant overall performance indicator here is the ratio of output related culture scores to input related culture scores which should not exceed 1.2 for balance. In addition, year-by-year business performance versus sector average can be used.

Indicators, based on the above concepts, are shown in Table 9.6 for illustrative purposes at the end of this chapter.

The foregoing paragraphs on Strategic Performance Indicators represent guidance on some of the areas which are likely to require SPIs and the form that they could take. In practice, the development of the detailed action plans lead to discussion on the methods to be adopted and the parameters to be measured for monitoring progress. The next section looks at the definition of action plans in each of the five strategic areas and provides illustrations of plan formats, typical critical issues and a broader range of possible SPIs than that listed in the above paragraphs.

Analysis and presentation of IBMD information

The final chapter provides a series of practical examples of the application of the concepts and processes contained in this book. This section brings together the various analyses of earlier chapters and sections of this chapter to illustrate the route for development of an IBMD plan with the target of strategic leadership. What the practitioner needs for this purpose is:

1. A listing of areas for priority action planning, covering business objectives, supporting issues for capabilities development and the priority development areas for development of strategic best practice. This statement is required for each of the five strategic areas.

2. A quantified approach which provides for monitoring progress in each of the above areas, so as to achieve a balanced approach to development.

3. A basis for presenting the IBMD master plan in overview form which can allow the results of periodic reviews of progress to be added.

The processes outlined in Chapter 5 provide a basis for definition of strategy for the business from which the two statements of key business objectives and key capabilities, requiring development to support the strategy, can be produced. The audits of Chapters 2–8 provide the definition of what constitutes strategic best practice (summarized in Table 9.1) and, further, an assessment of the perceived position of the business's practices in relation to best practice standards. This chapter provides a process by which a focus can be achieved on the key business objectives and supportive capabilities development, plus the identification of the key issues for development of strategic best practice standards — these are combined and summarized in Fig. 9.7.

The following paragraphs, illustrations and tables show how this information is combined into a practical plan. Tables 9.2–9.6 provide an example of the format for an integrated business and management development plan for each of the five strategic areas. The analysis contained in the summary of Fig. 9.7 discussed earlier can be used to identify the three key areas on Tables 9.2–9.6, namely:

1. The issues for establishing business objectives — the tables show examples of typical issues and an indication of the format for SPIs which appear to be most relevant.

2. The corresponding issues concerning development of supportive management capabilities. The indicators here will be based on the perception of current audit scores, based on the relevant audit issue

as indicated in the tables and as used in earlier chapters. (Where more than one audit is relevant, then an average score is used.)

3. A listing of typical best practice issues to follow Route A in Fig. 9.2, relating to each of the five strategic areas, is also given in each table. The scoring system employed is as above and the tables show the relevant audit issues as before.

In presenting the results in a practical summary form, it has been found to be beneficial to use percentage achievement for both business objectives and development of capabilities. In this case, therefore, 100 per cent represents:

- achievement of 'Present Strategy' business objectives
- achievement of best practice (Table 9.1) in the related audit issues.

Two charts have been prepared to illustrate the presentation of the IBMD master plan, namely:

- Figure 9.8 which shows a typical sector and the basis of integration of the overview and progress statements.
- Figure 9.9 which shows profiles for two hypothetical companies to illustrate the use of the overview to analyse gaps and to give visibility to priorities in business development.

The analysis shown in Fig. 9.8 develops a number of practical concepts which can be useful in the overview planning situation, namely:

- the need to make choices on the key business objectives — focus is an important issue in achieving results and, while it is possible to manage programmes with large numbers of issues in each strategic area, the senior management overview should be restricted to the key issues. The issues selected from tables are marked with asterisks in each table.
- the identification of key supportive capabilities from the tables which requires a practical debate on how capabilities development will contribute to the business results.
- a residue of issues concerned with the development of best practice. Inclusion of any in the overview should only be accepted if a 'notional', but quantifiable, business improvement is associated with the activity towards achievement of best practice, i.e., Route A of Fig. 9.2 has to be proven.
- the chart format which provides a straightforward basis for indicating targets for the IBMD programme — Fig. 9.8 gives an illustration of a 12-month improvement target.

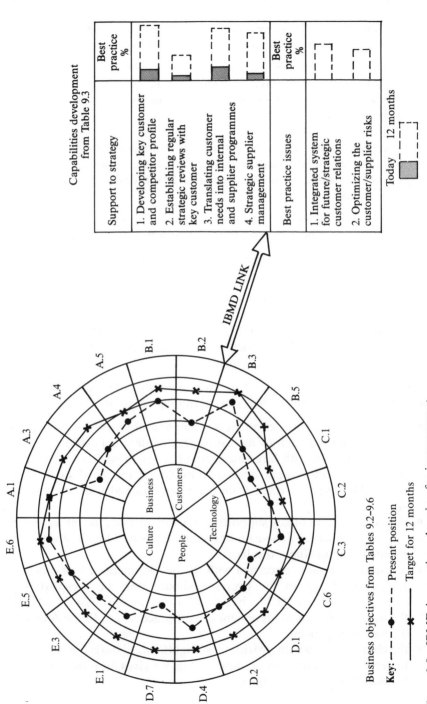

Figure 9.8 IBMD in practice: planning for improvement

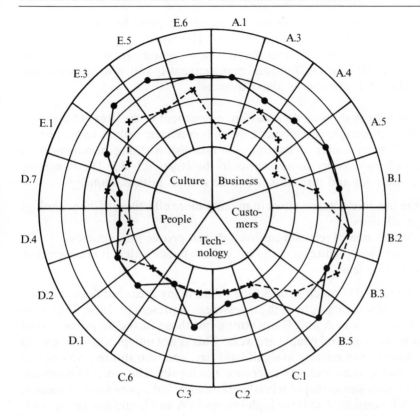

Key: – – –✕– – – Company 'A' — Engineering-based manufacture

————●———— Company 'B' — Service provider

Figure 9.9 IBMD in practice — inter-company comparison

The overview is also important in providing a picture of the overall development situation and has value both as a management appreciation format and for stakeholder communication. Figure 9.9 illustrates typical profiles for two hypothetical companies:

Company A: A company in the engineering-based manufacturing sector, which has had a significant influence in developing the industrial sector that it operates in today. Over recent years it has seen a decline in financial performance, market share and significant gains by traditional and new competitors. It has started to take action to redress the position.

Company B: A company in the service sector, providing a professional service to a large number of customers. The business has grown rapidly over recent years to the extent that it is now a significant force in its market sector. Most of the 'founder' management is still with the company but other staff turnover is above average.

Company A shows a poor current assessment in the areas of business results and strategic development, which is consistent with its recent history. The efforts by senior management to establish a strong customer-driven approach to recovery comes across in the issues B.1–B.5. The remaining areas are poor and three issues can be seen as critical, namely:

- the need for a major effort in making more effective use of technology in all areas
- the absence of relevant business-driven people programmes
- a historical picture on company culture issues which, if not corrected, could be fatal.

Company B is much stronger than A in many areas but does exhibit a number of warning signs in the assessment of present position. The issues in strategic areas A and B are strong but those in the areas concerned with technology and people are weak. This is not untypical of companies that have grown quickly to significant size, and who still rely on original operating systems and staff tolerance and loyalty. The issues in company culture show strong output related performance but a poor sense of mission — this is consistent with the high ratings in A and B and low ratings in C and D. If this business is to develop strategically, it will need to address three issues:

- the development of a sense of mission across all people involved with the business
- making better and full use of technology right across the business
- a rapid shift towards a more business-driven people development programme.

The above illustrations outline the practical nature of the process and its ability to provide the essential overview of an IBMD programme. The situations described are hypothetical, and do not cover a comprehensive range of situations. The final chapter provides guide-lines for application and use of the process in a range of practical business applications.

The process described in this chapter allows for a comprehensive, but relevant, and practical approach to producing an integrated business and management development programme for your business. It is both timely and essential in that it:

- recognizes best practice in the key strategic areas for the next decade

- updates a proven strategy process to take account of the demands from business development
- provides a systematic and orderly approach to assembling the critical information
- sets out a practical process for establishing an IBMD programme in terms which can be managed within day-to-day business activity.

The case histories included in the final chapter provide clear evidence that striving for strategic leadership in your business can be a stimulating, practical and manageable process.

The following statements outline best practice standards used to define the 'Excellent' rating in the audits contained in Chapters 2–8.

Table 9.1   Best practice inventory for strategic leadership

A. Customer Focus (Chapter 2)

1. Regular review of emerging customer strategic needs
2. Regular top level strategic dialogue with key customers
3. Product/service development focused on customer strategic needs
4. Regular review of technology needed to support customer strategic needs
5. Create most of current and future business with market leaders
6. Formalize strategic relationships with key customers
7. Test market and design for most demanding competition
8. Exploit balance of current and future business with key customers
9. All staff should be fully aware of customer needs
10. Internal customer policies should be as tough as for externals

B. Supplier Strategic Management (Chapter 3)

1. Conscious culture development by key suppliers
2. Existence of core of reliable and committed suppliers
3. Strategic relations in place with key suppliers
4. Strategic support relationships with key suppliers
5. Joint ventures in place for key new product and service ventures
6. Joint approach to search and acquisition of technology
7. Key suppliers seen as leading innovators in their sectors
8. Strong strategic culture which is customer driven
9. Regular reviews of supplier competitors for benchmarking
10. Regular joint strategy reviews with key suppliers

C. Strategic Use of Technology (Chapter 4)

1. Manage technology as an exploitable strategic asset across the whole business
2. Develop sub-strategies to exploit technology across the business
3. Ensure technological inputs to regular strategy reviews
4. Develop technology awareness as business opportunity at senior manager level
5. Create programme to search and access new available technology — exploit the technology gap
6. Systematically analyse potentially relevant technologies

Table 9.1 *cont.*

7. Establish cost-effective approach to global scanning for available technologies
8. Focus the use of technology to improve response to key customers' strategic needs
9. Ensure that bottlenecks in application sensed and rectified
10. Apply technology across all aspects of the business in products, services, processes and procedures

D. Environmental Issues (Chapter 4)

1. Seek to take leadership role in influencing standards and legislation
2. Products and services designed to achieve 'green' competitiveness
3. Close relationships with key customers and suppliers on environmental issues
4. Major attention is paid to environmental impact of processes/systems
5. In-house priorities on environmentally friendly systems/procedures
6. Existence of ongoing programme to replace sensitive materials and substances
7. Ensures that suppliers are aware of, and committed to, environmental strategy
8. Take a major environmental role in community projects
9. Involvement at national level in relevant sectors
10. All staff fully briefed in environmental mission

E. The New Strategic Management Process (Chapter 5)

1. Regular review and updating of the strategic process
2. Strategic analysis and scanning is a continuous process
3. Strategic analysis covers all functions and facets
4. Comprehensive approach to managing the relevant databases
5. All senior managers involved in the process
6. Strategic process should provide for flexible and dynamic response
7. Opportunities and risks reviewed on a continuous basis
8. Technology considered on a business-wide basis
9. Pro-active and joint approach to considering customer strategies
10. Strategy statement is unique, comprehensive and executive

F. Company Culture Development (Chapter 6)

Output related practices:

1. Business organized and funded to respond quickly
2. A number of strategic joint ventures exist with key customers
3. A number of strategic joint ventures exist with key suppliers
4. Make full use of technology available to whole business
5. Services/products support and add value to customer strategy
6. Funding of innovation is available on continuous basis for venture projects
7. Professionalism of employees is respected
8. Careful anticipation and opportunity search on environmental issues
9. Social policies and standards are exemplary
10. Regular and reliable business performance is the norm

Input related practices:

11. The business has a well developed 'sense of mission'
12. The whole company is committed to ambitious objectives
13. Structure is geared to business needs and is flexible
14. Communication is open and effective across whole business

Table 9.1 *cont.*

15. All processes and systems are streamlined and customer focused
16. People development is a key constituent in strategy
17. Existence of a business-wide sense of purpose and motivation
18. Effective leadership is accepted and understood by all employees
19. Systems and procedures are in place to manage risk effectively
20. Rewards reflect both personal and company achievement

Senior Management Capabilities (Chapter 7)

G. Board Capabilities

1. Board deliberations focus on culture development and strategic corporate issues
2. The board plays a major role in defining strategic vision
3. Strong board involvement in development of sense of mission
4. Active involvement by board in developing customer strategic focus
5. Board involvement in defining strategy for effective use of technology
6. Directors and chief executive lead key action plans
7. Board involved as agents for change
8. Communication to and participation by all stakeholders
9. Board oversees business-led management development
10. Decision support on key business issues used by board

H. Chief Executive Capabilities

1. Ability to integrate and set priorities in all facets of strategy
2. Uses strategic action plans at all levels in the business
3. Ability to be effective in developing strategic culture
4. Leadership role in effective business-wide use of technology
5. Active strategic role with key customers
6. Regular consultation programmed with strategic stakeholders
7. Takes lead role in key areas of implementing strategy
8. Ensures decision support for decision-driven management style
9. Continuous activity in developing top team capabilities
10. Involvement in strategy-led training across the business

I. IBMD (Chapter 8)

1. The chief executive has formal personal development programme
2. Active approach to culture and mission development
3. Significant development programme to create multi-discipline managers
4. Management development organized at all levels up to board
5. Training at all levels on customer relations and strategic customer development issues
6. Organized briefings/training in effective use of technology up to board level
7. Through career training at all levels is the norm
8. All managers participate in strategy formulation and implementation
9. All key action plans are led by top managers
10. Conscious effort to give all managers relevant skills at best practice standards

Table 9.2   Area A   Business results and overall strategic development

1. Typical areas for business development/objectives	Suggested monitors/SPIs
* 1. Financial performance — growth	Profit/sales, market value added/capital employed, funds growth/capital employed.
2. Financial structure	Investor mix, development support, gearing.
* 3. Business/product/service mix	Sales content in new activity, growth in high added-value business.
* 4. Key customer profile	Extent of business with market leaders, percentage business on total quality basis.
* 5. Market share	Extent of market penetration on new and existing products, performance ratios.
6. Internal innovation	Percentage of new business from internal innovation, rate of return, growth.
7. Formulating and following strategies	Percentage of new business development directly geared to formal strategy, reduction in timescale to achieve results.

2. Supportive areas for capabilities development	Best practice audit reference
1. Developing financial planning, control and asset management skills	Business results 1, Culture 10
2. Establish skills in pro-active stakeholder relations	Culture 14, Board 8
3. Product/service management	Business Results 2, Customers 3
4. Market planning	Customers 1
5. Market skills	Customers 8
6. Encouragement of change, evaluation and management of projects	Business 3, Culture 1, 6
7. Setting strategy, action planning review (updating processes)	Business 4, Strategy — various

3. Key additional areas for best practice development	Best practice audit reference
1. Establishing culture to promote rapid change	Culture 1
2. Developing a sense of mission	Culture 11
3. Processes, systems and procedures	Culture 15

Table 9.3 Area B Customer focus and supplier strategy

1. Typical areas for business development/objectives	Suggested monitors/SPIs
* 1. Establishing new business with the market leaders	Percentage of new 'activity' that comes from new customers, growth new/old business ratio.
* 2. Extent to which business is driven by customer strategy	Percentage of new development arising from customer strategy, product/service focus, geographic investment.
* 3. Extent to which internal innovation is stimulated by customer needs	Extent of development of processes, systems, facilities investment is customer focused.
* 4. Development of key supplier concepts and relationships	Ratios such as purchase values, supplier, number of suppliers, material cost savings.
5. Moving the supplier interfaces	Extent of reduction of in-house development costs, quality costs, improved speed of response.

2. Supportive areas for capabilities development	Best practice audit reference
1. Analysis of customer strategic needs, customer culture and mode for response	Customers 1, Culture 2
2. Review and decision taking on customer business projections/strategies, action planning and risk analysis	Customers 3, 4, Culture 5, 15
3. Translation of customer strategic needs into development of processes, systems, procedures, VFM concepts, etc.	Customers 9, 10
4. Management of programmes to gain new key customers — market/customer planning, strategy assessment, etc.	Customers 1, 2, Technology 5, 8
5. Pro-active supplier development	Suppliers 'X'
6. Supplier appraisal, risk assessment and management	Suppliers 'Y'

3. Key additional areas for best practice development	Best practice audit reference
1. Creating sound and continuous funding for development and innovation	Culture 6
2. Ensuring a 'strategic' organization	Culture 13
3. Managing customer created risk	Culture 19

Table 9.4   Area C   The effective use of technology

1. Typical areas for business development/objectives	Suggested monitors/SPIs
* 1. Making full use of technology to reduce development lead times, improve response, etc.	Extent of investment in concept definition, percentage reduction in time to customer, improvement in problem solving time.
* 2. Defining and implementing a new balance and focus on in-house technology programmes	Extent of search, acquisition of outside proven technology, technology programmes with key suppliers and changes in in-house activity.
* 3. Use of IT in all areas of company activity from concept to customer use	Percentage of systems which are IT based, extent of access to IT, literacy levels.
4. Increasing the impact of customer strategy on technology planning	Percentage of in-house, supplier and licence activity arising from customer targets.
* 5. The management of 'green' technology in the business	Development of green screening/planning procedures, extent of green features in processes, products, services, etc.
6. Board/top team time spent on management of technology	Simple measure of time on decision-taking, of customer/supplier visits, etc.

2. Supportive areas for capabilities development	Best practice audit reference
1. Understanding conceptual design concepts, product/service development, technology planning	Technology 1, 2, 5, 6
2. Strategic use of technology	Customer 4, Suppliers 'X' Technology 1, 2, 4, 5, 6, 7, 8
3. Exposure to the use of IT across all areas	Culture 5, 6
4. Apply concept design to whole business	Technology 3, 4, 10
5. Developing an understanding of customer technology and management practices	Customer 4, Technology 3
6. Environmental quality management and competitive assessments	Environment 'A', Culture 8, 9 Board 2, 5, IBM 6
7. The need for multi-disciplinary training	Board 5, IBM 3, 6

3. Key additional areas for best practice development	Best practice audit reference
1. Making strategy work in the use of technology	Culture 3, 4, 7
2. Establishing a 'technology rich' business	Culture 7, 11, 15, 16
3. Making green issues work to competitive advantage	Culture 4, 8, 9, 16

Table 9.5 Area D The effective use and development of people

1. Typical areas for business development/objectives	Suggested monitors/SPIs
* 1. Establishing a comprehensive business-led training activity	Extent of participation by professional staff, time spent in task-force situations, number of top team led development projects.
* 2. Improving the performance in management of change	Extent of training for change, levels of innovative suggestions, response time, action planning levels, audit ratings.
3. Using internal innovation for people development	Levels of innovation proposals, success rates, reductions in change time.
* 4. Creating effective multi-disciplinary managers	Extent of multi-discipline professional training, multi-skill levels in whole work-force, problem solving performance ratings.
5. Making best practice the company standard	Use audit ratings to assess progress in selected best practice areas.
* 6. Improving team results	Success ratios in operating performance, problem solving and putting task-force results into practice.

2. Supportive areas for capabilities development	Best practice audit reference
1. Understanding the concepts and practical application of integrated business and management development	Board 1, 3, 6, 10
2. Planning and managing change — problem solving, decision-taking and risk management	Board 6, 7
3. Multi-disciplinary training, e.g. technology for the non-technical manager	IBMD 3
4. Understanding the need for best practice and the routes to achievement	IBMD 1, 2 Culture 11
5. Programmes to improve team-work — planning, objective setting, problem solving, etc.	Board 2, 3, 4, 5, 10 IBM 2, 4

3. Key additional areas for best practice development	Best practice audit reference
1. Conscious programmes to grow people and teams	Culture 7, 16, 17
2. Making the organization effective	Culture 11, 13, 14
3. Establishing relevant reward systems	Culture 20

Table 9.6   Area E   Development of company culture

1. Typical areas for business development/objectives	Suggested monitors/SPIs
1. Establishing a sense of corporate mission	Customer supplier and employee attitude surveys.
2. Establishing best practice standards in environmental and social activities	Compliance with selected areas of 'green' development and initiatives in programmes of social significance.
3. Creating the reputation of being a (high) value for money supplier	Set standards to improve on best competition on main customer indicators.
4. Active programmes to enhance motivation and response of all employees	Aim for business-wide sense of dedication — monitor by group performance improvement surveys.
5. Establish sound communication with all stakeholders	Monitor response to targets set against all communication programmes, extent of support from external groups, etc.
6. Being praised as a consistent and creative supplier	Delivery record, extent of innovation for customer, competitive standards and profit record, response to change.
7. Keeping pace with the market leaders	Sales growth with market leaders, gaining new key customers.

2. Supportive areas for capabilities development	Best practice audit reference
1. Participation and ongoing development of the company mission statement	Culture 11
2. Developing and understanding procedures for enhancing value for money to customers	Culture 1, 2, 5
3. Development of an understanding of individual and team needs for motivation	Culture 2, 6, 7, 12, 13, 14, 16, 20
4. Stakeholder communication principles	Culture 14, 17, 18 Board 8
5. Setting creative total quality performance standards	Culture 10, Board 10
6. Development of constructive strategic relationship with market leaders	Customers 1, 2, 3, 10 Technology 5, 6, 7, 8 Culture 1, 2 Board 2, 4

3. Key additional areas for best practice development	Best practice audit reference
1. The extent to which key customers are market leaders	Customers 5
2. Focus of use of technology on the needs of key customers	Technology 8
3. The development of individuals and teams in the business	IBMD 1 to 10

MAKING IT HAPPEN

The challenge of tomorrow is sustained competitive change. Change driven by a conscious effort to try and anticipate tomorrow better than in the past. Change planned in a more determined, committed and realistic manner. Change supported by productive modifications to core management processes and essential changes in culture and capabilities. Where there's a will there's a way.

Guide-lines for making it happen

The accumulation of ideas in the preceding chapters is substantial. For some readers ideas will be new, for others timely reminders. Most importantly, the ideas provide timely triggers to action, making new things happen or old things happen in a more productive manner.

But what to improve first? How to build on proven strengths of an existing strategic management process? Chapter 10 is new to the second edition. At the request of readers of the first edition, additional guide-lines are provided to aid the effective selection and introduction of concepts and processes. Practical guide-lines are provided in the following areas. The areas relate to the boxes in the flow charts included at the beginning of Chapters 1-9.

Section	Topic
10.1	Assessing strategic readiness — a health check
10.2	Improving the strategy process
10.3	Introducing the strategic customer concept
10.4	Establishing strategic access and use of technology
10.5	Starting to manage suppliers strategically
10.6	Creating 'best practice culture'
10.7	Developing top team capability/synergy
10.8	Starting to integrate business and management development
10.9	Establishing best practice performance indicators
10.10	Managing strategic progress

Examples relevant to both service and manufacturing organizations are given. The situations are representative of the spectrum of situations to be found in each industry and in each country. The guide-lines given provide practical stepping stones to best practice. To provide a framework, we commence with the Chapter 1 Basic Audit, used as the framework for a business health check.

10.1 Assessing strategic readiness — a health check

The audit questionnaires included in Chapters 2–8 can be used as the basis for timely health and fitness checks for both manufacturing and service companies. The Chapter 1 audit provides the basis for an initial review to gain a first opinion. A combination of the audits included in Chapters 2–8 provides a more in-depth diagnostic view. The two approaches are illustrated by two situations.

A BASIC AUDIT OR HEALTH CHECK

A medium-sized service company appointed a new managing director with a brief to raise the business and management standards within two years from the second to the first division in the industry. From a previous company, the managing director recognized the value of an early strategy review with his new team as part of his learning process and to minimize any delay in starting the necessary improvement process. A two-day strategy review was held and the audit document, as included in Chapter 1, intro-duced to summarize views of the team at the end of the session. Figure 10.1 illustrates the result. The inner profile represents the current position, and the two concentric profiles the team's objectives for one and two years.

The team noted and responded to the challenge. Achievement was secured by significant changes in the focus and behaviour of the top management team, the involvement of all 100 staff in a total quality programme, and investment in IT and management capabilities.

Specific behaviour changes included:

1. Firm commitment to allocating time — monthly — to the discussion of strategic issues on a rolling basis.

2. Rigorous six-monthly strategy reviews to progress and refine the top team's vision and plans for the future.

3. Accountable action planning and regular follow-up between managing director and accountable executives.

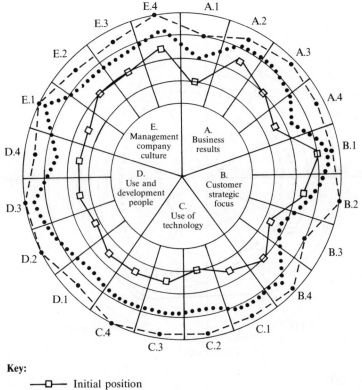

Key:

—□— Initial position

•••••• 1 year objectives

– –•– – 2 year objectives

Figure 10.1 A basic audit and annual objectives

4. More disciplined and tougher stance with non-performers who did not, or were not willing, to respond to retraining opportunities.

5. A conscious analysis of risks as opportunities on an ongoing basis. In the main the objectives were achieved.

Prior to the second annual review, two small businesses were acquired. The new business managers joined the strategy review. The opportunity was taken to repeat and update the profiling and objective setting exercise for the core business and the new businesses independently. Some major cultural gaps were identified and a programme of corrective action agreed.

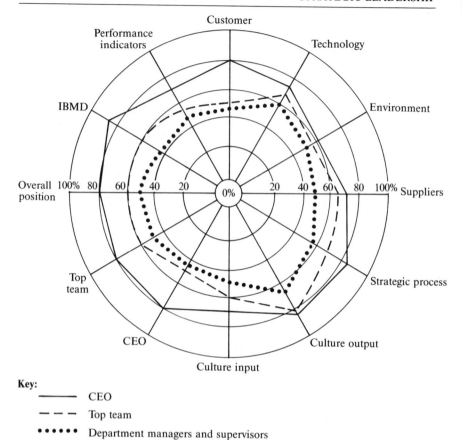

Key:

———— CEO

– – – Top team

•••••• Department managers and supervisors

Figure 10.2 An in-depth health check

AN IN-DEPTH HEALTH CHECK

The audits of Chapters 2–8 can be used to review:

- the preparedness of the business
- the perceptions of company strengths and weaknesses at different levels in the organization. This approach was taken by a major manufacturing company.

Three levels of perception were analysed. These are illustrated in Fig. 10.2 and are:

- the chief executive officer (CEO) who saw the company as being above average in strength in traditional 'response' areas but did not believe in the need for a structured approach to culture development, and did not see the need to mix business and people development

- the Top Team (chief executive's direct reports) reflected the CEO's perceptions in most outward-looking activities such as customers, suppliers, technology, etc. They differed considerably in the internal development capabilities concerned with strategy such as culture, chief executive role, own capabilities and IBMD
- the departmental managers and supervisors showed generally poor perception all round, compounded by poor communication.

The audit profiling approach showed up a number of issues which needed to be investigated, such as:

- How do the perceived strengths relate to the *realities* of best practice — are they really strengths?
- To what extent does the company use mission management, have clear operating policies and the disciplines of modern quality management? The signs are that none of these exist.
- Do the poor top team and departmental head ratings on chief executive officer, input culture and IBMD uncover a complete absence of modern training concepts or practices?
- What process does the company use to plan and implement strategic development?
- Why is there such a variation in the perceptions of the style of the chief executive?

The process provided a speedy and valuable diagnosis and the essential starting point for a viable IBMD programme.

The concept of a multi-level analysis based on the audits of Chapters 2–8 is of considerable value in constructing the approach for developing strategic relationships with customers and suppliers. In particular where the business is looking to select and develop key suppliers, the audit content forms a valuable basis for developing action plans.

There are numerous other uses for this concept in such areas as strengthening board capabilities through the appointment of complementary non-executive directors, and in the appointment from outside the company of senior managers.

10.2 Improving the strategy process

AUDIT CURRENT PRACTICES

Seminars, business school courses, books, articles and television programmes bombard senior management monthly with a variety of often conflicting views of what is the best way of thinking and planning for the future. So where to start? The options range from 'follow the neighbour' to 'reinvent the wheel'. Neither is likely to be effective.

The most sensible start point for many companies is to carry out a strategic review of the strategy process itself. The aims of the strategy process and objectives for strategy reviews are summarized in Chapter 5, pages 113 and 115; the basic strategic wedge analysis on page 125 and action planning on page 144.

The three processes can be conveniently integrated into a practical and searching strategy process audit as outlined below.

Step 1   Define what you need from a strategy process comprising: scanning, analysis, decision-making and implementation in 1993 onwards.

Step 2   Carry out a wedge analysis on your existing processes starting with the following questions:

The positives
- What are the strengths of our existing strategy process?
- How can we build on them?
- What have been the recent successes of the strategy process?
- How can we repeat and extend them?
- What are the natural opportunities coming up for improving the process?
- What can we do to take best advantage of those opportunities?
- What are the weaknesses of the way in which our key competitors think and plan ahead?
- How can we exploit the situation, particularly in relation to strategic customers, technology and supplier opportunities?

The negatives
- What are the weaknesses of our existing process? Which weaknesses are most critical? How can we best overcome them? What have been the recent failures? Why? How can we prevent them in future years?
- What are the forthcoming threats to our normal process? What can we do to reduce the level of risk?
- What are the strengths of the way key competitors think and plan for the future? What risks does this cause for us, particularly in relation to strategic customers?

Step 3   Decide on areas for most impact and leverage.
Step 4   Define specific improvement objectives.
Step 5   Agree an improvement action plan.
Step 6   Implement and monitor.
Step 7   Review improvement and slippages by pre-work and discussion
at the next two strategy reviews.

Common areas for improvement include pre-work, involvement of
both non-executive and executive directors and, where appropriate, an
advisory technology panel, opportunity and risk analysis, use of external
process leaders. W-planning to involve one or more sub-organizational levels
on an active and committed basis, the design of strategy review programmes,
implementation planning and implementation. Chapter 5 provides some
guide-lines in each area. However, in view of the level of interest shown,
we extend the guide-lines for W-planning in a number of situations in the
next section. Culture and integrated business and management development programmes are important improvement areas to support and
achieve successful strategy development and implementation. These
aspects have been discussed in Chapters 6 and 8. In view of their
importance, further guide-lines are provided later in this chapter.

Whenever a company reviews its strategic management processes, the
underlying question that needs an objective answer is *does our investment
of time and effort pay off in terms of improved results?*

EVOLVE A 'W'-PLANNING PROCESS

The concept of W-planning (introduced in Chapter 5, page 123, and
summarized in Fig. 10.3) is increasingly used by multi-subsidiary, multi-
divisional or multi-product group companies on a national or global
basis. Typical benefits include:

- deeper understanding, support and commitment to total group forward
  plans and, if necessary, short-term survival plans
- more detailed analysis and bigger net for innovative ideas to add perspective to broadly defined opportunities and risks
- tightened coordination and cooperation within international operations
  as opposed to loose federation with territorial barons
- improved international perspective of customer strategic needs,
  opportunities to access technology, location of key development projects,
  supplier potential and economic and competitive risks
- accelerated internationalism and development of central and decen-
  tralized directors and managers involved
- team building, focusing on competing with the competition v. in-
  company competition between businesses and functions.

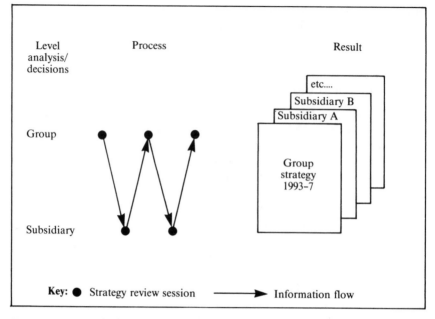

Figure 10.3 The basic W-planning process

Three situations are illustrated below. *The first* is a multi-national, improving world-wide strategic management; *the second* a bank, improving direction and creativity; *the third* the sharpening of forward planning for a university campus.

Tighter international management
The new managing director of a multi-national engineering and services company recognized that change was imperative in each of the company's markets. W-planning was phased in as illustrated below, involving four continents and some 20 subsidiaries.

Year 1   The group board arranged a series of three two-day strategy reviews a month apart. The managing directors of the three non-European contingent were involved in the third session. The value of the international perspective was recognized and the shallowness of headquarters' real knowledge of international customers, subsidiary company competence and competition highlighted.

Year 2   The group board again arranged a series of three two-day strategy reviews, this time two months apart. The group board took part in the first session. Between the first and second session local strategy reviews were held with the management teams of each subsidiary and region. The regional managing directors reported on opportunities and risks at the second group session in which they played a full part. Between the second and third session strategy reviews by emergent business streams were held and the results fed into the third group review. The strategic decisions resulting from the group review were communicated as agreed decisions, accountable actions and budgetary guide-lines.

Year 3   By now, directors and managers were becoming used to the challenge, openness and demands of W-planning and the shocks resulting from an international sharing of views highlighting more risks than opportunities. To strengthen central direction and coordination of action on risks as well as opportunities, the process in year three flowed as follows: group → business groups → group → subsidiaries → business groups → group.

Improving bank direction, creativity and profitability
A large bank with more than 1000 branches introduced W-planning to:

- provide direction to branches and financial services subsidiaries
- introduce business planning as opposed to budgets
- extend profit accountability
- stimulate creativity and contributions from bottom to top to improve total customer service, marketing, product development and productivity.

The multi-level W-planning process evolved over a period of three years to include all headquarters departments, regional management, branch teams, financial service subsidiaries and product management teams.

Strategic focusing of campus
The strategic focusing of university campuses is becoming increasingly important for many reasons, but mainly to:

- ensure research is focused on strategically important and fundable areas
- maintain academic programmes up-to-date and productive from student, staff and employer points of view
- develop further education/executive programmes that are relevant to industry/other user needs
- raise level of contract research to industry/government to a strategic as opposed to a problem-solving level

- accelerate technology transfer from academic research to commercial application
- broaden funding base for strategic development.

University structures can be complex structurally, both relationship-wise and culturally. However, the following process has been used to demonstrate the applicability of generic concepts.

Phase of W-planning		Level of analysis/ decisions	Involved	Output
I		Campus	Campus management team	Wedge analysis/ broad options
II	⇓	Academic schools	School teams -academic/ admin.	-"-
III	⇓	Streams • Academic research • Academic teaching • Further education • Contract research • Commercialization	Stream teams	Detailed analysis/ options
IV	⇑	Campus	Campus team	-"-
V	⇓	Technology transfer companies	Company teams	-"-
VI	⇑	Campus	Campus team	Integrated strategy, development/ funding plan

Similar W-planning processes have been found of benefit in service companies such as hotels to establish business management for each discrete saleable service group, major manufacturing companies in involving each manufacturing unit in developing and implementing an integrated manufacturing strategy, and even start-up situations with phased involvement of founders, funders and employee groups.

W-PLANNING IN STIMULATING PRODUCT STREAMS

Many companies faced with increased international opportunities, but also competition, have the need to strengthen and/or restimulate the management of key product groups. Many of the management concepts and processes of earlier chapters are vital. In particular, the benefits of:

- appointing profit accountable business stream or product group managers, who are prepared and capable to be *product champions*
- product management established as the *dedicated* management of specific products or services to *increase their profit contribution* from current and potential markets, in both the long and short term, *above that which would otherwise be achieved* by means of traditional approaches to the management of territorial sales activity, marketing, product development and productivity*.
- global strategy review to review, refine, redirect and revitalize the product group strategy and multi-functional, multi-territorial supportive team towards enhanced results, speedier product development, effective management of multi-national strategic customers, improved awareness and access to global in-house and external technology.

The latter can be approached in a number of ways, i.e.:

1. *An administrative approach* — based on detailed analysis of historic information and coordination of budgets; most communication by memos and letters, with little travel.

2. *A management approach* — based on coordination of operating plans; monitoring and controlling by exception; visits to communicate or request changes in priority.

3. *A leadership approach* — based on coordination through jointly developed and implemented strategy; frequent verbal contacts and visits.

   The leadership approach is likely to have most impact with top management support. For instance, a European-based multi-national group had expanded internationally through a series of investments and acquisitions in North and South America, the EC, EA (European Area) and Australasia as a stepping-off point to the Pacific Basin.
   A corporate strategy review identified one specific product group as offering the most exciting opportunity for global expansion through the established network of international subsidiaries. A product manager was appointed. He was accountable for the world-wide direction and co-

* Extract from *The Product Management Handbook*, McGraw-Hill 1989.

ordination of the product group which comprised five product lines and some 50 individual products. Prior to the appointment of the product manager, the larger subsidiaries were autonomous in terms of product strategy, product development, manufacturing capacity, supplier networks, international marketing and product support. Inevitably, product management — particularly with the strong new product champion — was initially seen as a threat to local authority and even national sovereignty.

The product manager had previously taken part in a national strategy review in his base country, and recognized the benefits of establishing an open dialogue with managers involved in the product range world-wide. He saw two options: to travel to each of the territories and attempt to sell the idea of a coordinated attack on world markets on a step-by-step basis, basis, or to invite all territories to participate in a world-wide strategy review to decide together: realistic objectives; how they would best be achieved; the areas where central direction and allocation of product development and manufacturing resources would be of benefit; where most market development direction and support would be of benefit; how best to manage global strategic customers; how best to trace, monitor and access best practice internal and external technology; in which countries to launch new products; in which countries to provide customer support; where best to design; manufacture or source product.

A product group strategy review was organized with agreement of corporate management. Essential features included:

1. Participants representing each territory and the marketing, product management, technical, manufacturing and finance functions.

2. Two three-day sessions at an international location with a two-month gap for additional analysis.

3. Pre-work including questions about:
   - strategic customers and needs (Chapter 2)
   - technology gap and opportunities (Chapter 3)
   - strategic supplier opportunities (Chapter 4)
   - product management culture (Chapter 6)
   - capability development needs (Chapter 8)
   - tomorrow's strategic performance measurements (Chapter 9).

4. An enriched multi-dimensional wedge analysis (Chapter 5) as the result of pre-work, discussion and debate. This was a sharing exercise that could not be replicated by desk research.

5. Agreement of global product strategy followed by territorial planning to support and speed implementation.

10.3 Introducing the strategic customer concept

This important concept represents the source of significant new business opportunities, but requires a significant extension and improvement of the way in which customer needs are identified, analysed and responded to. By definition, the strategic customer is one requiring/accepting help through innovative products or services to initiate and achieve significant changes in the nature, direction and extent of a corporate business or a personal/family lifestyle. Yet the position of many companies we have analysed since the publication of the first edition is illustrated by the typical abstract (Fig. 10.4) from the basic business audit questionnaire included at the end of Chapter 1.

Recognizing and responding to such needs requires new strategies, new products, new services, new ways of monitoring financial contributions, improved market intelligence, modified marketing and sales approaches and, most importantly, often a culture change and training.

The following 10 examples illustrate typical entry points for the strategic customer concept.

1. Add questions to strategy pre-work questionnaires, based on those included in Chapter 2.

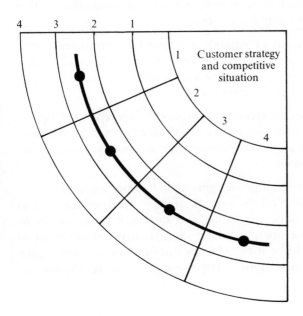

Figure 10.4 Segment of strategic profile

2. Make a discussion topic at strategy reviews to extend understanding and response to key customers, and test realities of technology-driven ideas.

3. Brainstorm product/service opportunities prior to, during, or as follow-up to the next strategy review.

    A brainstorming session, based on completing Table 10.1 has helped many companies achieve a deeper understanding of today's products and services, and a richer vision of tomorrow's opportunities. The analysis has been found to be useful to a range of banks, engineering and technology-based companies as well as government agencies at key stages in their growth.

Typical benefits achieved:
An engineering company with only one product business group and four component business groups recognized and exploited the potential for expansion through more product design and development, OEM manufacture and lifetime service concepts. Much of the technology required was already available or readily available.

A major bank recognized vulnerability in both personal and corporate business. Too many services fell in the problem-solving, crisis areas with significant gaps in the strategic area. Investment in raising the strategic thinking skills of senior bankers at head office and branches was as vital as strengthening of technology to customize the existing accountancy-driven computer systems.

An environmental testing company recognized the profit and image benefits of helping clients undergo environmental audits and develop environmental strategies as opposed to expanding the low-priced, problem-solving and crisis testing service.

A distribution company recognized previously unrecognized opportunities for offering a premium service to those customers preferring to manage products on a medium-term strategic as opposed to day-to-day crisis/operational basis.

A development corporation recognized the importance of understanding and focusing on the overall strategic needs of the area as opposed to purely short-term jobs and on the strategic needs as opposed to only the operational or short-term problems/crises of companies that might be attracted to look at the area as a future base. Changes in marketing resulted in larger and more secure investments.

Table 10.1 Review and expansion of product/service range

Customer support?	Crisis	Problem-solving	Operational	Strategic
What products are offered today?				
What products could be offered tomorrow (a) utilizing technology used in current products; (b) making use of unused, but available, internal technology; (c) by accessing and using/incorporating available external technology?				
What services are offered today?				
What services could be offered tomorrow (a) utilizing technology used in current services; (b) making use of unused, but available, internal technology; (c) by accessing and using/incorporating available external technology?				
What new technologies need to be accessed with urgency?				
What key capabilities would need to be developed to make the change in product/service profile indicate above?				
What is the scope for growth in	L M H	L M H	L M H	L M H
Profit?				
Volume?				
Cash flow?				
Business volume?				

© Strategic Leadership Partnership 1992

Key: L = Low; M = Medium; H = High

Table 10.2 Financial analysis by customer focus

Business Level	Sales %								Profit %							
	C		PS		O		S		C		PS		O		S	
	Now	3 Yr	Now	3 Yr	Now	3 Yr	Now	3 Yr	Now	3 Yr	Now	3 Yr	Now	3 Yr	Now	3 Yr
1.1 Company total products	5	3	20	12	70	60	5	25	0	3	10	15	90	53	0	35
1.2 Company total services	5	3	15	12	80	75	0	10	1	3	10	15	89	67	0	15
1.3 Company total	5	3	18	12	74	65	3	20	0	3	10	15	90	60	0	28
2 Product Group A	–	–	15	10	85	70	0	20	–	–	10	15	90	55	0	30
3 Product Group B																
3.1 Products	–	–	10	10	80	60	10	30	–	–	5	10	80	50	15	40
3.2 Services	20	10	60	50	20	25	0	15	10	8	50	40	35	27	0	25
3.3 Total	4	1	20	18	68	53	8	28	2	2	14	18	71	46	12	37

etc. . . . .

266

4. *Change financial analysis of products* — the strategic analysis outlined in the preceding section also needs innovation in the way sales and profit are analysed as illustrated in Table 10.2. Such an analysis has enabled companies to set and monitor the type of strategic performance measurements outlined in Chapter 9, page 231.

Such an analysis has proved to be more easily prepared and more meaningful where the brainstorming, analysis and recommendations on changes in product/service portfolios have been considered at business or product group level as part of a W-planning process that combines the vision and sense of direction derived from top management strategy thinking with detailed results planning at sub-level.

5. *Strengthen product/service specifications* — a key step in the implementation of strategy is the detailed specification of priority new products or services.

    The strategic customer concept provides a focal point for developing and challenging specifications. For instance:

    - require specifications to clearly define and separate the customer's strategic, operational, problem solving and crisis needs to be met
    - define quality and service standards in terms of those required by the customer to implement strategy decisions successfully
    - establish milestones ahead of customer's strategic deadlines
    - challenge specifications in terms of 'will a product or service defined this way give our customer and us a significant strategic advantage in securing major repeat orders?'

Additional steps that can be taken may include:

6. Sharpening strategic definition of market research briefs.

7. Improvement of sales-force market intelligence questionnaires/ reports.

8. Modifying marketing and sales approach to current and potential strategic customers.

9. Joint strategic reviews at director level between company and potential or actual strategic customer.

10. Adding a strategic customer dimension to Total Quality Programmes (TQM).

BEYOND TQM

Strategy and culture reviews continue to identify the importance of achieving step-changes in customer service throughout the total customer experience or direct/indirect interface with the company.

In parallel, many companies are disappointed with the achieved and sustained benefits of briefing groups, quality circles and total quality management programmes.

Success criteria identified include:

• chief executive accountability
• top management involvement in setting objective, initiating action, monitoring and corrective action
• a strategic as opposed to operationally initiated and implemented programme
• genuine involvement at all levels
• focus on *customer* not *company* view of quality.

Typical actions towards these ends include:

• consideration of customer needs at strategic level
• total customer management v. total quality management programmes
• multi-level strategy reviews that go beyond briefing groups and quality circles in the extent of information shared, and the intensity of ideas stimulated and considered
• total innovation programmes along lines referred to in the next section
• IBMD programmes as considered in Chapter 8 and in a later section of this chapter.

10.4 Establishing access to and making strategic use of technology

The development of technology strategy needs to take place at a number of levels in relation to most products and services. This can be illustrated by further analysing the example of the technology Route Map from Fig. 3.8 of Chapter 3.

The concept implies a hierarchy of technologies which can be expressed as follows:

Customers' technology needs

↓

Train technology system and sectors

↓

Key equipment supplier system and unit technology

↓

Outside sources of enabling technology

For the example chosen the train technology system and sectors require the phasing and integration of a number of related sector technologies, e.g., materials, power systems, suspension, etc. The development of key supplier strategic systems provides a basis for joint opportunity search, evaluation of options and commitment to courses of action for each major sector.

Of the examples shown in Fig. 10.5, the sub-sector elements are outlined for two sectors where development has to be kept in line with the requirements for the suburban train development windows. As the technology route mapping is developed at sub-system level, there will be clear indications of the need for enabling technologies which for electric drives would cover such areas as new developments in high speed power switching, low loss inventor technology, high temperature materials, control concepts, etc. Such information needs to be evaluated with care to determine the correct 'create v. buy' decisions for enabling technologies — these are the key to strategic success in manufacturing industries.

The above concepts apply equally to service sectors where two examples can be provided, namely, clearing bank (customer services) and food retailing.

The technology strategies for banking services need to be driven by three issues, which all involve technology strategies:

- the quality of customer services which involves making full use of available technology for in-house systems
- products for improved customer convenience — cash cards, smart cards, auto-tellers etc.
- the need to maintain absolute accuracy and security in all transactions.

The master route map needs to take all of these issues into account, backed up by sector analyses leading finally to consultants and suppliers who maintain the interface at best practice levels of enabling technology.

In the case of food retailing, a similar multi-level situation exists where the demands of the customer require:

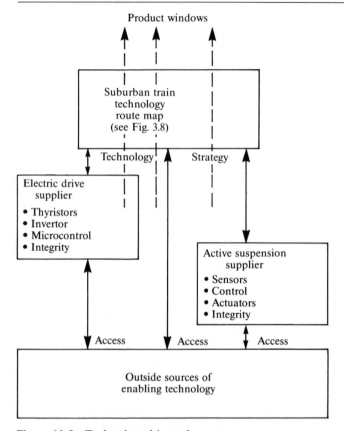

Figure 10.5 Technology hierarchy

- attractively displayed products and user-friendly purchasing
- good quality products which retain customer loyalty
- seasonal goods, available throughout the year, at a popular price
- food production methods which benefit the retailer's business results, e.g., sufficient shelf life in prime condition
- intelligent packaging to manage shelf life, pricing and charging.

As with banking, there needs to be a service standards driven technology route map which will embrace such issues as advanced EPOS concepts; but at lower levels the technology moves into the 'raw' products which could lead to considerations of genetic engineering and biotechnology within the strategic decisions of the major food retailer.

In each of the above cases, an objective basis will be achieved for allocating technology budgets between in-company, research establishments and university R&D, and licensed technology.

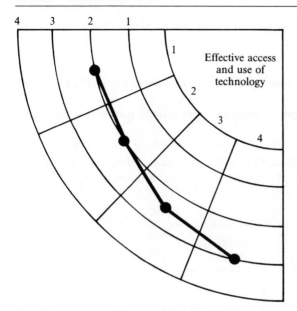

4 3 2 1

Figure 10.6 Segment of strategic profile

MANAGING THE IT GAP

The segment chart (Fig. 10.6) from the basic business audit at the end of Chapter 1 illustrates the position in companies in which technology, and particularly information/computer technology, is still directed and controlled by technical experts. As a result, the gap between available IT technology/best practice and average access/use for customer, business and suppliers' benefit remains wide.

Research by business schools and consultants increasingly emphasizes the need for software development teams to regain control of software development and hardware suppliers to improve reliability, flexibility and user-friendliness. These are 40 year problems now for some companies.

Important benefits of regular business strategy reviews and culture audits have been:

- the identification of IT as a critical issue at board level, both as an opportunity and significant risk area
- the stimulus of an IT strategic management process parallel with the core business strategic management process, with IT strategy reviews integrated into a W-planning process, as described in an earlier section, as well as in Chapter 5.

A process evolving in large and small companies in both the service and manufacturing sectors is illustrated in Fig. 10.7. The benefits achieved include:

- user as opposed to technical direction and ownership of IT strategy and investments
- comprehensive analysis of strategic, operational, problem-solving and crisis needs
- broader view of where relevant software, hardware, consultancy support and, most importantly, application best practice, might be found and accessed to achieve early profit-effective benefits from IT.

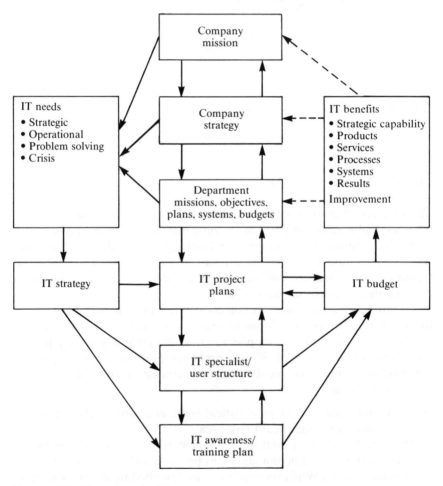

Figure 10.7 Managing the IT gap

Success criteria are observed to include:

- IT strategy reviews organized along lines of business strategy reviews with use of pre-work, mixed user/technical work groups, etc., to achieve openness, creativity and objectivity
- user sponsorship/steering group leadership of all significant projects
- joint involvement of users and technical experts in development of information architecture and risk management.

10.5 Starting to manage suppliers strategically

The development of successful strategic relationships with key suppliers is critical to the success in any business. The profile of capabilities, culture and preferred depth of risk-sharing relationships with suppliers can only come from having a detailed understanding of your own customers. In practice, supplier and customer strategic relationships have to be developed together, and it is therefore important to have a structured and secure approach to starting the supplier process.

Many companies find it useful to establish a task-force within the process of implementation of strategy, which has the assignment to develop technology strategy and to determine which elements of the subsequent action programmes are most suited to be part of a strategic relationship with key suppliers. As part of developing the action plans for technology strategy (outlined in the previous section of this chapter) the task-force will prepare preliminary route maps for potential key suppliers of products/ services or raw technology.

The route map will cover supplier technology or competence levels supplemented by a check-list of other features such as:

- financial performance required
- quality requirements
- attitude/performance in innovation
- training policies
- reliability record, etc.

The audit, therefore, will consist of two main statements to be used as the basis of evaluation of potential suppliers, namely:

- the ability to satisfy chosen technology/competence requirements as a key supplier
- the degree of compliance with the elements of the culture audit of Chapter 6.

At an early stage after the above evaluation, key suppliers should become involved in a review of the business strategy to establish where the interfaces can be drawn today and where they should be drawn for the future — essentially a 'make v. buy' risk analysis following the format of Table 5.8 as shown in Fig. 10.8. The obligations the buying company has on the supplier cover the following areas:

1. *Strategic* — working closely on strategic products/services and providing guidance in developing best practice standards.

2. *Operational* — providing clear guidance on requirements, prompt and professional commercial and financial support and comprehensive information.

3. *Problem solving* — professional and constructive support in dealing with deviations from agreed courses of action — working together to resolve problems.

The overall approach characterizes the policies followed by major Japanese companies when investing in new manufacturing operations outside Japan. The approach is generally to select carefully, provide full information and support to work towards best practice and to encourage key suppliers to work towards similar relationships with their suppliers. These are examples of this approach in other sectors. For instance, the policies of leading retail chains have pioneered this approach on a global basis. For most businesses today the low value cut-throat competition from a myriad of suppliers is well understood and largely discarded.

10.6 Add the culture dimension

From time to time probably all top management teams express disappointment with the resilience in changing marketing conditions of their strategy, the team commitment and progress in implementing agreed plans. Frequently, there is an underlying bottleneck present in good as well as bad times — that of cultural imbalance. In good times, however, the bottleneck is lived with, not overcome, and in poorer times, the bottleneck can lead to disaster.

In Chapter 5 we emphasized that strategy was about balancing opportunities and risks, and that more time was often required in areas of risk prevention and reduction.

Culture is undoubtedly a common risk area. Companies therefore find it of benefit to carry out a culture review from time to time and plan improvement action. The Company Culture Audit in Chapter 6, Table 6,

Possible problems	Likely cause	Impact (H,M,L)	Probability (H,M,L)	Preventive action Action	(H,M,L)	Contingent action Action	(H,M,L)
• Failure to meet technology milestones	• Technical failure	H	M	Develop alternative parallel solutions	H	Contact outside expert	M/L
	• Lack of relevant skills	M	L	-	-	Recruit if need arises	M
• Failure to meet quality standards	• Drawing errors	H	L	Check all	L	-	
	• Production process failure	M	L	Undertake failure analysis	L	Provide expert help to supplier	
	• Packages	H	L	Have alternative available	L/M	Use alternative	L
• Poor delivery in relation to	• Material supply delays to key supplier	H	M	Alternative sources developed	L	Use alternative	L
	• Inadequate operator training	H	L	Ensure full training used	L/M	-	-

Key: H = High; M = Medium; L = Low

Figure 10.8 Key supplier risk management

is designed to facilitate both the review and the action planning. Use of the audit includes:

1. Review of culture prior to planning changes in the total strategic management programme.

2. Completion of the next strategy review as a new and useful feature. The individual exercise can be completed overnight with collation, discussion and action planning the next morning.

3. Review of balance/imbalance between different business streams, functions or headquarters and subsidiaries.

4. Inclusion as a module in management development or team building sessions to provide objectivity and relevance to discussion about culture.

5. Evaluation of culture matches between potential strategic customers and company or company and potential strategic suppliers or actual customers and suppliers.

6. Evaluation of cultures as an extra dimension in merger and acquisition studies.

The challenge of culture change is illustrated in Fig. 10.9.

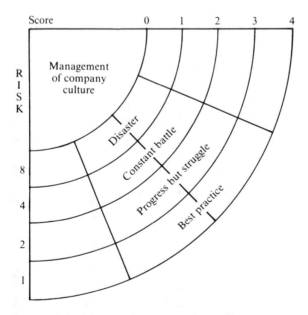

Figure 10.9 Segment from strategic profile

Unless top scores are achieved in the initial Company Culture Audit (Chapter 1, Table 1.5), action in this area may be long overdue. Examination of the actions planned, and the bottlenecks to progress, suggested a lack of cohesiveness in commitments and approaches. It was agreed that the culture of the companies needed review and that the timely available company audit introduced in Chapter 6, Table 6.1, would be used. For reasons of space the result of the culture review for the service company only is illustrated in Fig. 10.10, A and B.

The cause of slow progress in improving the business was self-evident. A culture development programme was initiated. Key features included an extension of the W-planning process, investment in an IBMD programme, and the start of a total customer management programme commencing with a thorough review of customer needs to determine what total quality meant in the eyes of the customer. The company recognized that the cause of slippage in many traditional Total Quality Management programmes was a too inward-looking approach.

The benefit of adding the culture audit can be illustrated by two representative situations. A manufacturing company (A) and a service company (B) both completed the initial audit questionnaire as included in the first edition of the book. This evaluated strategic readiness in terms of only four of the five areas currently included in Chapter 1, Table 1, namely:

A.   Business results and overall strategic development
B.   Customer strategy and competitive situation
C.   Effective use of technology
D.   Effective use and development of people, *but excluded*
E.   Management of company culture.

The profiles of both companies A and B are plotted on the profile chart in Fig. 10.11. Both profiles indicated the need for urgent action in business development areas, and also in the people support areas. Action plans were drawn up. Those in the people area are illustrated in Fig. 10.11 related to the four audit areas.

Progress reviews were planned for six months later. Various crises resulted in the reviews being delayed for three months. Both companies were disappointed with progress, particularly in the people area. The extent of progress is represented by the percentage complete column of the management development issue box in Fig. 10.11.

A. Culture Profile

Output factors	Score				Input factors	Score			
	1	2	3	4		1	2	3	4
1. Rapid change					1. Mission				
2. Strategic customer relations					2. Objectives				
3. Strategic supplier relations					3. Organization				
4. Strategic use of technology					4. Openness/effectiveness communication				
5. Value for money products/ services					5. Systems/procedures				
6. Continuous funding for innovation					6. Skills				
7. Growing teams + individuals					7. Spirit and innovation				
8. Environmental compatibility					8. Relationships				
9. Socially responsible					9. Risks				
10. Achievement business results					10. Rewards				

B. Culture Matrix

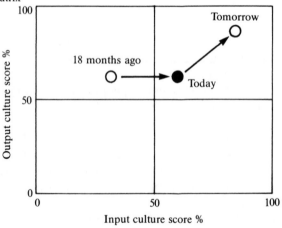

Figure 10.10   Result of culture audit

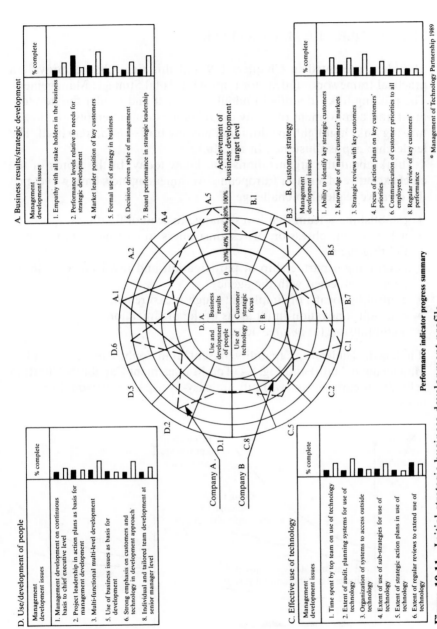

D. Use/development of people

Management development issues	% complete
1. Management development on continuous basis to chief executive level	
2. Project leadership in action plans as basis for management development	
3. Multi-functional multi-level development	
5. Use of business issues as basis for development	
6. Strong emphasis on customers and technology in development approach	
8. Individual and tailored team development at senior manager level	

A. Business results/strategic development

Management development issues	% complete
1. Empathy with all stake holders in the business	
2. Performance levels relative to needs for strategic development	
4. Market leader position of key customers	
5. Formal use of strategy in business	
6. Decision driven style of management	
7. Board performance in strategic leadership	

C. Effective use of technology

Management development issues	% complete
1. Time spent by top team on use of technology	
2. Extent of audit, planning systems for use of technology	
3. Organization of systems to access outside technology	
4. Extent of use of sub-strategies for use of technology	
5. Extent of strategic action plans in use of technology	
6. Extent of regular reviews to extend use of technology	

B. Customer strategy

Management development issues	% complete
1. Ability to identify key strategic customers	
2. Knowledge of main customers' markets	
3. Strategic reviews with key customers	
4. Focus of action plans on key customers' priorities	
6. Communication of customer priorities to all employees	
8. Regular review of key customers' performance	

Achievement of business development target level

Company A

Company B

Performance indicator progress summary

* Management of Technology Partnership 1989

Figure 10.11 Initial strategic business development profile

279

10.7 Developing Top Team capability/synergy

THE LEADERSHIP MISSING LINK

The ideas presented in Chapters 1–9 and this final chapter provide a practical framework of ideas for improving Total Strategic Management. The missing links identified undoubtedly exist and hinder the development and achievement of many organizations. But attempts to add the missing links highlight an additional missing link — *leadership* itself. The leadership gap is illustrated in Fig. 10.12.

Think about the organizations you know today. In the words of the chief executive of a major European government agency, have we yet met the creative leadership challenge of:

- establishing a team that loves change instead of fighting it
- achieving an obsession of responsiveness to customers rather than fighting them
- developing a partnership of participation and involvement with all people connected with the agency
- control by means of simple but tough measurements
- constant innovation in all areas of the organization
- a compulsion for *on time* action?

If not, is the leadership capability present? If in doubt, use Table 7.1 (Top Management Audit) and Fig. 8.4 (Top Management Capability Chart) to achieve an early overview. Both are easy to use on a personal or team basis.

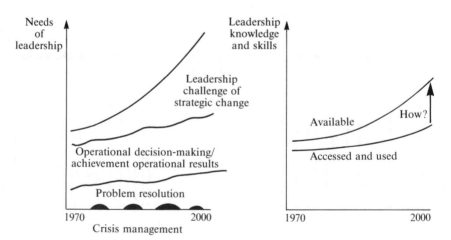

Figure 10.12   The leadership gap

If a gap exists, invest now in people and their development. Use a combination of experiences, as outlined in Chapter 8, with the emphasis on achievement-centred IBMD experiences explained further in this section.

DEVELOPING TOP TEAM SYNERGY

The Chief Executive Audit chart from the end of Chapter 7 provides a simple route to focusing on issues to strengthen top team performance. Often, particularly in companies which are performing badly under competitive pressures, there is a gap between the perceptions of the chief executive and other team members of the chief executive/top team standards. The gap is usually the result of the chief executive having a higher perception of his own and top team capability than those of the team members — the dangers are obvious. This is illustrated in Fig. 10.13.

In the example shown, the numbers are those of the Chief Executive Audit shown earlier in Table 7.3. This shows that the chief executive believes that he has strengths and can lead effectively in:

- developing culture and implementing strategy
- making effective use of technology
- translating key customer needs into company programmes
- following a decision-driven style of management
- providing well structured business-led training.

In reality, only the customer strength can be supported but is diminished in its effectiveness by the other issues.

The follow-up action has set out to provide programmes for development capabilities for both the chief executive and top team members plus actions to provide team development based on resolution of company strategic issues.

The company still relies on a traditional five-year-plan but this is now supported by a clear understanding of the supportive capabilities, the need for top team effectiveness and the recognition of the need to move towards best practice standards.

The analysis of Fig. 10.13 did not in itself lead to all of this action but has been the catalyst in moving towards a structured approach to business development and supportive people/team development. In particular the following approaches are found to be relevant:

1. *Culture development* — initially centred around the development of an acceptable mission statement, understanding of core business concepts, development of clear but compact business policies, and recognition of the role of TQM in developing culture.

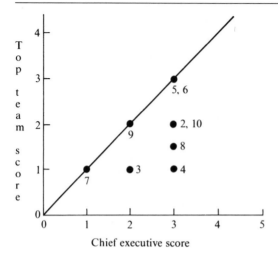

Figure 10.13 Synergy matrix

2. *Responding better to customer strategic needs* — through such routes as strategic definition with customers, close links with outside technologists, good and deep supplier relations and sound product management.

3. *Business-led training* — two main strands are most effective in this example. Firstly, develop the top team's capabilities as individuals and as a team, and second use the TQM programme to define company-wide training priorities.

The benefits of developing chief executive/top team relationships by this route do lead, in many instances, to rapid development of the business results.

As a footnote, all the audits contained in this book provide a basis for the 'vertical' development of the business in each of the areas covered by Chapters 2–8.

10.8 Starting to integrate business and management development

INTEGRATED IBMD

The position illustrated in Fig. 10.14 on the effective use and development of people segment of the initial company audit (Table 1.4 in Chapter 1),

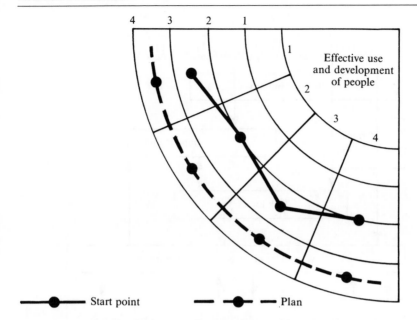

Figure 10.14   Segment from strategic profile

has been found to be representative of many companies in the process of realigning their management development to ensure that it is business-driven and integrated with the day-to-day management of the business along lines discussed conceptually in Chapters 5, 7 and 8.

Common characteristics of typical improvement programmes are:

- needs analysis from board level to supervisor derived from strategic change and capability needs
- move towards tailored programmes on independent basis or in co-operation with other companies with similar needs
- achievement-centred using projects derived from business critical issues
- all group management sessions seen as a management development/ coaching opportunity
- sustained investment in people and tougher action on non-performers.

Figure 10.15 illustrates an improved approach used by companies determined to move towards an IBMD approach.

The essential features in a typical manufacturing or financial services company are:

(a)   A sustained series of participative strategy reviews at six-monthly intervals preceded by appropriate searching pre-work.

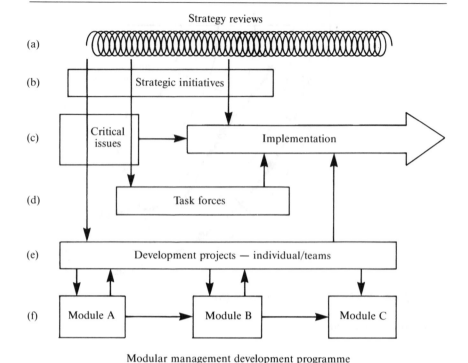

Modular management development programme

© Strategic Leadership Partnership 1992

Figure 10.15 Integration management development with business development

(b)   Confirmation, modification or incorporation of new strategic initiatives in strategy and implementation plan at each strategy review.

(c)   Action plan for critical issues confirmed or identified by strategy review. The action plan will typically include:

   c.1 urgent or phase 1 implementation of strategic development initiatives
   c.2 opportunity issues requiring analysis and preparation before finalizing and taking action
   c.3 risk issues requiring analysis and cost-benefit decisions before taking action
   c.4 removal of short-term problem to create clearer path for strategic change
   c.5 capability development issues.

Each critical issue would have clear accountability for results and timescales.

(d)   c.2, c.3, c.4 and c.5 may either be allocated to individual directors/ executives for personal or regular team action or specially formed task-forces.

(e)   Critical issues with less initial urgency suggest themselves as development projects for individuals or small groups as an integral part of a modular management development programme comprising projects and

(f)   a series of modules providing the knowledge and skills required to provide essential strategic and operational capability and the effective progressing of projects.

The use of projects as an integral part of management development has a number of benefits:

- aids achievement of IBMD (Integrated Business and Management Development)
- reinforces commitment to strategy
- critical issues benefit from new ideas and approach
- resolution of issues speeded up
- time pressures stimulate project holder to seek cooperation and support
- accelerates learning by early application of knowledge and skills
- peer pressures stimulate emergence of essential change champion
- cost-effective development as projects can achieve significant economic, time and cultural benefits whether modular development programmes are organized in-house or along the lines of the regular cooperative Kent and Sussex Management Development Programmes
- provide framework and stimulus for the development and collation of evidence required by managers working towards Management Charter Initiatives (MCI) awards.

In some situations, the strategic review and modular development programmes might best be integrated as the following two examples illustrate.

1.   A company was involved in the design, manufacture and marketing of products requiring the integration of a number of new technologies, acceptance of a switch to external access to key enabling technologies as opposed to solely in-house R&D, and a more customer- as opposed to technology-driven strategy. Top management comprised new MBAs and long-established technologists. There was a vital need for joint cooperation on an increasing number of projects. To date, infighting was rife; things moved slowly; leadership was scarce. The following leadership/team development programme was established combining a number of approaches:

Phase I	Day 1/2	Module A	In-house examination of leadership and membership of team skills by action learning
	Day 3/4	Module B	Outdoor exercise with day and night team and company tasks
	Day 5/6	Module B	Indoor review of experience and lessons learnt for running the company and design of strategic management process

Phase II   Strategic analysis including customer needs and technology gap
Phase III   Strategy review meetings
Phase IV   Implementation.

2. A government agency used a reverse approach to integrate, motivate and develop a new team:

Phase I   Introductory strategy review
Phase II   Team building session
Phase III   In-depth strategic analysis
Phase IV   Second strategy review
Phase V   Second team building session and implementation planning
Phase VI   Implementation.

The approach proved very relevant and timely. Most importantly, the culture changed from one of administration to one of leadership. Young business graduates, older professionals and near retirement administrators started to innovate on a continuous basis with, increasingly, a common direction.

CREATING FOCUS AND RELEVANCE IN IBMD PROGRAMMES

The detailed development of an Integrated Business and Management Development Plan was outlined in Chapter 9 and illustrated in Figure 9.8.

In practical situations the managers of the business may be faced with up to 40 or 50 objectives derived from the strategy/company plan, and up to a 100 points plan from the key capabilities audits of Chapters 2–8. The process for rating and profiling reduced these to a manageable number and in most cases the following picture emerges.

Business objectives — focused into four or five key issues from which around four key objectives emerge for each key issue.

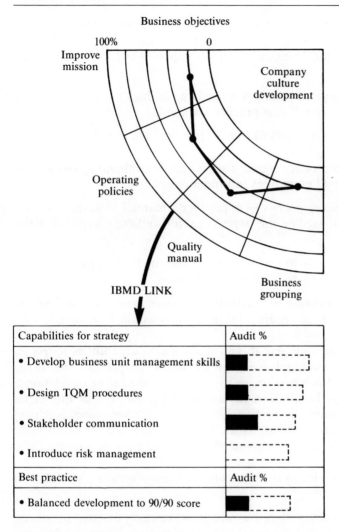

Figure 10.16 IBMD in practice

Key capabilities — the rating and profiling system reduces the number of relevant key capabilities for each business issue to some six or seven in number, of which about 80 per cent are concerned with implementation of present strategy.

Figure 10.16 gives an example of the end result of this process for a business in which competitive culture has been identified as an important business development issue. The segment plot shows the present position in relation to objectives for 12 months forward for four action plans. The tabulation shows the areas for development of key capabilities in terms of present position and:

- 12 months target for strategy related capabilities
- 2–3 years for overall best practice standards.

Specifically, the business objectives involved are as follows:

1. *Mission* — to produce, agree, discuss and disseminate agreed mission statement to all employees in nine months.

2. *Business operating policies* — to produce a manual of business operating policies (based on the 20-point culture audit of Chapter 6) within six months.

3. *Quality manual* — to update, reissue and brief all employees on the Company Quality Manual in nine months.

4. *Business Organization* — to establish the three main areas of company product activity as separate business units within 12 months.

The areas of development of key management capabilities reflect the needs of the business in relation to present levels of capability. The scoring system illustrated is based on an assessment of the rating in relation to the items directly involved in the audits of Chapter 6 plus the related issues in audits from other relevant chapters — the percentage is derived from ratings in relation to all issues. The best practice issue relates to the achievement of a balance score of 90/90 per cent from the culture audits of Chapter 6.

The process provides a number of advantages to a business involved in that:

- it identifies practical objectives which can be easily assessed for success
- it identifies capabilities in a fashion which gives every identification of training support
- implementing business action plans and related training can be pursued and monitored in parallel
- the end target for best practice standards is defined clearly.

USE IBMD TO MAKE 'INVESTMENT IN PEOPLE' A SUCCESS

Since the publication of the first edition of *Strategic Leadership* not only a commercial need but a strong political desire for business to increase investment in business-led training has grown in the UK. The Investors in People (IIP) initiative, managed by the area Training and Enterprise Agencies (TECs) is designed to establish a direct link between business objectives and training, and aims towards best practice standards. The four-part IIP national standard is defined as follows:

- an *Investor in People* makes a public commitment from the top to develop all employees to achieve its business objectives
- an *Investor in People* regularly reviews the training and development needs of all employees
- an *Investor in People* takes action to train and develop individuals on recruitment and throughout their employment
- an *Investor in People* evaluates the investment achievement and improves future effectiveness.

Each section of best practice is complemented with detailed statements on subsidiary issues, leading to a statement consisting of some 24 issues, supported by an IIP Tool Kit, including diagnostic audits and action planners.

IIP is a major advance for businesses in the UK in terms of the very large number of companies who are likely to become involved. Involvement is stimulated by subsidies and nationally recognized awards. The IIP concept occupies a middle ground in IBMD in that it:

- assumes that companies have realistic business objectives and plans as a start point — the authors' experience is that many do not
- lacks the breadth of inputs and analysis which would arise from an overall business strategy and conscious development of best practice as described in Chapters 2–8.

However, it is a start and for many represents a major advance. How then can the earlier chapters of this book provide solutions to those companies who are unable as yet to reach the middle ground, or those who aspire to greater heights? The chart of Fig. 10.17 shows how the concepts in Chapters 2–10 can be used to deal with those extremes.

In effect the processes of earlier chapters provide an umbrella for the IIP process and provide the essential links to expand its application and attraction to a full spectrum of companies covering the full range of management competence levels.

The next section relates to establishing best practice performance standards.

10.9 Establishing best practice performance indicators

The audit questionnaires of Chapters 2–8 defined best practice standards and Chapter 9 described the development of action plans to meet the

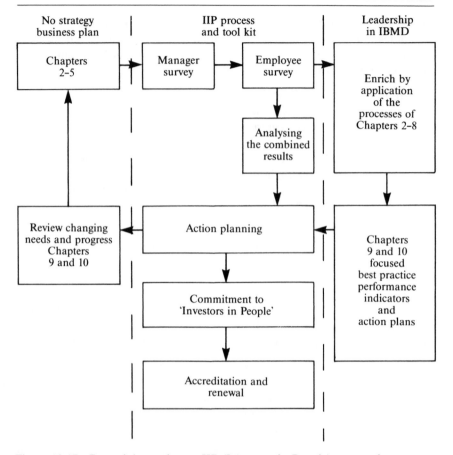

Figure 10.17   Potential to enhance IIP (Investors in People) approach

excellence standards. The chart of Fig. 10.18 shows an extract from a manufacturing company action plan, based on the analyses of Chapter 9, and covering a selection of:

- business objectives concerned with customer and supplier strategic relationships
- the best practice standards which need to be achieved quickly to match the needs of business development
- the broader areas of best practice which need to be developed to move towards strategic leadership (Route A in Fig. 9.2).

The quantification of best practice development is important but differs in practice to the measures used for business objectives. In each case the

BUSINESS DEVELOPMENT ISSUE: Customer Focus & Supplier Strategy

COMPANY:.. NAME: .... DATE: ....

1. Business development objectives	Position today %	Plan 1–2 years %
• To establish strategic contracts with two leading customers for each company business sector (number of contracts)	20–30	100
• To expand extent of internal innovation stimulated by customer needs (% of costs incurred)	20	60
• To optimize risk interfaces with key suppliers — reduce in-house R&D costs	100	50

2. Best practice capabilities for business objectives	Position today %	Plan 1–2 years %
• Development of customer strategic needs profiles (cover of all key players)	10	90
• Process to convert customer strategic needs into in-house actions (extent of issued procedures/training)	informal	90
• Creating system to stimulate customer-driven supplier strategies (extent of supplier R&D driven by us)	informal	75
• Managing supplier development programmes for our key customers (extent to which we direct suppliers)	0	100

3. Best practice capabilities development for leadership	Position today %	Plan 3 years %
• Development of internal capabilities to respond to full profile of customer strategic needs (full issue of relevant policies/training)	20	90
• Optimization of processes, systems and procedures to key customer profiles (regular optimizing reviews and meeting targets)	5	90
• Ensuring sound and continuous funding for in-house development and innovation (ability to satisfy in-house demands)	25	90

Figure 10.18   Best practice performance indicators

best practice development programme will be based on an action plan, the elements of which will relate to different issues in each of the audits of Chapters 2–8. Two examples from Fig. 10.18 illustrate this point, namely:

1. *Development capabilities to respond to the full profile of customer needs* — the action plan for this can draw upon the following audit issues:

Customer 1, 2, 3, 4, 6, 8, 9, 10
Supplies 1, 3, 4, 6, 7
Technology 1, 2, 3, 4   A total of
Environment 3   some 34 issues
Strategy process 1, 2, 9   and 136 points
Culture 1, 2, 5, 6, 10, 11, 12, 13   relating to
Board 4   relevant standards
Chief executive 5, 6
IBMD 5, 8

Each best practice issue needs to be evaluated on the basis of a listing of the relevant best practice issues and appropriate indicators. The summary of best practice performance indicators, Table 9.1, and the analyses illustrated in Tables 9.2–9.6 provide thought-starters for this process. However, it is recommended that all best practice development issues need to be evaluated in the detail shown above in a situational basis.

2. The process for monitoring progress towards best practice is to under-take a review of the audit ratings on a regular basis. Each issue should as far as possible have its own statement of compliance which can be established as a matter of fact at these reviews. It is worth noting that in most practical cases it is not possible to achieve 100 per cent best practice and, therefore, compliance/indicators are shown with target levels of 90 per cent. In the above example current and planned per-formance levels can be calculated as follows:

$$\text{Performance rating (\%)} = \frac{\text{Cumulative audit scores}}{136} \times 100$$

The example shown has been chosen in view of the importance of customer strategic relationships. It is worth noting that the process is of considerable value in the areas of IBMD and company culture in the light of the approach used to quantify progress described above. The scoring illustrated is a complex task that can be eased by the use of an appropriate software package. Some companies prefer to rate on a three-point scale — High, Medium, Low, or four-point scale — disaster, poor, good, excellent.

10.10 Managing strategy progress

Plans have been agreed. Persons have accepted accountability. Programmes are designed to develop their capability and the business/team culture. Action is launched. What next? Desired results or slippage?

Practical experience demonstrates that progress cannot be left to chance. An ongoing progress review process is required. A process which provides timely and time-effective opportunities for checking on progress and replanning when appropriate. The basic process outlined in Fig. 10.19 can facilitate effective progress reviews.

The process combines time-effective and timely team and individual reviews:

Team sessions to review, refine and agree strategy and action plans; each taking account of the up-to-date view of emergent opportunities and risks.

Timely and effective team and individual reviews to progress planned change. Questions will include:

- Are best practice standards now being achieved?
- Have planned changes and improvements happened on time and within budget? Did things happen as planned?

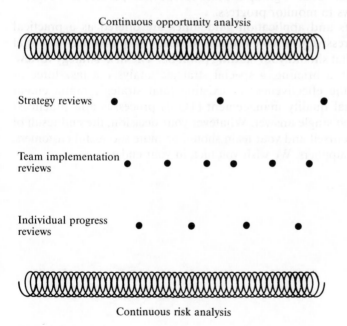

Figure 10.19 A continuous planning and review process

- Has time and effort been invested wisely?
- What can we learn from recent experience for the way ahead?
- What changes in objectives, plans and approaches to their successful implementation need to be considered?
- What new insights into opportunities and risks suggest that a rethink of the future is again required?

Progress is essential and possible. The authors are encouraged by the practical and often creative ways in which the concepts presented from Chapters 1–10 have been used by a wide range of organizations to improve their approach to Total Strategic Management (TSM). In spite of short-term pressures, time and effort have been allocated and more pro-active and professional management achieved. These are vital investments at a time when best business and management practice is necessary — not a luxury — for sustained success.

The way ahead

The rationale of this book has been to provide an aid to top management analysis, decisions and actions. The audits are provided to stimulate deeper enthusiasm for innovative strategic management. They are designed for individual or group use and can be incorporated into regular strategic reviews to monitor progress.

The concepts and application guide-lines are offered as a practical means of progressively moving towards the leadership practices essential for success. What should your starting point be? The next strategy review, a culture audit, a briefing, a special strategic analysis, a task-force or reflection on the effectiveness of existing total strategic management (TSM) and total quality management (TQM) processes and practices? There can be no single answer. Whatever your decision, the end result of the efforts by yourself and your team should be more successful customers, company and suppliers. We wish you luck in your endeavours.

POSTSCRIPT

Richard Handscombe and Philip Norman are collaborating through *The Strategic Leadership Partnership* and *The Management of Technology Partnership* in the continuous development of management process and diagnostic tool kits related to the main themes of the book *Strategic Leadership: Managing The Missing Links.* In this context, they will always be interested in news of readers' customer needs analyses and technology audits, ideas on the strategic process and corporate development performance indicators and innovative approaches to management development, and will give due credit in future publications.

The authors continue to be available to companies for management audits in company strategy sessions, workshops and top management briefings. They are also interested in contributing to international conferences, the continuous education activity of international business schools and professional bodies on the topics of strategy management of technology and management development.

By popular request a practical help line is provided to purchasers of the second edition. Readers should cut out and complete the attached 'Strategic Leadership Help Line Request' form and forward this to the following contact points:

Strategic Leadership Help Line Request

To: Richard Handscombe and   Philip Norman and Partner,
      Partner,   Rook House, Church Road,
      10 Gloucester Place   SNITTERFIELD
      WINDSOR   Nr. Stratford-upon-Avon
      Berkshire SL4 2AJ England   Warwickshire CV37 0LE
      Fax (0753) 863947   England
                                      Fax (0789) 731443

From: Name: Tel. no.:
      Position: Fax no.:
      Organization: Date of request:
      Address: Book obtained via
                                      shop/mailorder/seminar

Information, help, advice requested:

INDEX